Ian McPhedran is the Sy
News Limited. He has be
has covered conflicts in Burma, Somalia, Cambodia, Papua New
Guinea, Indonesia, East Timor, Afghanistan and Iraq. In 1993 he
won a United Nations Association peace media award and in 1999
the Walkley award for best news report for his exposé of the navy's
Collins class submarine fiasco. He is the author of the bestselling
books *The Amazing SAS*, and *Soldiers Without Borders*. McPhedran
lives in Balmain with his wife Verona and daughter Lucy.

TOO BOLD TO DIE

IAN McPHEDRAN
The Making of Australian War Heroes

HarperCollins*Publishers*

HarperCollins*Publishers*

First published in Australia in 2013
by HarperCollins*Publishers* Australia Pty Limited
ABN 36 009 913 517
harpercollins.com.au

Copyright © Ian McPhedran and Verona Burgess 2013

The right of Ian McPhedran and Verona Burgess to be identified as the
authors of this work has been asserted in accordance with the *Copyright Amendment
(Moral Rights) Act 2000.*

This work is copyright. Apart from any use as permitted under the *Copyright Act 1968,*
no part may be reproduced, copied, scanned, stored in a retrieval system, recorded,
or transmitted, in any form or by any means, without the prior written permission
of the publisher.

HarperCollins*Publishers*
Level 13, 201 Elizabeth Street, Sydney NSW 2000, Australia
31 View Road, Glenfield, Auckland 0627, New Zealand
A 53, Sector 57, Noida, UP, India
77–85 Fulham Palace Road, London W6 8JB, United Kingdom
2 Bloor Street East, 20th floor, Toronto, Ontario M4W 1A8, Canada
10 East 53rd Street, New York, NY 10022, USA

National Library of Australia Cataloguing-in-Publication data:

McPhedran, Ian
  Too bold to die\Ian McPhedran.
  978 0 7322 9023 8 (pbk.)
  978 1 7430 9763 2 (ebook)
  Heroes–Australia–Biography.
  Australia–History, Military–Biography.
  Australia–History, Military–20th century.
  Australia–History, Military–21st century.
355.0092294

Cover design by Heath McCurdy
Cover image by LS Paul Berry © Commonwealth of Australia, Department of Defence
Typeset in Bembo Std by Kirby Jones
Printed and bound in Australia by Griffin Press
The papers used by HarperCollins in the manufacture of this book are a natural, recyclable
product made from wood grown in sustainable plantation forests. The fibre source and
manufacturing processes meet recognised international environmental standards, and carry
certification.

5 4 3 2 1   13 14 15 16

for Roy Burton

Contents

Glossary	ix
Prologue: Afghanistan, September 2, 2008	1
Introduction: From the Trenches to the Taliban	5

Very Special 'Z' Men

1 Operation Copper: Five Hundred to One	13
2 Headhunters and Blowpipes	22
3 Behind Enemy Lines	33
4 The Stoic	52

Baptisms of Fire

1 Over the Rhine: Typhoon to POW	61
2 Kokoda: Guns to Garlands	69
3 Korea: Coming of Age	79

Vietnam: The Bitter Years

1 Too Busy to Die	93
2 The Nick of Time	106
3 Live Aid	114
4 A 40-Year Campaign	122
5 A Kaleidoscope of Ugliness	133

6 Emus Do Fly 148

7 The Spearhead 160

8 Responsibility 177

9 The Perils of Hindsight 188

Afghanistan and The Age of Terror

1 For Valour 199

2 Gallantry at Derapet 211

3 Towards Ana Kalay 218

4 A Bad Valley 227

5 Too Stubborn to Die 240

6 The Golden Hour 248

7 Weighing Up Valour 256

Saving Lives

1 Into the Fatal Sea 271

2 A Clandestine Swim 280

3 Burning Bridges 289

4 Too Bold to Die 298

5 Eye of the Storm 311

Acknowledgements 323

Index 325

Glossary

AME	aeromedical evacuation
ANA	Afghan National Army
APC	armoured personnel carrier
ARVN	Army of Republic of Vietnam
CDF	Chief of Defence Force

Commendation for Distinguished Service
(for distinguished performance of duties in warlike operations)

CG	Commendation for Gallantry (fourth-level award for gallantry in action replacing Mentioned in Despatches MID)

Commendation Medal for Valour
(mid-level US award for sustained valour in the face of the enemy)

CMF	Citizen Military Forces
CO	Commanding Officer
CSM	Company Sergeant Major
CT	counter-terrorist

DCM	Distinguished Conduct Medal (Imperial award for gallantry in the field by non-officers)
DSC	Distinguished Service Cross (for distinguished command and leadership in action)
DSO	Distinguished Service Order (for meritorious service in war)
EMU	Experimental Military Unit
GC	George Cross (highest Imperial award for gallantry by civilians)
HDML	Harbour Defence Motor Launch
HMG	heavy machine gun
IED	Improvised explosive device
KIA	Killed in action
MC	Military Cross (to officers for acts of exemplary gallantry)
MEAO	Middle East Area of Operations
MG	Medal for Gallantry (for acts of gallantry in hazardous circumstances)
MH	Medal of Honour (highest US award for heroism in battle)
MID	Mentioned in Despatches (for gallant or meritorious action in the face of the enemy)
MM	Military Medal (Imperial award for bravery by non-officers in battle on land)
MTF	Mentoring Task Force
NCO	Non-commissioned officer
NVA	North Vietnamese Army
RAAF	Royal Australian Air Force
RAN	Royal Australian Navy
RAR	Royal Australian Regiment
RHIB	rigid hull inflatable boat

RMC	Royal Military College, Duntroon
RPG	rocket-propelled grenade
SAS	Special Air Service
SASR	Special Air Service Regiment
SC	Star of Courage (for conspicuous courage by civilians under great peril)
SG	Star of Gallantry (second-highest award for heroism in battle after the Victoria Cross of Australia)
SEALs	Sea, Air, Land Teams (US Navy)
SIEV	Suspected Irregular Entry Vessel
SMG	sub-machine gun
SOCOMD	Special Operations Command

Silver Star Medal (third-highest US award for gallantry in action)

TAG	Tactical Assault Group
UCG	Unit Citation for Gallantry (group decoration for extraordinary gallantry in action)
VC	Victoria Cross (for valour in the face of the enemy)
VC	Vietcong
XO	Executive Officer

Prologue

Afghanistan, September 2, 2008

The battle in the isolated valley in southern Afghanistan had been raging for close to two hours and Special Air Service (SAS) Sergeant Troy 'Simmo' Simmonds was almost spent.

Just when he thought things couldn't get much worse after being shot in the back and the foot, he and two other Australians were blasted by a rocket-propelled grenade (RPG), which their mates initially thought must have killed them.

Adding to his woes, a round from a Taliban AK-47 had smashed and disabled his carbine. Realising he had ceased to be 'combat effective', Simmonds knew he had to focus on only one thing — surviving what had become a deadly fighting withdrawal.

'I'd already been shot twice and had shrapnel all up one side of my body, I was deaf in one ear and there was just nowhere I could go. I closed the door and turned around — it was like, ting, ting, ting [bullets ricocheting], all around me,' he recalls. 'So I went under the car and I dropped on my arse and just went on my elbows underneath the car.'

He remembers thinking, 'If I can get under the car maybe the other side isn't as bad.'

When he was halfway under, bullets were hitting the ground and ricocheting off the chassis. 'That's how bad it was on both sides. I was in this sort of weird cocoon of safety.'

Simmonds, who was the commander of SAS patrol callsign India 3, was also desperately seeking a moment of clarity to analyse his tactical situation amid a very sound Taliban rolling ambush. He knew five of his mates had been shot, the enemy fire was increasing and the convoy still had several kilometres to go to escape to the sanctuary of an American base called Anaconda, about 80 kilometres north-east of home base at Tarin Kowt.

After considering his team's situation he indulged in some close self-examination. His camouflage pants had been blown off by the RPG, he had two bullet wounds and was fragged [wounded by shrapnel] all up one side, but could still move. 'I was like Robinson Crusoe, I had rags everywhere, bloody rags all over my legs and there was blood everywhere. I didn't even know where I got hit, I had this weird sort of burning feeling in my guts. I thought, "Am I going to die any second? I don't know."'

Suddenly his worst nightmare became even worse as the vehicles began to move off towards Anaconda. He grabbed the underside of the Hummer and held on for dear life.

'There was no way I was going to let go. It dragged me for quite a way, there were all these boulders, it was quite rough ground, so I had to let go and dodged the diff [differential],' he says.

He emerged into the daylight and within seconds the ground around him had erupted with tiny dust clouds and the loud 'ping' of rounds hitting stone.

'Getting up from lying in a supported position wasn't as easy as it normally was — instant old man sort of syndrome,' he says wryly.

Parts of him wouldn't move due to his wounds and he was caught in the middle of a serious gun battle without a weapon to fight back. 'I was cactus, I just wanted to get my pistol out and start having a shot at people. I got myself on my feet, hobbling like an old man. I was off after the vehicle, luckily they weren't speeding. Just as I got to the vehicle there was an RPG burst just above us so I went down and they all got fragged a bit, but they were OK.'

Around this time, Sarbi, the explosive ordnance detection dog that would make global headlines when she turned up more than a year later, disappeared after the blast that wounded her handler.

Simmonds couldn't get onto the Humvee and none of the men on the back were in a fit state to help him, so he staggered around the vehicle as the small arms fire reached a crescendo. No sooner did he reach the front than rounds began pinging across the bonnet. Numerous enemy fighters had him in their sights and his every move was framed in lead coming from both sides of the vehicles. The only place he could ride was jammed between the bonnet and the bull bar on the front of the Hummer so he dragged himself aboard.

'I'd already seen the guy that got shot in the head and I thought, "If I catch one in my head I'm gone,"' he recalls.

The vehicle had a big link tow chain draped around the bull bar. 'I wrapped the chain around my head to provide some protection. I thought maybe if a bullet hits my head it might ricochet off the chain.'

He curled himself into the smallest possible target wearing his crown of chain and hung on for the longest ride of his life as the convoy headed for the narrow exit at the end of the valley. When a radio intercept revealed that the insurgents had planted a bomb somewhere along the route the vehicles were forced to drive in a big 'S' pattern. So when they sped out through the narrow pass they were up on two wheels, with Simmonds gripping on for dear life up the front.

The battle of Ana Kalay was one of the most intense contacts involving Australian special forces troops in Afghanistan. While bigger battles would follow, the large ambush in the valley of Khas Oruzgan left one American dead and nine of the 13 Australians in the contact wounded, including one critically injured with a sucking chest wound and another with bullet holes through both thighs.

Trooper Mark 'Donno' Donaldson would receive the Victoria Cross for Australia for rescuing a local interpreter that day, and four other diggers would be given gallantry awards.

Months later, in January 2009, Donaldson fronted up with his wife Emma and daughter Kaylee to a pristine Government House in Canberra to receive his VC from Governor-General Quentin Bryce. His spick-and-span appearance was a far cry from his putrid state at Ana Kalay.

Dressed in American combat camouflage uniform riddled with bullet holes, sporting a wild red beard and with a dead American soldier's blood coursing down his head from a helmet he had grabbed in the heat of the battle, he had made a fearsome sight on the killing ground where some 70 insurgents lay dead.

Australian soldiers exhibited great valour and leadership on the battlefield that day. Some were rightly rewarded with high military honours. Others missed out altogether.

Introduction

From the trenches to the Taliban

Standing in the overgrown remnants of an old Australian trench at the Nek, the ghosts of hundreds of young men from Victoria and Western Australia are all around.

The Nek was the small land bridge between Australian and Turkish trenches at the northern end of the Gallipoli battlefields. Dozens of lads from farms and towns thousands of kilometres away in a peaceful and prosperous land took their final breaths there, as they clambered out of their sanctuary to face a wall of lead.

What were they thinking as the whistles blew and they knew it was time to die?

There is sometimes a fine line between courage and stupidity, and there are few places in the annals of Australian military history where that line is more blurred than at the Nek. In just a matter of minutes in the early morning of August 7, 1915, 234

Australians were slaughtered and more than 140 wounded by Turkish machine guns. That level of carnage was common on the Western Front, where British generals regarded their young men as mere cannon fodder, but for Australia it was a tragedy that would haunt the nation and come to symbolise the futility of war.

The charge was dramatised and brought to a new generation of Australians in Peter Weir's 1981 film *Gallipoli*. It captures the innocence of the farm boys who joined the Light Horse for the adventure of a lifetime then died violent deaths on the ridges of the Gallipoli Peninsula.

The most shocking thing about the Nek is the size of the piece of ground that 600 dismounted Australian troops from the 3rd Light Horse Brigade were supposed to capture. The front is just 80 metres wide and the advance had to cover just 30 metres of ground. The official historian Charles Bean described it as 'three tennis courts'. Bean would later write, 'The flower of the youth of Victoria and Western Australia fell in that attempt.'

Taking up most of the old battlefield, the Nek cemetery contains the remains of more than 300 Australians who fell on and around August 7.

The attack involved four waves of 150 men each, from two regiments of the 3rd Light Horse Brigade — Victoria's 8th Light Horse Regiment and the Western Australian 10th Light Horse Regiment — who were due to advance two minutes apart following a naval bombardment of Turkish positions. The naval guns missed their target and a lack of coordination saw the attack delayed by several crucial minutes, giving the Turkish gunners enough time to return to their weapons and slaughter the Australians as easily as shooting fish in a bucket.

Three waves went over the top before the carnage — described by the commander of the 10th Light Horse Regiment,

Lieutenant Colonel Noel Brazier, as 'bloody murder', was cancelled, although elements of the fourth wave didn't hear the order and went over the top to meet their maker.

The charge at the Nek has been compared with the charge of another 'brave 600' from the British Light Brigade during the Crimean War. Bean summed it up best when he wrote: 'Behind the glorious charge of the Light Brigade there is a story of inadequacies, incompetence and bitter personal rivalries. The action at the Nek was no different. Yet still we marvel at the courage of those who took part.'

Bean was at pains to highlight the valour of the individual soldiers involved in the face of the bloody-mindedness and incompetence of their high commanders.

Australian troops had been known to defy orders from stupid officers, and their disdain for British class-based regimentation was well documented, but at the Nek they didn't falter. They had a job to do and somehow, despite the piles of fresh corpses strewn across the 'three tennis courts', they continued to climb from the trenches to confront certain death.

Courage under fire is the ultimate test of a soldier's mettle. Nowhere has it been displayed more vividly than at Gallipoli and Lone Pine. While the light horsemen were being slaughtered at the Nek, diggers from the 1st Brigade were engaged in a fight to the death to capture Turkish trenches just 160 metres from their front, on a ridge marked by a solitary pine tree.

At the Lone Pine Memorial today, the hundreds of sun-bleached headstones stretching across what was no-man's-land to the Australian trenches on the western side are testimony to the dreadful losses incurred between August 6 and 19, 1915, when 2000 Australians were killed or wounded while inflicting an estimated 5000 casualties on the Turkish forces.

Such was the ferocity of fighting at Lone Pine that seven Victoria Crosses were awarded when the dust and smoke had cleared. In one captured Turkish trench, Lieutenant Fredrick Tubb of the 7th Battalion from Longwood in Victoria, and Corporals William Dunstan of Ballarat and Alexander Burton of Euroa, fought with such valour against overwhelming odds that all three were awarded the VC.

According to an archaeological survey of the site conducted in 2012, the trench is most likely located underneath the bitumen of the main access road as it passes just behind and to the east of the Lone Pine Memorial.

During a tour of the battlefields in September 2012 with the survey team, Department of Veterans' Affairs historian Richard Reid led a party of officials and journalists through the bush to point out where trenches, many by now less than 50 centimetres deep, intersect with tunnels and firing points. Turkish snipers had the area well covered from their positions just 50 to 100 metres away.

Both sides dug deep tunnels, burrowing beneath the trenches to provide access for troops to attack the enemy or to lay explosive charges to blow up the trenches above, along with anyone unlucky enough to be in them. Reid described Gallipoli circa 1915 as a huge mining camp, with every inch of ground occupied by young men who would forge the Anzac legend, and their Turkish opponents.

From Gallipoli to Afghanistan, generations of Australian troops have risen to the occasion. Some go above and beyond the call of duty, ignoring the threat of imminent death to confront an enemy machine gun or to rescue a wounded mate. These are the men who stand above the crowd. They are the Victoria Cross holders who have passed a test few confront.

Yet for each VC winner who is officially bestowed with hero status by a grateful nation, there are dozens who are never recognised, whose valour dies with them or whose deeds are overlooked by a system of honours and awards that has been riven with quotas, personality politics or simple human frailty.

The Australian War Memorial has a list of more than 70 soldiers recommended for but not granted VCs during World War I. Many didn't receive any award for their courage — even after being recommended for the nation's highest honour.

Sandwiched between the global conflict of World War II and the early stages of the Cold War and its threat of nuclear Armageddon, Korea is a conflict that has been all but forgotten, despite some harrowing battles and remarkable acts of valour.

And in no war more than Vietnam did politics muddy the public's understanding of the skill, courage and endurance of the 60,000 Australians who fought in the jungles, including the 520 who died in the unwinnable conflict. Despite four Victoria Crosses and hundreds of other gallantry decorations, the mythology of national heroism accorded to other veterans still largely eludes Vietnam vets.

Allowing returned troops to become political scapegoats was a grievous error that successive Australian governments resolved never to repeat in the modern period of high-tempo military activity from East Timor in 1999 to the present day.

Three young Australians, Trooper Mark Donaldson and Corporal Ben Roberts-Smith of the SAS Regiment, and Corporal Daniel Keighran of the 6th Battalion Royal Australian Regiment, have been awarded the Victoria Cross for Australia. Dozens more have received high-level valour awards, including the Star of Gallantry and the Medal for Gallantry, all to unambiguous acclaim.

They include some special forces operators from the SAS and Commando regiments whose names and citations are kept secret, and who may never receive (or want) public recognition.

Many more who fought with courage, perseverance and boldness have missed out altogether. Yet their actions, too, have translated the intangible concept of valour into practical reality.

That is the nature of war, and reflects the fog that enshrouds every contact with the enemy and most recollections of battle when it comes time to tally the awards and anoint new heroes.

VERY SPECIAL 'Z' MEN

Chapter 1

Operation Copper: Five Hundred to One

Even at 93 years of age the flame burns bright in Mick Dennis's eyes as the old warrior looks back on one of the most remarkable solo efforts by an Australian commando during World War II.

As he sits in the kitchen of his tiny war veterans' flat in Maroubra in south-eastern Sydney, it is not at all difficult to imagine Mick as a super-fit, muscular 20-year-old sapper causing havoc behind enemy lines and cutting a swathe through the young ladies at dance halls across Sydney's eastern suburbs.

An accomplished wrestler, swimmer and surfer before the war, Edgar Thomas 'Mick' Dennis was recruited into the 'Z' Special Unit as a covert operative trained to go behind enemy lines and live off the land.

'Z' Special Unit was the forerunner of today's Special Air Service Regiment (SASR), and many of the tactics, techniques and procedures developed by 'Z' during World War II, including guerrilla warfare, water operations and parachute insertion techniques, are still used by the modern–day SAS and Commando regiments.

Late on a dark April night in 1945 a high–speed navy Harbour Defence Motor Launch (HDML) delivered Mick and seven other 'Z' men to Muschu Island off the north coast of New Guinea. With him were Lieutenant Alan Gubbay, Lieutenant Thomas Barnes, Sergeant Malcolm Weber, Lance Corporal Spencer Walklate, Private Ronald Eagleton, Private Michael Hagger and Private John Chandler.

Their mission, codenamed Operation Copper, was to find out the status of the enemy's large naval guns on the island as well as the strength and disposition of the Japanese force, and to capture a prisoner for intelligence officers to interrogate, then return him.

The eight men rowed ashore in collapsible kayaks known as folboats, but the current swept them away from their designated landing beach to an area surrounded by dangerous reefs. Unfortunately two of the boats were swamped and much of the men's gear, including weapons, radios and torches, was lost overboard.

Only Mick Dennis managed to secure his primary weapon, an Austen (Australian Sten) sub–machine gun, and eight magazines (160 rounds) of ammunition. During his early army training an instructor had drummed into young Mick that when the fighting started the only friend he would have was his weapon.

'A tough old sergeant major said to me, "You've got a lot of mates, but you've only got one friend and that friend is your gun or your rifle, whatever weapon you have, never let it out of your possession." That's the only reason I'm alive today, that sergeant major saved my life, because if I had not had my gun with me at all times I would have had no chance of ever surviving.'

The message stayed with him and he was never separated from his weapon throughout the entire war.

After the eight men had regrouped on a beach and concealed their boats in the scrub, they set off in search of the enemy's big guns and to hopefully bag a prisoner. Mick was given the job of interrogating the first Japanese soldier they nabbed, but the man simply knelt down and bowed, so Mick was ordered to shoot him. A second prisoner managed to undo his gag and shout to his mates before he could be silenced.

The mission was aborted, and the eight operatives went bush to try and evade the enemy force, numbering about 500. They also needed to signal the HDML that would be cruising offshore the next evening, but all the torch batteries had been saturated when the boats were swamped, so there was no way to signal the rescue boat.

After an aborted attempt to escape on a raft, four of the men decided to put to sea on logs to try and signal the aircraft that would be flying over in a set pattern every morning. They were never seen again.

As the remaining four men walked back towards the higher ground they ran into an enemy ambush and Mick Dennis was separated from his three mates. This was the last time he would see the men, who were captured and eventually executed. Mick set off on his own to begin a one-man harassment campaign and to try and reunite with his mates. Each man had been issued with a cyanide pill and Mick always kept his dry and handy just in case he was captured.

'I thought I would head back to where the Japanese camp was in case the boys had been captured,' he says. 'On my way I saw three Japanese about 50 yards away, one had been wounded and the other two were sort of helping him move. I opened up on them and I killed them. I thought, "I'm in trouble now, what am I going to do now?"'

He knew that with about 500 troops on the tiny island he would eventually be killed or captured. He thought, 'Oh well, I can't get off the island. I'm gone, I'll probably get killed eventually so I will kill as many of them as I can.'

True to his pledge, he killed an estimated 20 enemy during the next five days as he tried to figure out a way of getting off Muschu Island.

Mick's first priority was preserving ammunition, so he seldom fired his weapon on automatic but almost always on single shot. 'One shot, one Jap' was his mantra. Fortunately he was equipped to stick to it — a good shot, he had won the Lone Pine shoot at the Long Bay range in Sydney soon after he joined the army.

His Sten gun was not as reliable as his preferred weapon, the Owen sub-machine gun, but Mick managed to keep it functioning, to deadly effect.

He walked to the far side of the island where he found a couple of large enemy camps and an excellent hiding place about 100 metres from the biggest of them.

'It was a very good, very good beautiful hiding spot, no one would ever look for me there so that's where I stayed,' he says.

At one point he saw a Japanese officer with a child in his arms. 'I thought I couldn't shoot him.'

Being so close to the camp, he was tormented by cooking smells. They became almost unbearable when a pig was roasted on a spit as Mick sucked on a Horlicks milk tablet or chewed a date or nibbled on some rock-hard army chocolate. Each man on the ill-fated mission had come ashore with one 24-hour ration tin, and after several days Mick's was starting to run a little thin.

Water wasn't a problem, and as every soldier knows you can go a long time without food but you can't last long without water.

During his many forays into the interior Mick mostly managed to avoid trouble. He finally escaped from the island after he stole a long timber plank used by the Japanese as a gangway on a barge. He found some vines to tie his meagre possessions on to one end and launched the 'board' into the water in the direction of the mainland, about four kilometres away.

'I could see the mainland on the horizon, as far as I was concerned, and I headed out that way. About 20 minutes later it was quite darkish and up come the moon so I could see by the moon that I was heading in the right direction.'

His surfing experience at Clovelly and Coogee stood him in good stead as he paddled the plank across the open ocean towards the New Guinea coast.

'It [the plank] started to sink so all I could do then was lie on the back part to keep the front up where the gear was. Eventually I couldn't even lie on it, I wanted to save what was on it ... especially my gun, so I had to put my arm across it and paddle one way, then the other side.'

Throughout his all-night paddle Mick's thoughts turned to his beloved mother, Susan Violet Dennis. She came from a large property near Cobar in western NSW and was the rock of the Dennis family. On the night of his long swim his mother, who was staying at Cobar, woke with a start and told her other son Phil she had dreamed Teddy (Mick) was in the water.

Mick was one of six surviving children of Susan and Alexander, who was a senior police prosecutor with the NSW Police. His dad died at 47. Mick recalls the day as clear as a bell. The kids had been to the movies the night before and as they got up in the morning everything was very quiet. His mum was in the kitchen making the kids' lunches and Mick noticed she had been crying.

'I looked over and said, "Mum what's wrong? You've been crying."'

'She said, "Yes, you lost your daddy, daddy died last night." Here she was in there getting our lunches cut ready for school, a wonderful woman.'

After a marathon all-night swim in the fluorescent tropical waters and a close encounter with some large marine creatures that could have been sharks, Mick washed ashore at dawn on the New Guinea coast between Aitape and Wewak.

The ocean held few mysteries for Mick Dennis, who was a powerful swimmer. His sister Clara had been an Olympic gold medallist in 1932, and swimming was second nature to the Dennis kids.

'I was a good swimmer, I could do the 50 in 27.2, that's pretty fast, and my sister, she was an Australian champion, she did the same time as I did, she was a very good swimmer,' he says.

As he scrambled ashore he noticed a Japanese heavy machine gun post in a hut on stilts just above the beach. Fortunately it was not manned, although the gun crew arrived just after Mick got off the beach and into the jungle. 'Another half hour I would have been a gone goose.'

As he made his way inland up a steep path he met two enemy soldiers coming down the other way.

'They saw me with my gun and they panicked and dived off the path. Luckily for me they went the wrong way and there was a sheer drop off that side and they both tumbled over the cliff,' he says.

A little further on he found a hut with three Japanese in it. He shot one dead, wounded a second and the third took off. The temperature was dropping as Mick went higher and he managed to souvenir a Japanese great coat from the hut.

'I thought, "I'll grab that overcoat, I'll use that for warmth." And when I got down onto low ground again down towards the creeks and the river, I just took off the coat. I thought, "If I don't, then my blokes might shoot me."'

Mick encountered two more Japanese patrols and he managed to kill several more enemy soldiers before disappearing into the jungle to leave the enemy firing at shadows.

On about the third day he heard more voices yabbering away, then suddenly a voice boomed out, 'Tell those blokes to shut up, there is a whole bloody Japanese army out there.'

Mick realised it was an Australian patrol with native porters, and when he saw a felt hat he knew he was safe.

He yelled out, 'Ahoy there, patrol!'

There was total silence before a voice called, 'Who's that?'

'I yelled out who I was,' Mick recalls. Then he asked, 'Who's that?'

The reply came, 'Sergeant Osmond, 7th Commando Company.'

'Is that you, Fatty?' Mick asked. 'It's Mick Dennis. I'm coming out, I've got my gun up in the air. I'm holding my gun up in the air.'

As he came out they rushed over to help him.

'Poor old Fatty, I hadn't seen him for three years, but it was a great relief,' Mick says. 'They took me up to camp, which was about another ten minutes' walk, and I had a cup of tea and they gave me some bread and jam and it lasted around about two minutes and I brought it all up again. I had nothing in my stomach.'

Remarkably, when he was found Mick still had three full magazines of ammunition in his webbing. He had killed more than 20 enemy soldiers with fewer than 100 rounds of ammo.

After several days of intelligence debriefing and a special parade and booze-up, Mick was winging his way back to Sydney via Townsville and Brisbane. His war was over and his story had already reached the newspapers. It would become the stuff of 'Z' Special legend and the subject of a couple of books, including *The Guns of Muschu*, written by his nephew, Don Dennis.

Mick was awarded the Military Medal, for 'great courage and initiative' on Muschu Island off Wewak on the northern New Guinea coast between April 11 and 17, 1945. It was presented by the Governor-General, Sir William McKell, at Admiralty House on Sydney Harbour on a stinking hot summer's day in 1948. The dignitaries kept the soldiers and their families waiting in the heat so the men resolved to teach the GG a bit of a lesson.

'It was 102 degrees and I had my wife and little baby there and there wasn't much cover at all, and everyone is getting a bit cranky,' he says. 'So a few of us got together that were getting the awards and decided that when he shakes our hands we would give it to him and squeeze as hard as we could. He would have had sore hands for a week, I'm bloody sure of it.'

Mick regards acts of bravery as random occurrences often combined with a great deal of luck.

'I don't think it's born in you, it's not drilled into you, it's just something that happens on the spur of the moment. You know what you are going to do and you do it,' he says. 'I couldn't get off the island, I was probably going to get killed eventually so, I'll kill as many as I can, and that's what I did. I did a few things that people would have said were brave, I got stuck into them and I was very, very lucky I got away from them. I've been lucky all the time.'

Mick, who has been married three times and fathered six children, doesn't regard his conduct as being particularly brave, but pure survival instinct.

'I had the advantage because they didn't see me, I saw them and when they came into view and they were close enough I shot them,' he says.

His closest shave came when he was surrounded and hiding under a palm tree and a Japanese solder touched the fronds that were sheltering him with his bayonet. 'If he'd seen me I was going to shoot him. I would never have lived, they would have been all around me.'

One thing that Mick Dennis did resolve was that he would not be taken prisoner under any circumstances. It was kill or be killed and he would die either from an enemy bullet or he would swallow the cyanide.

'I killed plenty of them and I'm not bloody sorry either.'

Chapter 2

Headhunters and Blowpipes

Jack 'Snow' Tredrea was 24 years old when he jumped from a Liberator bomber into the wilds of North Borneo on March 25, 1945, to begin one of the most daring and successful covert operations by Australian troops during World War II.

As a highly trained member of the top-secret 'Z' Special Unit, young Jack, an apprentice tailor from Adelaide, had been selected as one of eight 'Z' operatives to parachute behind Japanese lines in an operation codenamed Semut 1 (*semut* is Malay for 'ant').

The men's orders were to gather intelligence and harass Japanese forces, ahead of an invasion led by the Australian Army's 9th Division scheduled for June that year. The mission was under the command of the eccentric British explorer, adventurer and pre-war Borneo hand Major Tom Harrison. Its objectives were to win the trust of the local tribespeople and former headhunters, the Kelabit, and to recruit and train them to kill the battle-hardened Japanese jungle fighters.

The operatives, along with eight 'storpedoes' — special cigar-shaped containers of stores designed to break open on impact — were dropped into an area known as the Plain of Bah, south-east of Labuan Island in Brunei Bay, where the invading 9th Division force was due to come ashore. Their objective was a village called Bario and from there they would spread out and recruit and train their native forces.

Jack was working for an Adelaide tailoring firm when he joined the Citizen Military Forces, or CMF, in 1939 as a medic. A few years later, in mid-1943, he was a sergeant instructor at the 3rd Training Battalion in Melbourne when a notice appeared on the board calling for six volunteers with medical knowledge to join a 'special' unit.

He was first in line at the interviews and he was pleasantly surprised to learn they were being conducted by Lieutenant Colonel, later Major General, Sir Samuel Burston, Director-General of Medical Services.

'He looked at me and I looked at him; he said, "Where have I met you?"'

'I said, "Where did you get your uniform, Colonel?"'

He had recognised Jack from the tailor's, where the young man had assisted with the making of the Colonel's uniforms.

Jack was duly selected for 'special' duty and he and the other recruits reported to a mansion on St Kilda Road called Airlie where 'Z' Special had its headquarters. From there it was on to Fraser Island in Queensland to begin their specialised jungle training. During one of his brief leave periods in 1943 Jack married his sweetheart from Adelaide, Edith Bongiorno.

By late 1944 it was apparent that Operation Semut would proceed. After a final visit with Edith in Melbourne, Jack and four of his mates, and their storpedoes, caught the train to Brisbane and on to Leyburn to learn how to jump from a Liberator bomber. They had done several jumps from the side door of a Dakota transport plane, but the Liberator was different.

'Z' Special had six RAAF Liberators attached to the unit in a group designated 200 Flight to provide specialist air support to the covert troops. Unlike the Dakota, the Liberator had no side door and the men had to exit the aircraft via a short slippery dip and out through the camera hatch in the floor. The other key difference was that in a Dakota they exited at about 90 miles (145 kilometres) per hour compared to 140 miles (225 kilometres) per hour from a Liberator.

Parachuting was a primary skill for all 'Z' Special operatives and most had many jumps under their belts before they were called upon to do it behind enemy lines. Jumping from a fast-moving aircraft several thousand feet above the ground is not for everyone. Jack recalls a padre who turned up at Richmond RAAF base near Sydney, where he was undergoing basic parachute training from a Douglas Dakota DC3. The padre wanted to be the padre of the parachute battalion so he had to learn how to be a parachutist.

'Once you get to the door you take up your position and you've got the guy that gives you the warning sign to go,' Jack says. 'Well, the padre got to the door and he was standing on the door and the red light came on and the controller said, "Right, get ready!"'

The terrified padre crouched down but couldn't bring himself to jump even after the light turned green.

'[When] the green light had been on for a few seconds, finally the sergeant kicked him in the arse straight out the door. He never came back the next day,' says Jack with a chuckle.

The eight men who were selected for Semut 1 flew from Australia to the unit's forward base on the island of Morotai in the Halmahera group of Indonesia's eastern Maluku Islands. From there they conducted several reconnaissance flights over northeast Borneo in search of a suitable drop zone for the team and their stores.

During one flight, Jack and Major Harrison identified a promising-looking rice paddy close to the village of Bario. The flight from Morotai to Borneo was only just within the range of the Liberators, so Harrison decided to move the group to the American airfield at San Jose on Mindoro Island in the Philippines — two hours' flight time closer to Borneo.

'The very first morning Harrison lined us all up alongside one of the planes and told us what our destination was, what we were going to do,' Tredrea recalls. 'We were parachuting into Borneo to gain as much intelligence as possible for the invasion by 9 Divvy, and as well as that the other main job we had was to get the natives on side with us.'

During the briefing Harrison took out a tin and gave each man a small red rubber capsule. 'I looked at mine and said, "What are these?"

'He said, "They are cyanide capsules." And if we got into any trouble, we were to take it before the Japs got us.'

Many 'Z' operatives were captured, tortured and executed by the Japanese, including ten beheaded following the ill-fated Operation Rimau raid on Singapore Harbour, which took place in October 1944.

'I've never forgiven them [the Japanese] for that,' Jack says.

The two Liberators lifted off from Mindoro early on March 25, 1945, with Major Harrison and Sergeants Fred Sanderson, Doug Bower and Keith Barrie in the lead aircraft followed by Kiwi Captain Eric Edmeades, Warrant Officer Rod Cusack and Sergeants Jack Tredrea and Kel Hallam in the second Liberator.

Due to low cloud, the second team missed the drop zone, landing several miles away. They had to hack their way through the jungle back to the village, where they married up with their mates and their stores, which had been carted in by some helpful locals.

They set up headquarters in the village long house, which had 37 doors to accommodate 37 families. That night they were guests of honour at a welcoming party where they sampled the delights of the local rice wine known as *borak*.

'They welcomed us with open arms, they turned on a drinking and dancing session that night and I can tell you truthfully there was seven very drunk Australians and one pommy,' Jack says. 'Most of us lay down in our clothes and slept on the floor of the long house. Kel Hallam was the unlucky one — he took his boots off and in the morning he found the dogs had eaten them.'

Late afternoon on the second day at Bario saw the headman for the entire Kelabit tribe arrive to meet with Harrison and his men.

'To this day we don't know how he knew we were there, but he pledged the whole Kelabit population would help us in any way they could,' Jack says. 'Harrison impressed upon him that in no way were the Japs to know that any white man had come back in. We wanted at least a month to allow others to come in, for more arms to arrive and for us to semi-train the natives and arm them for their benefit as well as our own.'

As it turned out, security was so good that it would be two months later, in mid-May, before the Japanese got wind of the presence of the allied operatives in their midst.

'That just shows you how good that population were. They were wonderful people and to this day, and I've been back twice, as far as they are concerned the Australians are number one. They treated me like a bloody king when I went back last time,' Jack says.

On the third morning Major Harrison said to him, 'Snow, there is an old guy in the Kelabit quarters that can't walk, go in and have a look at him, see what you can do for him.'

'So I went in there and he was laying down on the floor and he couldn't walk,' Tredrea says.

The local men wore only a length of cloth around their waist and under their groin to cover their genitals. After he scraped away the accumulated dirt and filth Jack found a golfball-sized lump on the man's groin.

'I got some hot water and cleaned it, I think there was a quarter of an inch dirt to get rid of; I got down to one, a spot in the centre that looked a bit lighter colour than the rest of him and I went and got my kit. I asked Keith Barrie to hold his shoulders and Kel to hold his feet and I lanced it. As soon as I lanced it all the pus in the world came out so I compressed it, cleaned it as much as I could, filled it with powder, slapped a bit of sticking plaster on the cut and said, "I'll see you tomorrow." The next morning he came tottering out, walked towards me, "*Chuon* Doc, *terima kasih, terima kasih*" [thank you, thank you] and from then onwards until I left Borneo I was called Chuon Doc.'

More than 65 years later Jack returned to Borneo and was greeted by headlines in the local papers: 'Chuon Doc returns after 65 years.'

After four days Harrison divided the team and ordered each member to go off in a different direction to recruit local men into a guerrilla force that they would train to attack isolated Japanese patrols.

Jack Tredrea left Bario for a five-week tour of the long houses of the Plain of Bah, with half a dozen women carrying his medical and other supplies. Harrison had ordered all the other local men to stay behind to begin training.

Tredrea lived on rice and the occasional bit of monkey or pig meat and travelled through the jungle treating minor ailments, including boils and dysentery, and gathering men for the guerrilla force and intelligence about the Japanese. After five weeks he returned to the headquarters with 30 local Iban recruits, telling Harrison he would need ten days to recover from his mission. It had left him badly chafed and exhausted.

The native fighters were schooled in the use of modern weapons such as the Bren machine gun and the Owen gun and guerrilla tactics, and in return they taught the soldiers how to use their primary weapon – the blowpipe and poisoned darts.

By the third week of May the teams were ready to begin attacking enemy patrols. Tredrea and his team were sent towards a place called Malino in Dutch Borneo where there was a healthy number of Japanese waiting to be picked off.

There was another reason why he was sent into Dutch Borneo — to investigate what had happened to a Dutch missionary friend of Harrison.

'The Japs had apparently massacred his whole family as soon as they arrived there, and Harrison wanted me to find out, if I could, who was responsible for turning them in and where they were buried,' he says. 'I did find out which camp they were massacred at and that they were buried in the jungle. There was nothing you could do about it, but that was the husband, wife and four children.'

Travelling down the wild rivers of Borneo in local dugout canoes was quite hazardous, and during the first week they managed to lose the radio overboard while shooting down some rapids.

The bush telegraph in Borneo was extraordinary. Jack would usually know 24 hours in advance about the movements of a

Japanese patrol and where the best ambush sites were. In their first contact his team killed all 20 members of an enemy patrol.

'I went back to the boat. To my horror the boys came back carrying the heads, I thought "Oh shit", but it was a cultural thing, they were headhunters in the old days, and so you know, you just had to go with it,' he says.

Headhunting had been taboo for decades, thanks largely to Christian missionaries active throughout the archipelago, but it underwent a major resurgence in 1945 under 'Z' Special supervision. The impact on already worn-out and hungry Japanese troops of finding hundreds of their comrades throughout North Borneo dead and minus their heads must have been unnerving.

The Kelabit people regarded Semut 1 and the Australians as the new authority that would not only permit but actively encourage a return to the sacred headhunting raids of their songs and legends. The news spread throughout the jungle and headhunters from miles around volunteered to join the 'Semut tribe'.

By June 1945 headhunting was so popular in North Borneo that anyone associated with Japanese forces, including Malays or Chinese, were considered fair game. Fortunately Semut 1 could maintain discipline, and apart from one unlucky Malay collaborator, only the heads of enemy fighters were targets for Harrison's native force.

A bounty of five gilders was paid for each Japanese head.

'Believe you me they got some heads. To allow them to go back to headhunting was one of the best things we could do for them,' Jack says. 'It did cause a few problems because a couple of times there were a few Chinese heads there as well.'

In late May Jack Tredrea got word from his native scouts about a large force of Japanese soldiers holed up in a former Dutch timber town. After scoping it out he found about 60 enemy living in six huts at one end of the village. He sent a map back to Harrison and requested a strafing raid on the huts. Six long-range P-38 Lightning fighters arrived at the agreed time and took out about half the Japanese force with their cannons and machine guns.

Jack had set up an ambush along the river where the escaping Japanese duly headed, and he and 15 of 'his boys' managed to eliminate most of the survivors.

Jack took out half a dozen himself with a heavy machine gun and was awarded the Military Medal for his courage under heavy fire that day.

His citation reads:

Sgt Tredrea was a member of the first SRD [Services Reconnaissance Department] party to be parachuted into Central Borneo in March 1945, for the purposes of establishing an intelligence network throughout Sarawak. From the first he showed remarkable energy, unselfishness and devotion to duty.

In early June a large force of Japanese (approx. 200) endeavoured to come up the Mentarang River by way of the Semamoe to establish themselves in the interior. Sgt Tredrea with 30 native troops so effectively removed all canoes, food, guides and porters that the enemy were forced to withdraw.

During the withdrawal Tredrea with his native guerrillas attacked the column relentlessly at Buntoel, Long Boeloeh and Semoeloemowg, always leading the attacks in person.

On one occasion during these engagements he led seven natives armed with SMGs [sub-machine guns] in a direct attack on a Jap HMG [heavy machine gun] which was silenced and all six of the enemy killed at the post. At the end of June and July he operated with small forces against large odds to clear the enemy from the lower Segaja always leading attacks personally regardless of his own safety. At all times he has proved himself a fearless soldier and a gifted leader of men.

During Operation Semut 1 the four men in Harrison's team and their native fighters accounted for 1001 Japanese dead; Jack took just one prisoner.

'I sent him back to Harrison more or less as a joke. One of my boys took him back with a note for Bob Long and I said, "After you've got what you can out of him, take him into the jungle and lose him,"' Jack says. 'After the war I said to him one day, "Bob, what happened to that chap I sent back to you?" He said, "I took him out and handed him over as a POW."

'He said, "Jack, I couldn't take him out and shoot him, he used to cook our meals, clean our guns, cut my hair, he was too bloody valuable." Oh dear, there were some funny things that went on.'

Jack Tredrea stayed in the North Borneo jungle for seven months until the third week of October 1945, two months after the war had ended. He paid off 15 of his boys and the other 15 rowed him around the coast to Tarakan for the start of the long journey home to Australia.

The boys stayed the night on Tarakan and were fed and refreshed with a few bottles of beer before Jack paid them off. The commanding officer said he had been expecting him and that he had a 'priority 1' trip back to Australia.

Aircraft seats out of post-war Tarakan were scarce, so Jack went by Liberty ship to Morotai and the next day was on a plane bound for Brisbane.

After making his way to headquarters in Melbourne, he was debriefed and discharged and was finally on his way home to

Adelaide, to Edith and his young daughter, who had not yet met her dad.

He had left Australia weighing ten stone six (80 kilos) with a 17-inch (45 cm) neck and as fit as a mallee bull. He arrived back weighing just eight stone and barely able to walk, but carrying some wonderful souvenirs, including his blowpipe and parang knife. The war trophies occupy pride of place at the army museum at Keswick Barracks in Adelaide.

Jack returned to his tailor's job where he spent the next 50 years, including the last 28 as the owner of the business. He and Edith were married for 64 years. They raised two daughters, and Jack now has four grandchildren and nine great-grandchildren.

'I made suits for every South Australian governor from 1947 until my retirement, so I had a pretty good lucky life.'

Chapter 3

Behind Enemy Lines

Living hard was part and parcel of Fred Otway's life from a very early age. Little did he know as he struggled through a poverty-filled childhood that one day the hardships that had forged him would help to keep him alive in the jungles of East Timor and elsewhere as a commando and 'Z' Special Unit operative during the fight to save Australia from the marauding Japanese Imperial Army.

Fred's early years around Pinjarra in Western Australia were tough. The son of a drunkard railway-sleeper cutter and a sickly mother, he was born in 1920. By the time he was eight, he and his four brothers and one sister had been removed from their parents and sent to live in institutions in Perth after their mother contracted tuberculosis.

Fred, the second youngest, was sent to a Salvation Army Boys Home in the inner-city suburb of Nedlands. It was a grim existence and 92-year-old Fred recalls, with the clarity of someone who has known real hunger, being permanently famished and having cracked feet in winter because he had no shoes.

When he was 12 years old Fred remembers the wife of the manager coming down the path and blurting out, 'By the way, your mother has died.'

'Just like that,' he says.

Young Fred had never even had a letter from his mum and was never able to write to her to say hello, to tell her to get well and that he loved her.

'No kid in that home ever wrote a letter and no kid ever received a letter. They [the supervisors] got any letters that came and just told us, "Your father wrote to us",' he says. 'What a terrible thing it must have been for that woman to be in that house, or in that place, wherever it was. They separated us because it was a contagious disease, living there for eight years and no contact with her family, just waiting to die.'

At 14 Fred was sent to work on a poultry farm. He lasted six months, sleeping in the feed shed and eating in a corridor of the main house, never at the table of the farm owners.

One day he said, 'I'm sick of working my guts out for you, I'm going back to the home.' So he went back to Nedlands and they immediately sent him to another farm as virtual slave labour.

His second job was on a mixed farm where at least he was taught some skills, including harnessing and driving a team of eight horses. The sleeping arrangements were no better and he dossed down in a flea-ridden hessian bed as he toiled six days a week for the paltry sum of two shillings. The only reason he got Sundays off was so he could wash his clothes.

'There was no 40-hour week back then and you worked longer in summer than you did in winter.'

At 17 Fred was finally reunited with two of his brothers, Jack and Charlie, and the trio worked an unsuccessful mining lease together before they went travelling, jumping freight trains, with all their worldly goods, including the mandatory frying pan in a sugar bag, slung over their shoulders.

Eventually Charlie got a job on a dairy farm in Coolgardie and Fred snared a start as a general hand in a boarding house in Kalgoorlie for 'ten bob' a week and his tea.

His next job was as a barman in a pub at Leonora, where there was a nickel rush on. After returning for a brief stint in the mines, Fred eventually made his way back to Perth and enlisted in the army in May 1941.

Due to his bush upbringing and his ability to live off the land, he was transferred from the training camp at Northam north of Perth across to the 2/2nd Independent Company at Wilsons Promontory in Victoria. The British commandos ran a training camp there to teach fresh recruits the dark arts of commando warfare — from demolitions and hand-to-hand combat to guerrilla warfare and how to recruit and train the locals.

Fred says the 2/2nd was very different from any other unit in the Australian Army. He didn't like the rigid formality and spit-and-polish traditions of the 'big army', but he loved the informal approach of the commandos.

'In the 2/2nd you might be a captain, but you are just Bill or Tom, that's all, nothing else, just one of us, we were all the same. Each depended on the other, none of this bloody army stuff saluting, yes sir, none of that stuff,' he says. 'We were free and easy and the unit was allowed to do what it liked, it wasn't under the command of any battalion. We were under command of the brigades, but we did what we did ourselves. When you were on patrol, you made your own decisions.'

By late 1941 things were looking grim for Australia as Japan overran Asian nations at will. After the bombing of Pearl Harbor the authorities realised Timor would be a vital piece in the Japanese imperial puzzle as the knights of bushido moved resolutely down through the islands of South-East Asia towards what many saw as the main prize — Australia.

Fred and his mates were shipped out of their camp in Katherine, south of Darwin, on a cattle train and then on to Kupang in Dutch West Timor before the final leg into Dili in Portuguese East Timor in mid-December 1941.

The 350 or so Australian commandos joined other allied fighters from the 2/40th Battalion and British and Dutch units to form Sparrow Force, which would harass and occupy an entire Japanese division in Timor for a year.

Unfortunately the army's knowledge of tropical diseases was rudimentary at best, and the men, dressed in shorts and light shirts, succumbed en masse to malaria.

Just before the Japanese arrived in Timor in late February 1942, the commandos decided to leave Dili and head for a healthier environment in the hills to the south of the capital. The town is built on a narrow coastal strip and immediately behind the built-up area the mountains rise almost vertically to provide a natural barrier to the interior and the island's south coast.

The high ridges overlooking Dili made ideal observation posts for the diggers and their comrades, who included local fighters drafted to the cause. Visitors to Dili today can clearly see how vital the high ground was to the Aussie guerrillas of Sparrow Force by visiting the Commando Memorial at the village of Dare high above the town. The views from the memorial to the 2/2nd Company (double red diamond insignia),

WWII 'Z' Special Unit operative Jack Tredrea: (right) with friends during a top-secret mission behind Japanese lines in Borneo.

Jack Tredrea

(above right) Tredrea proudly wears his 'Z' Special Unit insignia at home in Adelaide.

James Elby

Former commando and 'Z' Special operative Roland Griffiths-Marsh looking dapper (above left) prior to Operation Semut 1 in Borneo, 1945, and (above right) not long before his death in December 2012. Griffiths-Marsh spent several months behind enemy lines in Borneo and returned home a shadow of his former self due to disease and malnutrition.
Roland Griffiths-Marsh

WWII Royal Air Force fighter pilot George Clissold (right) with his South African mate Ainsley Cook and another friend during a skiing trip to France in early 1945. Not long after Clissold was shot down and became a POW.
George Clissold

Members of the 2nd/2nd Independent Commando Company in East Timor, 1942. They spent more than a year living among the East Timorese people, harassing and spying on the Japanese invaders. Fred Otway

'Z' Special operative Sapper Mick Dennis (above) with his Mother and sister, gold-medal swimmer Clara Dennis. Mick Dennis (left) Dennis at the unveiling of an honour board at St George Leagues Club that features his comrade, Spencer Walklate, who was killed on Operation Copper.
Kristi Miller, News Limited

Fred Otway's tough childhood prepared him for the job of a secret soldier operating behind enemy lines during WWII.
Ian McPhedran

(right) Twenty-one-year-old Sergeant Douglas Herps and Lieutenant Henry Hollingsworth during parachute training for 'Z' Special Unit missions during WWII. Douglas Herps
(Below) Herps with his much treasured framed navy ensign — signed by many of his 'Z' Special mates — at his home in Sydney's Woollahra. John Feder

Former 'Z' Special Unit operative Norm Wallace with a Japanese flag signed by the Australians who were present for the Japanese surrender at Ranau on September 23, 1945. Ian McPhedran

Some tools of the trade used by 'Z' Special operatives during World War II. They include a native Parang knife, silenced Sten gun, magnetic limpet mine, Australian-designed stiletto dagger and a knuckle knife. One of the medals is a Distinguished Service Order belonging to Captain Robert Page, who was executed by the Japanese after the ill-fated Operation Rimau raid on Singapore Harbour. Roland Griffiths-Marsh

Fuzzy wuzzy sculpture at the Kokoda museum.
Ian McPhedran

Len 'Griffo' Griffiths and other veterans of the Kokoda campaign received a hero's welcome when they arrived in the village for the 70th anniversary celebrations in September 2012. Ian McPhedran

Commanding officer of Special Operations Command Australia, Major General Peter 'Gus' Gilmore pays his respects to 'Z' Special Unit operatives Private John Whitworth and Lieutenant Scobell McFerran-Rogers, who died during an operation behind enemy lines in Sulawesi in 1945. Their remains were identified after extensive research and their graves formally dedicated in September 2012. The Bomana war cemetery on the outskirts of Port Moresby in Papua New Guinea holds the remains of 3823 Commonwealth soldiers, including 700 that remain unidentified. Stephen Cooper

WWII 'Z' Special Unit veteran Henry Fawkes, and his daughter Janine, at the graves of his comrades. Ian McPhedran

2/40th Battalion (double blue diamonds) and their local helpers take in a panoroma of the coastline, the town and the roads leading up into the hills.

During the East Timor independence battles in 1999 the Dare area would once again take on crucial tactical significance as Australian troops moved inland in pursuit of pro-Jakarta militia thugs.

Following some alcohol-fuelled skylarking in the town prior to the Japanese invasion, the Australians had been banned from taking their rifles into Dili, and they only found out the enemy had arrived when a supply truck carrying 17 diggers was intercepted by a Japanese patrol. The men were all shot and bayonetted, and only one, Keith Hayes, escaped with his life. He was treated and sheltered by locals, including a middle-aged woman called Donnabella Martins, who nursed him back to health using mudpacks and banana leaves to heal his wounds.

The Australians eventually split into small bands of guerrilla fighters and would spend most of 1942 and 1943 killing and harassing the enemy across East Timor.

'You can do plenty of damage even if there is only four or five of you,' Fred says. 'As a guerrilla fighter there are certain rules to be observed and number one is you cannot exist without the support of the civilian population. You don't interfere with them, you don't interfere with their women, you don't interfere with their customs and if you want food, you pay for it, which the Japs didn't do.

'I had information about one native boy that was helping the Australians; they [the Japanese] wiped his whole little village out. That was how the Japs worked, trade on fear, "This is what will happen to you if you help the Australians, if you give food to the Australians."'

37

The threat of death or torture didn't deter most of the hardy and God-fearing East Timorese, who remained loyal to the Aussies throughout the war.

Respect for the locals and paying their way whenever possible were basic tenets of Australian special operations during the war. According to Fred Otway, every time the Australians killed a goat or got some rice, they gave the farmer a chit that he could later convert into silver or gold courtesy of the Australian Government. Unfortunately this system didn't always work and many Timorese were left out of pocket, but this did not stop them from risking their lives to support the commandos in their quest to rid the island of the invader.

Many veterans of Sparrow Force spent decades after the war fighting for justice for the East Timorese people in return for their vital help in the campaign to save Australia. In 1999 the Prime Minister, John Howard, provided the ultimate 'thank you' when he encouraged the Indonesians to leave the island and the international community to step in and to help bring independence to East Timor (Timor Leste).

During its year-long guerrilla campaign, Sparrow Force killed about 1700 Japanese troops and delayed Japan's eastwards advance. Fred Otway took to army life like a duck to water. Finally, at the age of 21, he had found a home.

After returning from Timor and with yet another serious bout of malaria under his belt, Fred was sent to New Guinea in June 1943 to chase and harass the Japanese again. From Port Moresby the men of the 2/2nd were flown up to a place called Bena Bena near Goroka in the Highlands where the Japanese were expected to try and take the airstrip in order to attack American bombers on their runs from Port Moresby to Wewak.

'Our task was to give the impression that we were 2000 strong rather than 200,' Fred says. They accomplished their mission and the Japanese force withdrew towards the north coast.

About this time he got word that his old commanding officer from Timor, Captain Dave Dexter, who had been seriously wounded in New Guinea and had joined 'Z' Special Unit in Melbourne, was looking for volunteers. Regarded as a fine officer, Dexter was well liked and trusted by the men, so in October 1944 Fred and eight of his mates from the unit decided to make the move.

After completing parachute and submarine training and learning how to operate a variety of boats, Fred Otway was sent back to Timor to train the locals and to observe the Japanese, who by then controlled the island.

'A lot of the natives were with us, some were against us, they'd be telling the Japs where we were, setting up the ambushes and so forth,' Fred says. 'The Australian Government decided that we would help Portuguese civilians to escape from the occupied island. I'll never forget how we were loading these nuns up and we were all naked, except for our boots. We weren't going to get our clothes wet so that once the boat had gone we could lay down in the wet soil but keep our clothes dry. We didn't mind wet boots.'

Some Portuguese didn't want to leave and they took the Japanese at their word that they would be placed in a secure enclave and looked after. Fred says it was nothing more than a concentration camp and many Portuguese, including five children, starved to death or succumbed to disease. Despite being from a neutral country, nine Portuguese soldiers were executed during his time there.

Looking back, Fred says he enjoyed being in East Timor because he regarded it as a civilised place when compared with New Guinea.

'I hated New Guinea. There wasn't even anyone to talk to, whereas in Timor you could talk to the locals, including the women,' Fred says. 'There were plenty of people there; it was really like being in Brisbane, only you'd have to go out and do a bit of fighting every now and then — simple.'

After the war, Fred Otway retrained as a painter and decorator, and in 1956 he moved to Brisbane where he settled with his family. A motorcycle accident put paid to his ambition to be a politician, so he spent the next 22 years working for the Queensland Government.

* * *

Norm Wallace turned 17 at about the same time as he was recruited into 'Z' Special Unit in early 1943. He had lied about his age when he joined the army at just 16.

Possibly the youngest person to ever join the nation's most covert military unit, Norm was a paratrooper and signaller when he was sent to the unit's new training base at Fraser Island in Queensland. He became friends with several of the operatives who conducted the unit's successful raid on Singapore Harbour under Operation Jaywick — using the *Krait*, a converted fishing boat — and Norm was chosen to go to Western Australia to prepare for the second Singapore raid, codenamed Operation Rimau, using so-called 'Sleeping Beauty' motorised submersible canoes. The one-man vessels were designed to allow a lone frogman to enter an enemy harbour to attack shipping and then return to the mother ship.

The Sleeping Beauty measured about four metres long and 75 centimetres across and was built from mild steel. It was powered by a five-horsepower electric motor run off four six-volt batteries. Many operators likened the experience of piloting one of the vessels to riding a torpedo. The mini-subs had a top speed of just 4.4 knots and could dive to a depth of 15 metres, with a range of about 60 kilometres. The operator controlled the craft using a joystick connected to a rudder and hydroplanes. He wore a dry suit and breathed using a re-breathing device. To get his bearings the operator would need to come close to the surface.

Fortunately, like the Sleeping Beauties, Norm never made it to Singapore Harbour. 'It turned out there were a lot of people training for that particular op, and I along with a number of others didn't go on the op,' Norm says. 'I cut my finger on coral, got a poison finger out of it, upset a bit of the scheduling, that's what happened. Most of us didn't go on that op which as it turned out was a bit favourable.'

The submersibles were sent to the bottom of the sea when a Japanese patrol boat compromised the mission. Ten of the operatives were captured and beheaded by the Japanese and the remaining 13 were killed in action. Rimau was an unmitigated disaster.

'Z' Special was undergoing all sorts of training in preparation for whatever roles the powers that be might throw at them. Then, as now, the special forces brought highly specialised skill sets and remarkable motivation and training to the command table.

In Norm Wallace's case the focus was on underground operations and how to exist in a cave system while using the caves as a base. 'We were going up [to New Guinea] to live in caves and descend upon the Japs from there, or to observe from a safe place to be in, whatever was required, so we did that at those caves outside Rockhampton, which I believe now are a bit of a tourist resort, and you had to do various types of tests to find out if you were claustrophobic,' he recalls.

The training included learning how to wriggle through holes in the underground system without knowing where they would lead.

'You certainly got tested in those situations,' he says.

There was also training in advanced unarmed combat and lessons in Malay and Pidgin English. 'They even imported a number of New Guinea locals down to train with us.'

Soon the anticipation turned to disappointment as rumour after rumour about a big 'job' was met with stony silence and more training. Thanks to advances in aircraft design and munitions many of the demolition tasks once undertaken by 'Z' operatives were by then being done by aircraft.

But one job that could never be left to the aircraft was rescuing people. In August 1945 Norm and his crew got the call to travel to Borneo in search of survivors from the Sandakan prison camp and death march.

Just six of the 1787 Australians imprisoned survived the ordeal. They were Warrant Officer Bill Sticpewich, Private Keith Boterill, Lance Bombardier William Moxham, Bombardier Dick Braithwaite, Private Nelson Short and Gunner Owen Campbell. Braithwaite and Campbell escaped before the other four were picked up by an allied patrol.

The remainder of the Australians and 641 British troops were murdered by their Japanese captors or succumbed to disease. About 1260 Australians perished on the brutal death marches from Sandakan camp to Ranau.

By the end of July 1945, just before Wallace and his mates arrived in Borneo, only 38 Australians remained alive. These men were summarily executed days before the war ended on August 15.

Norm's commanding officer had landed by submarine several days before him and the rest parachuted in to search for survivors. After they found the first two Australian ex-POWs it was clear they would be lucky to find many more. Ultimately four others were recovered and were flown out on a RAAF Auster aircraft from a tiny airstrip cut out of the scrub.

The operatives were horrified by the stories of murder and wanton cruelty inflicted by the Japanese jailers and especially by the fact that prisoners had been executed just days before the surrender. The men also came across pockets of pitiful enemy troops on the verge of starvation. Tempted as they were, the Australians never committed a single atrocity against their murderous foes.

'We realised we could have killed the ones we found in various stages of dying and so on, because we searched everywhere and you'd find a pocket of Japanese here, half dead and so on, but we reckon if we did that, we'd be as bloody low as them, so we did not do anything like that whatsoever,' Norm says. 'We searched the Japanese and their camps for stuff belonging to POWs.'

Once the four prisoners were evacuated, Norm and his mates were told they would not be flown out and would have to hike for several days through the jungle to a larger airfield.

During their hike they encountered hundreds of Japanese troops fleeing to the coast. Having heard the stories from the Aussie POWs, the Australians understandably felt no great fondness for them, but they gained some insight into their strange thinking and ritual cruelty. In one instance a group of Japanese soldiers came down the track, and the operatives removed all their bullets but left them their weapons so they could at least bluff their way past the bloodthirsty native headhunters, who were not so merciful.

'They got down along the road and one of their blokes, they weren't in good condition either, one of their blokes collapses,' Norm says. 'So the officer in charge goes up and sticks the boot into him to try and get him up on his feet. He doesn't get up, so the officer just takes his gear off and leaves him there. They carry on and are laughing and joking with each other and they just left him there to bloody die.'

Norm Wallace was so disgusted by what he saw as the cover-up of the atrocities committed at Sandakan and on the death marches that he didn't even collect his own war medals until well into the 1990s.

'It was kept quiet, when we came back, because we were not supposed to speak about anything. To a certain extent we spoke a bit. I used to tell people … as to what had happened at Ranau [but] people just turned off. There were a lot of stories told about the war, I was just another soldier loud mouthing about something or other, so nobody was listening.

'After the war, I'm speaking about '46, '47, we were well into the stages of being nice to the Japanese, we had to make sure the Japanese didn't go towards the Russians, we had to be nice to them. Didn't know we executed some of their war criminals. The reality of what occurred, I think, was deliberately suppressed from the Australian people.'

* * *

For Douglas Herps, the life of a 'Z' Special operative was a mixture of fear and the downright bizarre. The Alstonville, NSW local was the youngest of three sons of Western Front veteran John Herps and his wife Sophia to go to war.

Speaking in the living room of his comfortable home in Woollahra in Sydney's eastern suburbs, beneath an Australian ensign covered in the signatures of 'Z' Special men, he recalls the day he was recruited.

It was one fine day in 1941. A physical fitness, unarmed combat and weapons trainer, he was working at the Jungle Training Centre at Canungra near Brisbane when Captain Luke McQuinn, wearing a 6th Division transport patch, turned up out of the blue and asked him if he would be interested in joining a special unit.

'Bear in mind we are on six shillings a day and I didn't have any money at all, every penny I got from my army pay was going to my mother, I was giving her the maximum,' he says.

Captain McQuinn told Douglas he would be eligible for an extra four shillings a day once he was parachute qualified. If he went into action he would get another 12 shillings a day danger money.

'I thought, "I'll be in that!" And so to be honest, that's why I went into it — for the money,' he says. 'He told me to go up and get my bag and meet him in 20 minutes, so I did.'

More than half a century later, Douglas received a phone call from one of his old Canungra mates who told him everyone there had thought he was absent without leave because no one said where he had gone.

From Brisbane he travelled north to Fraser Island where a top-secret training camp known as Fraser Commando School had been established for 'Z' Special Unit. It was part of the Services Reconnaissance Department of Special Operations Australia — the dirty-tricks department of the Allied Intelligence Bureau.

Fraser Island was no ordinary army training camp. Among other traditional skills such as weapons handling, Douglas was taught how to ride a horse, and pack and handle a pack horse, given Malay language classes, and trained in explosives and advanced unarmed combat skills.

The operatives were schooled in how to navigate and handle the folboats, used to insert troops from submarines, and the fast patrol boats known as snake boats. They were also taught how to recognise enemy ship types from their silhouettes and aircraft from their shape and sound. 'Z' worked closely with another clandestine organisation called 'M' Special Unit that included the coastwatchers, who lived behind enemy lines for months on end and reported on ship and aircraft movements. Just like modern-day SAS troopers, they also learned how to parachute, at the Richmond RAAF base near Sydney.

During their folboat training, Douglas and his mates were sent about 20 kilometres up the Mary River, near Maryborough, to simulate a night attack on a shipyard. 'I can recall getting ashore, mud almost up to our hips and we went into this shipbuilding place and we laid dummy charges all around,' he says. 'When the people turned up to go to work the next day they suddenly saw these charges and they ran out of the shipyard.'

The realistic nature of their training meant that even the local police were kept in the dark until after the event.

More than 1000 soldiers passed through the Fraser Island facility but only about 330 operatives ever went behind enemy lines on operations. Douglas Herps was forbidden from telling anyone, even his mother, what he was doing. He still recalls her bursting into tears when he turned up for his brother's wedding, a highly trained 21-year-old elite soldier, with his sergeant's stripes and parachute wings on display.

'She thought I was safe, the young one was safe, she wondered what the hell I was doing. When she wrote to me, she used to write to SRD — Services Reconnaissance Department. It was a post office address in Melbourne.'

The department also ran a 'research station' at Mount Martha on the Mornington Peninsula. 'They had all sorts of odd bods down there, and I can recall sitting down talking to a fellow who was from J Arthur Rank, the film studio. He'd been sent out from England and his job was to make false documents. I was staggered to find this out,' Douglas says.

The demand for fake documents was not as great in Australia as it was in Britain, where male and female agents from the Special Operations Executive were being parachuted into France and elsewhere all the time, so the document artist ended up spending a lot of his time on the beach sketching seascapes.

Other departments at Mount Martha conducted all sorts of weird and wonderful experiments, and on one occasion some of the lads got hold of a special dog fragrance that was being tested. During a party one night they smeared the scent, supposed to simulate a bitch on heat, all over an officer's car and found it really worked. Every dog from miles around was trying to hump the car.

The security net around 'Z' Special was so tight that when Douglas came down with severe tonsillitis on the eve of a parachute mission, he was provided with an armed guard and sent to Melbourne by train.

'The fellow stayed with me until I was put in hospital in Melbourne,' he says. 'It seems strange that I went to Melbourne and that's how I went back to training at Mount Martha [with an armed guard], because I knew all about the operation. I never gave it much thought at the time but that was the way "Z" operated.'

As it turned out, the tonsillitis saved his life, as the plane carrying the men on the secret mission crashed on Labuan Island off the coast of Borneo, killing all on board.

After the war Douglas travelled to Labuan to pay his respects. 'I thought, "That's where I should be" — there was the seat number. It was strange looking at the graves, because I've still got my tonsils.'

Finally the time came for Douglas to undertake his first mission behind enemy lines under Operation Agus 5. On this six- to seven-week job in Borneo, the objective was to befriend and recruit the locals and to report on enemy troop movements as the war drew to a close.

Douglas was dropped off the coast of Borneo by a navy snake boat with two other 'Z' Special operatives in August 1945. A sailor on the boat handed him the Australian navy flag and said, 'Give 'em heaps, Herpsie.'

'He was looking at me as if to say, "You poor bastard".'

A healthy stash of gold sovereigns helped the 'hearts and minds' operation immensely. The Japanese handed out paper money that meant nothing to the locals. Every 'Z' Special operation included as many gold sovereigns as the men could carry.

'The gold sovereigns were worth about seven pounds each,' he says. 'I remember we went to the locals and asked them for some food, did they have any food? They were starving too, of course, but they had chickens. I did a deal with one woman who I asked to sell me some chickens. I said, "When we need them I'll come and get them." I don't think we ever got a chicken but she got the money anyhow.'

He says people think you are a hero for operating behind enemy lines, but he freely admits he was scared stiff every waking moment. 'You don't know where the enemy is coming from'.

Every member of 'Z' Special was ordered to operate without rank or any insignia that would identify them as Australian special operators. If captured by the Japanese they all knew they were supposed to swallow their cyanide pills.

He also knew many of the captured 'Z' operatives had been offered up by locals. 'If the locals knew we were there, then we had to assume that the Japs also knew.'

The natives built a thatched sleeping hut for the Australians, but they never used it and always slept outside. 'I slept in the jungle because we'd been taught if you were given ten seconds start you had a chance to get away,' Douglas says.

At one point they thought it would be a good idea to get a cook so they went into a village and kidnapped a local cook. 'We sneaked in and grabbed him and he was screaming the place down because it turned out he wanted his wife to come too. When we got him back we found out he was a pastry cook; he did our cooking for us. People were wonderful to us, that's how we survived.'

Douglas was also fortunate to have a soldier called Frank 'Shagger' Haley as his signaller. Years after the war his widow Clare called Douglas to ask him what her husband's nickname or callsign had been.

So he said, 'Oh, Frank, of course.'

But she said 'No, no, it wasn't Frank.'

'Well then, "Signalman".'

'No no,' she said. 'Go on, you can talk to me.'

Douglas says, 'Keep in mind she is in her late 70s, living with her sister who was a nun and they are in a Catholic nursing home, and she said, "What did you used to call him?"'

He finally said, 'We used to call him Shagger.'

'I thought that's what it was,' she said. 'Do you know we had 11 children?'

Just like the modern-day special forces troops, 'Z' operatives carried unusual or non-standard issue weapons including Colt 45 pistols, carbines, Bren guns and an American-made dagger. They didn't look like other soldiers and often wore long paratrooper-type boots. They were often inserted by parachute or by submarine, snake boat or flying boat. In many instances during operations the men adopted the clothing and weapons used by the local people, including the parang and the blowpipe in Borneo.

Going native is an integral part of guerrilla warfare and living with and like the locals is a key element of a successful guerrilla campaign.

On a jungle track during Operation Agus 5, Douglas came face to face with an enemy soldier he describes as 'the biggest Jap I have ever seen', who slashed his leg with a dagger. The soldier might have been a Korean, as they were bigger and stronger than their Japanese colleagues. Either way, the incident left Douglas with a serious leg wound.

Contact with the enemy was not what the mission was essentially about, but despite their best efforts to avoid the Japanese, as the war came to an end they were forced to deal with plenty of surrendering enemy troops. They included a large boatload of about 40 who gave themselves up to Douglas and his two mates.

'I gave them a blast of the Bren gun over their heads, because if they had known we were only three men we didn't know what they might do,' he says. Just a few days later the team was picked up by flying boat and soon after were back home in post-war Australia.

Fast-forward to 2013 and Douglas Herps — just shy of his 90th birthday — is still fighting. For years he has been trying to preserve the *Krait* as a permanent memorial to the men of Operation Jaywick, many of whom were his mates, and to the 'Z' Special Unit more generally. The vessel belongs to the Australian War Memorial but is on permanent display at the National Maritime Museum in Darling Harbour, Sydney.

Douglas believes — and he has strong data to support his claim — that the vessel will eventually rot in the water. He wants it moved to dry land and displayed in a purpose-built museum that could also house a collection of other 'Z' Special equipment such as folboats, specialised weapons and vehicles, and other unusual and interesting gear used by the secret soldiers.

He found a strong ally in the director of the Australian War Memorial, Dr Brendan Nelson, who vowed to lobby the NSW Government to find a site to display the *Krait* and other items that are kept in the memorial's vast storage facilities.

Chapter 4

The Stoic

Corporal Roland Griffiths-Marsh could scarcely believe his eyes when he first witnessed native fighters in Borneo practising the bloodthirsty traditions of their headhunting ancestors.

He had parachuted into central Borneo in June 1945 with a team of fellow 'Z' Special Unit operatives under an operation called Semut 2, to gather intelligence and harass the enemy ahead of an invasion by the 9th Division.

Headhunting, long outlawed in the wild jungle, had well and truly made a comeback in Borneo by mid-1945 thanks to the deeds of the secret Australian soldiers from 'Z' Special Unit. They placed a bounty on every Japanese head taken and were constantly amazed by the plentiful but gory harvest.

For Roland Griffiths-Marsh, who had fought for four years as an infantryman with the 2/8th Battalion through campaigns in Libya, Greece and Crete, the savagery displayed by the wild men of Borneo came as a shock and the nightmares never really faded.

He emerged from the jungle five months later a wounded skeleton of a man, struck down with amoebic dysentery that almost killed him. He had trained a native force and learned their customs and traditions, and even carried his own blowpipe and poisoned darts that he would eventually donate to the Australian War Memorial.

Griffiths–Marsh spent his final years in quiet retirement on Bribie Island with his wife Helen in a small bungalow in a street set well away from the tourist buzz along the foreshore. Bribie Island, between Brisbane and Noosa Heads in Queensland, is a very popular retirement destination. In fact the entire southern Queensland coast from Coolangatta to Bundaberg is a mecca for retirees from around the nation, many of whom are former military personnel.

His soldier's bearing remained strong in 2011 despite his ailing health and his 88 years. This was a man to be reckoned with. Showing that the fire still burned in the belly of this former tough soldier, he was campaigning passionately to have the insultingly low two-dollars-a-fortnight 'decoration allowance' — a medal winner's bonus to the veteran's pension — brought up to date.

When he received his Military Medal in 1949 the allowance had been five shillings and sixpence a fortnight, when the average wage was 40 shillings a fortnight – a ratio of eight to one.

Today the two dollars-a-fortnight allowance yields just $52 a year when the average wage is more than $1000 a fortnight – a ratio of 500 to 1. This compares to a decoration allowance of $2000 a year for a Victoria Cross winner. Griffiths–Marsh said the allowance had been frozen for more than 40 years and was nothing more than a bad joke.

'Even prisoners in jail have had their allowances adjusted up seven times since then,' he said. 'To me it seems so unconscionable, perhaps I have a different code.'

His wartime exploits demonstrate a code of courage and honour he believes was instilled in him at a very early age. His mother was born in Haiphong in Vietnam's Red River delta, the daughter of a French colonial administrator, and his father was a New Zealand-born sea captain. The fourth of eight children, Roland was born in Penang, Malaysia on April 22, 1923.

When he joined the Australian Army in 1939 he was just 16 years old. He used his brother's name and lied about his age to enlist in the infantry. After fighting in the Middle East and across the battlefields of the Mediterranean, he found himself in the top-secret 'Z' Special Unit.

His survival and soldiering skills, combined with his upbringing in Indo-China and his proficiency in Malay and French, made him an ideal candidate.

Griffiths-Marsh was finally presented with his Military Medal for 'bravery and devotion to duty in Central Borneo' by the Governor-General Sir William McKell in Melbourne on March 3, 1949.

His citation reads:

Cpl Griffiths parachuted into Central Borneo to join a Services Reconnaissance Party on the ground in early June 1945. He was at once sent to the Padas River sector and thence to Sipidang and Sindumin where with enterprise and skill he quickly formed a small guerrilla force to harass the Japs escaping through the area. He showed a quick grasp of native mentality and a real ability to lead native troops and in a very short time he produced good results. In this area he killed 34 Japanese and captured four. In August he took charge of blocking the track from Sapong estate west to Mahaman, in conjunction with 9th Australian Division, which he carried out with marked success killing a further four Japs and capturing valuable intelligence reports and maps. During these operations Griffiths lived wholly on native food and covered large distances on foot through dangerous country. At all times his bearing and conduct were of a very high standard.

The understated language of the award citation barely does justice to the hardship and dangers faced by the men of Operation Semut in the hostile, disease-ridden jungles of Borneo. Very few of the 'Z' Special operators were wounded by enemy action, but most suffered terribly from disease. Griffiths-Marsh returned home a broken man thanks to his terrible bout of amoebic dysentery, not to mention the invisible mental wounds suffered by many soldiers.

'In my day there was no such thing as post traumatic stress disorder, yet I was unemployable for about five years after the war,' he said. 'I used to be very irritable, very angry; I would knock a fellow down if he looked at me sideways, you know. Fortunately they have much greater remedial techniques now than in my day. I paid for my own medication, I was told I was cured, I spent three months in hospital with amoebic dysentery.'

The mental terror stayed with him for the rest of his life. In his mid-80s, Roland had a major breakdown and was admitted to the Keith Payne mental health unit in Brisbane.

'They recognised the symptoms straight away and I became sane again,' he said.

During his time with 'Z' he also suffered the added tension of a strained relationship with his commanding officer, Major Tom Harrison. The pair disliked each other immensely, so Roland was often sent out on missions alone during Operation Semut rather than in the usual two-man team.

'He was obviously going to get me killed and he was the most incompetent commanding officer I have ever seen.'

Their animosity could be traced back to a training exercise through the High Country of eastern Victoria, a three-day hike to test new equipment. At the end they arrived at a pub where Roland charmed an attractive lass who had also caught Harrison's drunken eye. Later that night Harrison knocked on her door and was humiliated when Roland opened it and told him to get lost. From that day onwards, Roland claimed, Harrison tried to make his life a misery.

Griffiths-Marsh summed up valour as 'the courage to cope with great adversity'. He believed that a good upbringing and a well-developed sense of responsibility were essential foundations for a person who would go on to perform acts of bravery.

Despite the extreme risks he and others had faced during Operation Semut he didn't regard operating behind enemy lines for months on end with a band of native fighters, whom he had trained, as being particularly courageous.

To him, 'bravery' was a word that should be used only very rarely. He said he had seen a person jump into a fast-flowing river to rescue a child and had read about men fighting off man-eating sharks to save strangers. 'That is brave.'

One of the bravest things he witnessed occurred during the Libyan campaign in North Africa. His unit was pinned down by German machine-gun fire and was sustaining serious casualties. A stretcher-bearer was shot and killed as he tried to rescue a wounded man, so Roland's mate, Jock Murray, raced to the wounded soldier's aid and knowingly exposed himself to the enemy's machine guns.

'Jock Murray just knelt down beside the injured man and attended to his wounds. He knew he was under heavy machine-gun fire and most of us were getting wounded and so on, but he deliberately, instead of cowering in the ground, in a hole in the ground, or what have you, he did this deliberately,' Roland said. 'He knew he would be a target but he acted regardless.'

Nothing in Murray's personality or demeanour leading up to the battle had provided any indication that he would act so selflessly, he explained. 'You would be surprised how the most unlikely of men turn out to be brave men, courageous men.' In his view, courage had more to do with having a sense of obligation instilled in you as you grew up.

Of his own childhood and the time he spent on his father's ship on the Singapore run, he said, 'I was brought up on a diet of Greek. My father was a keen historian and his library on board the ship was full of Greek mythology. I remember the story of a Spartan boy who took a baby fox to school, put it in his gown, and the baby fox started to eat his stomach. Spartan kids were taught to be very hardy, and without a murmur he didn't interfere, didn't interrupt the class or anything and he died. Stoicism is the word I'm looking for, stoicism, so I was brought up that way.'

That is what motivated him to join 'Z' Special Unit where the chances of surviving its high-risk operations were not always very high.

'I was told, "There is a good chance of not coming back," but I was an experienced soldier and we didn't know the atomic bomb was over the horizon. We thought the war would go on for a couple more years,' he said. 'We thought the Japanese were going to invade Australia so I attribute my actions to a combination of stoicism and upbringing and a sense of responsibility. If that is bravery, well that's bravery.'

But he was also concerned that the military awards system had become politicised.

'Either our soldiers are getting braver or our politicians are getting canny, because there is no question at all a Victoria Cross is a political armament of the politician,' he observed in 2012.

Roland Griffiths-Marsh passed away peacefully, his family and friends by his side, on 29 December 2012.

BAPTISMS OF FIRE

Chapter 1

Over the Rhine: Typhoon to P.O.W.

George Clissold barely even saw the German jet aircraft as it streaked past the flight of Royal Air Force Typhoon fighters.

It was 1944 and the 19-year-old Australian fighter pilot from Kempsey in NSW was serving with the RAF at Volkel airbase near Eindhoven in eastern Holland, flying Typhoon fighter-bombers on ground attack missions on the German side of the Rhine River.

His flight was cruising along at a comfortable 300 miles (480 kilometres) an hour near the Dutch–German border when a jet-powered Nazi aircraft literally shot past them as if they had been standing still.

'I thought to myself, "What in hell! There is not much hope for us if too many of these things are produced,"' Clissold says.

If controversial British Bomber Command supremo 'Bomber' Harris had not knocked out the jet production facilities as part of his merciless bombing blitz of enemy cities, Clissold says Germany would almost certainly have won the war.

In late June 1944 George Clissold's 245 Squadron moved from Britain to the continent in support of the allied eastern advance towards the Rhine River and the German homeland beyond. On June 5, 1944, the day before the D-Day landings, the squadron was engaged in a successful attack on the Joburg radar station near Cap de la Hague, Normandy, and on June 10 it joined an attack on the headquarters of Panzer Group West, in which the group's chief of staff, General von Dawans, was killed.

From Normandy the squadron moved north-east towards Holland and eventually took up residence at Volkel where its role was to attack German ground forces, especially tanks and armoured fighting vehicles, along the nearby Rhine.

By September 1944, the Allies were desperate for a breakthrough to shorten the war and even finish it by the year's end. The supreme allied commander, American General Dwight D. Eisenhower, was keen to pursue the retreating Germans all the way to Berlin. British commander Field Marshal Bernard Montgomery wanted first to take out the enemy's industrial heartland in the Ruhr and to stop the growing number of V-2 rocket attacks on London.

Operation Market Garden was conceived to satisfy the aims of both senior allied commanders. It would take 41,600 airborne troops, one armoured division, two infantry divisions and an armoured brigade to capture several bridges over the Rhine before the final push into the Ruhr and on to Berlin.

Also involving British and American gliders carrying troops, weapons, equipment and stores, it would be the largest airborne operation in history up to that time. But it failed and the war extended into a sixth year; Germany was on the ropes but not down for the count.

By March 1945, the allied advance was accelerating and George Clissold and 245 Squadron found themselves flying missions in support of Operation Plunder, the allied crossing of the Rhine, which began on March 23.

Just two days later Clissold's Typhoon was hit by ground fire and the young Australian pilot scrambled to jump free of the burning aircraft.

The war-torn plains of Western Europe were a long way from his carefree bush childhood at Kempsey and his grandmother's house at Rockdale in Sydney where, as a lad, he used to sit on the balcony with binoculars to watch the planes landing and taking off at nearby Mascot aerodrome and dream of flying.

At 18 he joined the Royal Australian Air Force and after initial training at Tamworth and Wagga he received his wings. He was sent to England with 30 other newly minted pilots on board the 28,000-tonne cargo ship *Dominion Monarch*.

He spent an enjoyable final leave at home in Kempsey with his family and his sweetheart, Eugenie, before boarding for the long voyage to Liverpool via New Zealand and Panama. The air force boys had the job of manning the Oerlikon 20 mm anti-aircraft guns on the ship's upper deck, and after Panama that meant shifts of four hours on and four off all the way across the Atlantic.

Young Clissold's favourite snack on the ship was cheese on toast — many a dogwatch shift was cheered by the warming glow of hot melted cheese on toasted bread. But by the time they arrived in Liverpool the flyboys were keen to sample the local fare so they piled in to the best restaurant they could find.

'I saw Welsh rarebit on the menu and I thought it was bloody rabbit and I said, "That's for me," and I ended up with a plate coming out with bloody cheese on toast again,' he says with a laugh. 'And that was my arrival in England.'

The war was in full swing and George and his fellow pilots were dismayed to find that in 1942 there were more pilots in England than aircraft. After two months travelling around southern England he was posted to Cambridge to keep his hand in by flying de Havilland 82s for a month.

Then it was on to Ternhill flying Miles Masters and Avro Ansons before being posted to Grangemouth near Falkirk in Scotland to begin operational training on the legendary Spitfire. By now used to the setbacks of military life, George Clissold was transferred to a satellite base called Balado Bridge to fly Lysanders and Martinets, towing target drones for the Spitfire pilots to shoot at.

During this time he logged 300 flying hours and was promoted to pilot officer before being sent to 59 Operational Training Unit at Milfield in Northumberland to convert onto Hurricane fighters.

After stints at several bases to convert to Typhoon ground attack fighter-bombers he was finally posted to 245 Squadron for the 'real thing' and sent to the south of England to learn the art of low-level ground attack flying and hitting targets with the fighter's arsenal of rockets and bombs.

The Typhoon began life as a long-range high-altitude interceptor to replace the nimble Hurricane, but its design made it better suited to low-level ground attack missions. It would become the most successful ground attack aircraft of the war.

'We weren't allowed to fly any higher than the spire on the Salisbury cathedral and as you can imagine the Typhoon going over at ground level, virtually, what that did to all the land girls driving horses around,' he says. 'We thought it was a laugh but it wasn't, and the English people during this period were fantastic to me.'

He watched the D–Day crossing from the cockpit of a P–40 Tomahawk fighter. 'The water was white with all the ships going on D-Day to France,' he recalls.

George finally joined the squadron at Volkel in Holland. By good fortune he was back in England having aircraft serviced when the base was attacked and badly shot up by German aircraft.

It wasn't all fear and loathing during the squadron's stay at Volkel, where they lived in a Catholic college and were looked after by local nuns. At one point George and a few mates, including his lifelong pal, Ainslie Cook from South Africa, flew down to the French Alps for a fortnight of skiing below Mont Blanc.

By early March things were heating up as the allies prepared to launch their final major offensives across the Rhine. On March 25, 1945, Clissold and his comrades took off for a regular mission under Operations Plunder and Varsity, the allied advance across the great river, which included paratroopers and heavy weapons landed on large gliders. Many gliders were destroyed as they came down in wooded areas or ran into trees or fences, killing many on board.

The squadron had been attacking tanks and half-tracks on the German side of the river the day after the operation began when Clissold's Typhoon was hit by ground fire.

The engine had taken a round and was on fire so he had no choice but to bail out as the flames licked the cockpit and singed his face. The flight lead, his South African mate Cook, was yelling down the radio, 'Get out Cliss, get out.'

He didn't have to be told too many times, but bailing out of a Typhoon is not a simple matter. Many a pilot had broken his back trying to escape using conventional methods. The trick was to jettison the cockpit hood, stand on the seat, pull back on the stick, undo harnesses and wires, and then place the plane into a steep dive to be virtually thrown out of the cockpit and clear of the machine.

'It was one of the most beautiful sensations I could ever have, floating down, but they were shooting at me all the way down,' he says. 'I didn't get hit, although I landed a bit roughly and damaged my knee.'

He hid in a drain, but was eventually captured by four German soldiers who were more interested in the workings of his service pistol than in him.

'I was very pleased when the ammunition ran out,' he says.

Pilot Officer Clissold was taken to a nearby camp where he was treated for facial burns and interrogated before being moved to a railway station to be transferred to the Prisoner of War camp Stalag XI-B at Fallingbostel in Lower Saxony, east of Bremen and north of Hanover.

As he stood on the platform beside carriages marked 'Eight horses or 50 men', he noticed a flight of Typhoons, ironically from his own 245 Squadron, preparing to attack the train.

'I looked up into the sky and there were six Typhoons circling above ready to come down on the train, because trains were one of the main targets for us, and at that stage I left the group being put into the train and got under the platform of the station,' he says.

George later emerged to a scene of utter carnage, with dead Germans and POWs littering the platform area.

Eventually the surviving prisoners were loaded onto another train and arrived at Fallingbostel where they stayed for a month with thousands of other allied prisoners from the Rhine campaign and earlier battles in Crete and Greece.

A month or so later they were informed that the camp would close before the advancing allied armies arrived and about 2000

POWs would have to march south-west to the city of Cologne, about 350 kilometres away.

After a few days and a number of attacks from the air, George's injured knee was acting up and he and a mate decided they would take their leave from the group and make their own travel arrangements.

'You have a comfort stop when you are being marched, so we went behind one of the largest trees we could find, an Englishman and myself, and we had a few biscuits and things. We had to carry a bit of newspaper as if we were going to the toilet and we went to the furthest tree and just stayed there actually, and the troops moved off and left us,' he says. 'We headed in a different direction and came to a forest and we were sleeping under the pine needles one morning when two men came. They'd seen our boots sticking out of the pine needles apparently, because we slept near the edge of the forest. I thought we would be shot for sure, being escaped prisoners. But they turned out to be two young Polish farm labourers who were quite sympathetic to us and said in sign language, "Stay there until it is dark and we will take you down to stay in the attic of our house," and this occurred and they gave us a bit of potato and a bit of milk.'

The pair remained there for several weeks until advancing British forces were told two British officers were hiding in the house. A tank was dispatched and the very relieved pilots were taken back to British headquarters and eventually released to their former units, but not before being treated to a festive feast by their hosts.

'They gave us plum pudding and some of the richest food you've ever seen and we'd had next to nothing, so I was as crook as Rookwood, couldn't keep anything down,' he says.

Eventually George returned to his squadron but was barred from further operational flying in case he was taken prisoner again.

He would be at grave risk of being shot for having previously escaped.

He was back in London for VE (Victory in Europe) Day on May 8, 1945. With another fellow from Kempsey whom he had met the previous day, he was sitting on the Queen Victoria statue outside Buckingham Palace when the royal family emerged from the balcony to wave to the joyous crowd.

The homewards journey mirrored the cruise over in late 1942, back through the Panama Canal to Wellington in New Zealand and on to Sydney Harbour. As the ship sailed up the harbour, Eugenie, the love of his life with whom he'd walked home from school in Kempsey and who was in the Women's Land Army, was standing on Middle Head waving a towel.

'She was in signals, so she was able to pick up the time I was arriving back easily,' he says.

They were reunited that evening and spent the next 64 years happily married, including 52 years living in the home they built at Peakhurst in southern Sydney.

Chapter 2

Kokoda: Guns to Garlands

Len Griffiths stood proud and tall as he marched into the village of Kokoda in New Guinea almost 70 years to the day since he first set foot there during World War II.

Instead of Japanese machine-gun and sniper fire, Len and his mates from the Kokoda 70th anniversary veterans' tour were welcomed on November 2, 2012, by bands of local people in native dress singing and dancing for their honoured guests. The ecstatic welcome was a far cry from the fight to the death they had endured on the Kokoda Track in 1942.

'Griffo', as he is known to his legion of mates and acquaintances, was as bright-eyed and bushy-tailed as any 90-year-old has the right to be as he marched, ramrod straight, on to the steamy Kokoda village oval with garlands of flowers around his neck, an Akubra on his head and the inappropriate 'non-tropical' dark government-supplied suit barely generating a sweat despite the brutal humidity.

Kokoda veterans are made of tough stuff.

As he shook hands with local children and revelled in his rock star welcome, Len was thrilled to meet two 90-year-old Papuans, Francis Simeni and Dickson Hango, who had served on the track as 'fuzzy wuzzy angels'. They were porters who had hauled supplies to the diggers and carried wounded soldiers out of the battle zone that most who fought there describe as a 'bastard of a place'. The angels saved countless lives and are regarded as just that — angels — by the men who fought on the track.

'They did a magnificent job, there is no question about it,' says Griffiths. 'We couldn't have done the same things ourselves, no way. No shoes, no boots, they were bare footed, see their shoulders up here are raw, the skin is all worn off. They did a magnificent job but so did the Australians.'

Like most diggers who fought in the New Guinea campaign, Len Griffiths is in no doubt that Japan intended to invade and occupy northern Australia and that victory in New Guinea would have provided an irresistible springboard to achieve that aim. Based on evidence found in archives in Tokyo, Australian academics and historians, such as the eminent Professor David Horner, have argued that the enemy never planned to invade Australia and too much importance is placed on the Kokoda campaign.

But the soldiers who stopped the Japanese advance, captured their special 'Australian' currency, and found the written plans on enemy corpses, confirming their worst fears, won't have a bar of it.

They are men such as Bede Tongs, who won his Military Medal by taking out a machine gun at Templeton's Crossing. Tongs was also in Kokoda to mark the 70th anniversary. He said the only reason Japan didn't invade was because she was defeated.

'We knew damn well that Australia was in dire straits,' Tongs said. 'We knew the Japanese would continue on to invade Australia like the Germans intended to invade wherever they went. It was natural for us because when the war started against Japan, Australia was a jewel in the crown. Those who don't believe it should stand in the middle of Bomana Cemetery and tell those blokes.'

And so it was to rousing applause from the veterans that Minister for Defence Materiel Jason Clare told the audience at Kokoda, 'The men who died here were fighting to defend their homes, their families and their country.'

The Bomana War Cemetery, on the outskirts of Port Moresby, is the final resting place for more than 3000 Australians who made the ultimate sacrifice during the New Guinea campaign. The beautifully groomed and landscaped cemetery between the mountains and the sea is a fitting memorial to the young men who slogged it out through malaria-infested jungle across the Owen Stanley Range to the steamy north coast of the hostile land, battling a fanatical enemy, debilitating diseases and a brutal environment.

Len Griffiths was a member of the 3rd Battalion, made up mainly of men from the fine wool country of the NSW Southern Tablelands, from Goulburn to Cooma and across to Yass. A Queanbeyan local, Griffiths came from a large family of eight children (five girls and three boys) that, like many others, had battled through the Great Depression by eking out a subsistence living on a two-acre block.

'We had chooks and turkeys and all the ground was taken up with vegetables such as potatoes and pumpkins, and we were rather lucky in that respect, we had an old cow, plenty of milk, cream, we were never short.'

Number six in the offspring pecking order, young Len joined his siblings on the five-kilometre walk to Queanbeyan High School and back every day until the family's need for cash dictated that he should leave school and get a job. In summer the daily trek to school included a swim in the Queanbeyan River on the way home, but in winter it was a freezing, windy journey through the bitter cold. Every Sunday the eight kids would line up for their weekly scrub in a large bath that was kept in the spare room.

His first job, as a 15-year-old, was with a local hardware firm called Hayes and Russell, starting in the timber yard stacking timber for 48 hours a week for the princely sum of 12 shillings and sixpence. He paid his mum half his wage for board and lodging and even managed to save some pennies from the remainder. He was promoted to work in the hardware store before he moved on to join a local contractor carting materials for the War Memorial construction project in Canberra.

'We had two Bedford trucks and we'd put eight ton of bricks on each truck, but we had to go to the brick yards out there at Yarralumla to get the bricks out of the kiln,' he recalls. 'We would load them onto the truck and take them to the War Memorial and on the way back we would call in at the Wellington Hotel for a quiet beer.'

Griffiths developed the taste for a cold beer at a tender age and it stays with him to this day. As the temperature soared during the 70th anniversary functions he would often whisper, 'I could do with a bloody beer.'

After a stint with another contractor and then as a general hand at the American Embassy, 18-year-old Griffiths joined up in 1941 and was sent to Greta army camp near Newcastle for his basic infantry training.

The trainees had no idea where they would end up, but most of the speculation centred on North Africa. Drilled in open desert-style warfare, they thought they would be off to the Middle East to relieve the 6th Division.

Once on board their Dutch cattle ship/troop carrier the men began to get an inkling that they were headed towards New Guinea instead. 'You could see these ships, they were going that way and all of a sudden they made a left-hand turn. You could see these bloody ships turning around.' Theirs followed suit, turning left off the NSW coast and heading north towards New Guinea.

By then it was May 1942 and the waters between Sydney and Port Moresby were infested with Japanese submarines. Just days after Len's ship sailed, the Japanese launched their daring mini-submarine raid on Sydney Harbour.

The diggers arrived in Port Moresby and camped near the aerodrome. A Japanese air raid on their first afternoon provided their first taste of war. They were immediately put to work on the docks unloading ships filled with supplies for the battles to come, and received a little jungle warfare training around Moresby — not exactly jungle territory.

Fighting on the Kokoda Track began on July 23 when the Australian 39th Militia Battalion and the Papuan Infantry Battalion met Japanese forces at Awala. Griffiths clearly recalls the day that he and his mates were sent forward on to the track.

'It was a hot stinking day and for some unknown reason they gave us two bottles of beer. Now you can imagine what it was like out in the open. It was DA or Dirty Annie as we called it,' he says, laughing. 'It was our first beer and most of us were a bit tiddly after a couple of bottles of the warm liquid.'

The battalion was trucked to Owers' Corner to begin the march up to Imita Ridge, the last natural obstacle on the track, where they were ordered to dig in to meet the Japanese advance that was closing in on the road link to Port Moresby.

'It rained and it rained nearly every day,' he recalls. 'An inch of rain, you could set your clock by it. At 3 o'clock in the afternoon, down came the rain, if you weren't wet with rain you were wet with perspiration, but we got by. I'd see some chaps when they took their socks off, their skin used to come off … It was hard going.'

They slept mostly on the ground and sometimes in a slit trench. 'They called them slit trench, but you couldn't dig a slit trench in the jungle on account of all the vines. You'd get down about that deep [a few centimetres], and that was a slit trench!'

The final section of the journey was the infamous 'golden steps', more than 2000 timber stairs cut into the mountainside by engineers to speed up the ascent onto the ridge itself.

The allied high command back in Brisbane was furious that the Australians had been pushed back to within a few miles of Owers' Corner and they were ordered to hold the line at Imita Ridge 'at all costs'.

However, the Japanese invaders had quite literally reached the end of their tether by this stage, and when the Australians launched a counter-attack on their position they found it abandoned. It was September 18, 1942, and the battle for New Guinea had turned — the counter-offensive back across the Kokoda Track had begun.

Griffiths was a member of an initial 100-man force sent out to attack the Japanese positions at a place called Ioribaiwa. 'We went up and found the Japanese were gone and then we moved forward and that was the start of the end, you might say, with the Japanese, as we followed them right through to Kokoda and on to Sanananda.'

Jungle warfare was a cat-and-mouse game, with intermittent fighting every three or four days as the diggers adapted to their unfamiliar surroundings and to fighting in jungle terrain, and indeed to the jungle itself.

'Oh, it was frightening,' he says. 'Night-time is the worst time in the jungle, because all the creepy crawly things come out and the fire flies, millions of them, they light up the air and the noise was pretty deafening. It's not a pleasant sight, or feeling, at night-time. At least during the day you can see a little bit, but it wasn't real good.'

The diggers didn't take long to adapt. 'We knew we were going to go forward and so we just had to get used to it.'

The slog across the majestic Owen Stanley Range was a truly daunting prospect. '[We were] buggered,' Griffiths says. 'You'd look up and you'd slide back, take another step and slide back again. The mountains are fantastic. When we were at Templeton's Crossing we were up 6500 feet [nearly 2000 metres], that's in the jungle, so you are wet during the day and wet during the night, so it wasn't a very pleasant feeling but you had no option, you had to keep going.'

Japanese snipers presented one of the major hazards.

'Oh, they had snipers,' he says feelingly. 'They were really good too, they had this high-powered bullet. One of my mates got killed at Templeton's Crossing and they couldn't find out what killed him, they had to have a post mortem, irrespective of being a soldier, and they found out the bullet went through his neck and broke his neck, and came out the other side just like a little pin hole, so a very high-powered rifle they had.'

Constant hunger was a given. 'We used to get a tin of bully beef, that's for a full day's ration, sometimes you didn't even get that. And the dog biscuits as they call them, like a Sao biscuit but as hard as that table. What we used to do, we used to get plenty of milk, Lactogen, used to come in big tins, we'd get the Lactogen, get our Dixie, put our milk in it and put the dog biscuits in that, so you'd break them up, they'd be soft and you could eat them,' he recalls with a chuckle.

75

Griffiths never made it to the north coast and the historic battles at Buna and Gona. Malaria, dengue fever and diarrhoea were the main afflictions for the diggers. After about 100 days on the march, he was struck down with malaria at a place called Popondetta, between Kokoda and Buna on the coast.

'When the Japanese arrived it was a native camp, I suppose we call it, and they had every conceivable thing there, their huts were beautiful, everywhere was neat and tidy and all their vegetables that they grew and that sort of thing, but the Japanese came along and burnt the whole lot down and raped the [women].'

Griffiths was flown back to Port Moresby for treatment. 'I had a very pleasant time in nursing hospital and they fixed me up, and that was it,' he says.

By the time he was well enough to get back into action, his battalion had been disbanded. So he was sent to a place called Nadzab near Lae on the north coast where the Americans had built a major airfield that became the headquarters of the US Fifth Air Force and the RAAF.

Used to the privations of the Kokoda Track — he says the natives called it 'track' and the Americans 'trail' — and a constant fight for supplies, Sergeant Griffiths was shocked by what he found at the American stronghold. The kitchens were all stainless steel, there were two transport planes assigned to fly to Townsville every day to pick up fresh meat and other supplies, and there was an endless supply of beer and whisky.

'When the Yanks left Nadzab they buried their beer supplies and they reckoned there was a million cans of American beer underground,' he says. 'One day our colonel said there was something wrong with the natives; they were getting around like zombies. They had found some of the beer and were helping themselves. He ordered us to get some trucks, load up as much of the beer as we could find and get the engineers to blow it up. God knows how many cans of beer went up in the explosion. Yankee beer is only about 2.2 per cent but the natives, once they had it, well, it used to bowl them over.'

Griffiths was the platoon sergeant in 18 Platoon, and he finds it very difficult to single out individuals for acts of valour or courage on the Kokoda Track. As far as he is concerned all his mates were VC winners.

'You couldn't pick one out and say he'd done better than the other bloke. The courage of the soldiers — and they were mostly 18- to 20-year-olds — was just remarkable,' he says. 'They were brave men, none of them shirked their duty, one protected the other and you just kept going, otherwise, well, you are dead meat. "Up and into them, get at the so and sos," that was the attitude.'

As the campaign wore on, the fighting changed from vicious close-quarters combat to harassing and sniping as the Australians pursued the starving enemy towards the coast.

The Japanese troops became so hungry that they seemed to have resorted to cannibalism. On one occasion, when he found some dead Australians in gun pits, Len saw evidence that the enemy had been forced to eat human flesh.

'When we went through there they had lost their sinews under their arms and part of their buttocks were missing, and the calf muscle was missing,' he says. 'They [the Japanese] were starving. I don't think the Australians would have done the same to the Japanese, I don't think, it's not like the Australian soldier … [but] if you are starving and miles from nowhere you'd probably do anything to get something to eat.'

The incident angered the diggers and the natives too, he says. Having chased the Japanese across the Owen Stanleys for 100 days, the men in Len's platoon were not short of motivation, but the sight of their fallen comrades being butchered as a food source fired them up. 'We thought, "What a lot of so-and-so, what are we fighting against, cannibals?" You know, it just makes you think.'

In the end, for the men who fought the Kokoda campaign it was the mantra for all wars — kill or be killed.

'I suppose when you come to think of it, for a 20-year-old or 18-year-old it was a fairly good experience. You learned a lot by it, who you could trust. Made you think … I don't think the Australian people realise what we were up against.'

For him, it was all about teamwork and courage. 'Whatever you done, you helped one another. At the start it is frightening, but eventually you had to get used to it otherwise you were a dead person. Seeing your mates killed was very distressing. You had lived with them, drank with them, shared personal stories with them and suddenly they were gone. You couldn't do anything about it; you just had to keep going. It wasn't a pleasant experience, but that goes for any war, not only that one. All wars are no good.'

During the celebrations in Port Moresby the guests of honour were Prince Charles and his wife Camilla, the Duchess of Cornwall. The royals stayed at the same hotel as the Kokoda veterans, overlooking Jacksons International Airport, and when she heard that the diggers were in town Camilla requested a 'meet and greet'.

Len Griffiths, who is a genuine larrikin, took an immediate shine to the duchess and told her she would always have somewhere to stay (with him) if she ever visited Canberra.

Chapter 3

Korea: Coming of Age

The Korean War of 1950 to 1953 is Australia's least known military conflict. Thanks to the legend of Breaker Morant, even the Boer War is better known than Korea, famously dubbed 'the forgotten war'.

Despite the fact that 339 young Australians were killed and more than 1200 were wounded fighting under the United Nations flag, the war occupies very little space in the pantheon of Anzac and the legend of the digger. Yet Australian troops in Korea probably did as much actual 'digging' — shifting earth to create trenches to shelter from artillery barrages — as their Anzac forebears did at Gallipoli.

More than 17,000 Australians served with the United Nations Multinational Force to defend South Korea from communist North Korea and its Chinese backers. The war was marked by some of the last massed infantry charges in history. The Australians fought pitched battles to hold the line along the 38th Parallel against vast waves of Chinese infantry from the north.

For 21-year-old infantry Lieutenant Jim Hughes, from Murray Bridge in South Australia, Korea would confirm everything that he had been taught at the Royal Military College, Duntroon. But nothing could have prepared him fully for the bitter warfare and dreadful conditions he would encounter in the hills north of the South Korean capital, Seoul.

Being the son of a light horseman — his father Bill fought with the 9th Light Horse at Gallipoli — meant that Jim Hughes had some insights into warfare, but Korea in 1951 was a very different proposition from the Dardanelles in 1915.

The military gene ran strongly in the Hughes family, and both Jim and his brother Ron, who also attended Duntroon, would rise to the rank of major general in the Australian Army. Along the way, Jim would serve with the elite SAS in Borneo and would be awarded the Distinguished Service Order in Vietnam.

In the post-World War II era of the late 1940s there had been little sign on the horizon of the troubles that lay ahead. Jim clearly remembers his headmaster at Adelaide's prestigious St Peter's College saying there would be no military action ahead. And as he graduated from RMC in 1950 there was still little indication that Australian troops might be deployed to fight on the Korean Peninsula.

'Even the week of our graduation I recall the commanding officer of the staff cadets sitting on a table — which was unusual for him to do — talking to us, saying, "You blokes will have nothing."'

Lieutenant Hughes was assigned to the 1st Battalion Royal Australian Regiment (RAR) based at Ingleburn barracks on the outskirts of Sydney. The battalion had been hollowed out after it returned from post-war duties in Japan.

'They'd come back 18 months before from Japan, and the soldiers had just wasted away,' he says. 'They had an administration company, headquarters company it was called then, they didn't have any rifle company, they had no men, so it was boring, frustrating, and really I wondered what we had got ourselves into. Then the Korean War continued and we were on the reinforcement list and slowly but surely we got there.'

Hughes joined the 3rd Battalion RAR at its base on the Imjin River, north of Seoul. The main task for the new arrivals in August 1951 was reconnaissance patrols of two to four days across the river to see what the Chinese were up to in the lead-up to a major UN operation planned for October.

The Imjin is Korea's seventh largest river and it flows basically from north to south, crossing the 38th Parallel to join the Han River downstream of Seoul. When it rains the sedate waters transform into a raging torrent — several soldiers drowned attempting to cross what is known as 'the river of death' due to the large number of corpses it carries down each year from the impoverished North.

During these initial patrols, Lieutenant Hughes and his four Platoon troops were introduced to one of the terrors of infantry warfare — being in open ground during an artillery barrage. Soldiers caught above ground by indirect fire often say they were 'digging in with their eyelids' in an attempt to get below ground level and away from the lethal, razor-sharp shrapnel.

'When you are caught on a slope and there are no holes to get into, and I just happened to look across at the platoon sergeant after the first shelling and said, "Sergeant, you've got a dirty face." He said, "You should see yours, sir." We were all trying to get into the ground. I never knew what being under barrage was. It was all very well, the idea of how guns are used and ammunition is used, but you've got to be under one to understand. You know that if a shell lands on you that is the end of you.'

In response to the incoming shells, the Kiwi gunners from the New Zealand 16th Field Regiment fired 50,000 rounds back over the UN troops at the enemy in support of the operation.

There were minor contacts throughout August and September as both sides harassed each other, testing resolve and ability. As October approached, the battalion received word of a major offensive, codenamed Operation Commando, involving the newly formed 1st Commonwealth Division. The division's 28th Brigade, which included 3 RAR, would carry the lion's share of the load.

Their objective was a high feature known as Hill 317 (Maryang San) that would give UN forces command of the valley in both directions. Taking Hill 317 was regarded as a vital strategic objective for Commonwealth forces because if the enemy could be driven back a few kilometres they would lose contact with the Imjin River. Two previous attempts by American troops to take the hill from a well dug-in enemy had failed.

Trucks transported the battalion to the stepping-off point, where four companies formed a bivouac before moving off at 3 am for the march up to the frontline. As they awoke from their restless slumber under their half-blankets — there were no down-filled sub-zero sleeping bags in 1951 — a pea soup fog greeted the diggers.

'The fog was very thick and as the sun came up the fog got thicker,' Hughes recalls. 'We had rehearsed how to move at night so I hung on the bayonet of the bloke in front of me, someone hung onto my bayonet and we all wore white stuff on our backs so you could see us. Half a dozen of us had compasses so we'd stop regularly for a check and luckily we were going north, luckily the river was on our right, because there was a big bed in the river. I had to go parallel to the river, not on the bank, but we were up on the bank so the navigation was easier than I thought.'

The going was painfully slow and the men knew they were skirting enemy positions so they were being very quiet, 'tiptoeing, in fact'.

They reached the rendezvous point and established an all-round defensive position as they waited for the rest of the troops, before Bravo Company — to which Hughes belonged — launched its first attack against Chinese positions on the other side of two small hills.

'We got them, luckily, while they were having their breakfast. Always a good time to get people,' Hughes says.

The Australians lost three killed during the initial action; they killed a number of enemy themselves and took five prisoners before they dug in at about ten o'clock in the morning after being joined by Alpha Company. This location became the pivot point for the operation over the next few days.

On day five — Friday — Charlie Company was ordered to occupy the top of Hill 317. Fortunately the Chinese had decided to withdraw, so the mission was completed without incident despite the steep terrain.

Bravo Company, under the command of Captain Henry Nicholls, was then ordered to take a feature beyond the summit of Hill 317 known as the Hinge. As the first two platoons passed it, the Chinese triggered an ambush and attacked the company headquarters. That was the start of an intense day-long battle.

'We spent the day being shelled, mortared, running out of ammunition, not being able to get our casualties out; the enemy trenches didn't suit us because they faced the wrong way, we had to try and organise it,' Hughes says. 'On the way back we had our first problem — we had a grenade fight that started the ball rolling.'

For their gallantry and leadership under fire both Hughes and his commanding officer Captain Nicholls were awarded the Military Cross, and several non-commissioned officers received the Military Medal for their brave efforts.

That night, October 7, the Chinese launched three counter-attacks from the front and flanks with battalion-strength forces to try and win back the Hinge from the Australians. The diggers beat back each assault with accurate small-arms and machine-gun fire as well as brutal hand-to-hand combat, using bayonets and their bare hands. As their ammunition ran low they resorted to kicking and strangling their attackers. During the night, the Chinese would throw hand grenades at the Australians, who would pick them up and lob them back.

Finally the Chinese were routed by accurate artillery fire and forced to withdraw three kilometres. During five days of intense fighting the Australians lost 20 dead and 89 wounded. Chinese casualties included at least 283 killed (but possibly hundreds more) and 50 captured.

'During the night [our support troops] were bringing down ammunition for us,' Hughes says. 'If they could they would take a casualty back, but we had more casualties than they had stretchers.'

One of the dead diggers was a soldier who had returned to the platoon just a few days earlier and had been due to go home at the end of October. 'We all said to him, "You are a fool, go back to the Q store and be a storeman." "No," he said. "If 4 Platoon go to war then so do I."'

Jim Hughes gives a great deal of the credit for 3 RAR's victory at Maryang San to the hardened platoon sergeants. Many of them, such as Pat O'Connell, who won the Military Medal, were seasoned World War II veterans.

Throughout the action, 4 Platoon's strength was down to 20 men and by the end it had dwindled to just 15. As a platoon commander, Hughes says his job was simple — if he did the right thing by the platoon, he would keep them alive.

A close encounter with the enemy came as he was making his way to company headquarters for a meeting with his commander. 'I was carrying a rifle only, and making my merry way and I suddenly found a well-worn track and I thought, "I'll follow that,"' he recalls. 'Lo and behold, who comes around the corner but two Chinese soldiers very happily talking away. I just picked up the rifle, put it horizontal and threw it at them and ran.'

Clearly neither of the enemy soldiers was expecting to come face-to-face with an Australian officer. 'If they'd been switched on, they should have been carrying their rifles loaded and ready to go. So should have I, but as it was they both got clobbered in the face.'

After some 21 hours of intense fighting, the Chinese withdrew and a truce was declared to allow the enemy force to clear the field of dead and wounded.

'When the sun came up we took a look, we were then told not to do clearing patrols, not to engage the Chinese, let them clear their battlefield. I've got to be fair and say I certainly put two outpost people to watch them — I didn't want to be surprised. They reported back, "Yep, they are all busy doing what they can, collecting the wounded and so on." We never counted the dead, the Chinese dead, but there were a lot.'

The King's Own Scottish Borderers Regiment replaced the diggers on Hill 317 the next day, October 8. They lost the feature to a Chinese counter-offensive about six weeks later.

In another quirk of the honours and awards system, the Aussies discovered in 1990 that the British unit had received battle honours for their work on Hill 317. 'They got the honour for losing it and we didn't get one for winning it,' Hughes says drily.

Fortunately the situation was rectified, and in 1994 3 RAR was finally awarded battle honours for Maryang San.

According to Hughes, the word 'withdraw' was never even uttered during the fight. His conscious thought in the heat of battle was, 'We have to survive this, we've got to win this.' The two, he says, went together. 'If we survive, we win it.'

After the battle he wrote the following in his diary: 'We'd survived, we'd given our best, we were tired but very proud Australians, members of 3 RAR in general and B Company in particular. The soldiers of B Company were tenacious, they showed great initiative and courage, individual acts spontaneously for the common good, whenever a problem arose.'

Former army officer and Vietnam veteran Professor Robert O'Neill's official history, *Australia in the Korean War, 1950–53*, describes the battle for Maryang San as probably the greatest single feat of the Australian Army during the Korean War.

The other major battle involving Australians was at Kapyong on 22–25 April, 1951, where 39 diggers died and 59 were wounded.

Courage and teamwork were the key factors in Operation Commando, according to the commander of 3 RAR in Korea and later Chief of the General Staff, General Sir Frank Hassett. Or as Jim Hughes put it, 'We were there, and we were there to stay.'

Also serving at the battle of Maryang San was Bill (later Sir William) Keys, who would become national secretary and national president of the RSL and a powerful advocate for Korean and other war veterans.

Looking back after more than 60 years, Jim Hughes says, 'I would like to think I'd been trained to lead a platoon in battle and get the best out of the men as part of my platoon, which is part of the company, which is part of the battalion. And I think with very few exceptions, all the platoon commanders were RMC graduates this time. We were lucky. A couple of the others were World War II officers, they had the same approach.'

He says bravery is not about making a conscious effort to do something courageous. 'You were there to do your job. If anybody says to me they were never scared, they were a liar,' he says. 'I mean I've never told anyone they are a liar but I feel they are a liar. All that ammunition, all that metal falling around you, you have to be scared. I think it is a natural reaction. I would like to think that our training helped us to control our fear as such, but as I said I didn't take unnecessary risks.

'When the shelling was on, don't worry, I had my head down like every other member in the company! I certainly wasn't wandering around. Being scared is normal, a man who says he's not is lying, and I believe that my responsibilities helped me conquer that or get over it, and not think about it. I was responsible for them [and] we as a collective platoon had been successful in keeping the rest of the company efficient and alive. You look after your own. You look after your mate.'

Courage was all around Hughes in Korea and soldiers from 3 RAR were awarded eight individual awards from the battle of Maryang San. He witnessed some incredible acts of bravery, but for every one of those he says there were several that he didn't witness.

'I think some of the bravest things I couldn't see, because they were done at night-time, and that was the problem, and there are certainly enough stories about the … night patrols in particular, who suffered tremendous casualties.'

As for separating those who win a VC from the rest, he suggests, 'Well they could be some of the people who suddenly feel that they've got double the height or double the weight or "Those shells, those bullets won't touch me, but I gotta help my mates out." I think that is the basic thing.'

A basic humanity, a willingness to put their own lives at risk to help others without thinking about their own.

'Yes, so therefore those VCs who survived, to me must be very lucky men, because I think back to World War I and World War II, so many of them did not survive. I only knew one VC from Vietnam and he didn't survive, but I knew him as a rifleman in Malaya in 1959 and he was just a happy-go-lucky, very efficient soldier.' That was Kevin 'Dasher' Wheatley, who had served with 3 RAR in Malaya.

'He was just a very good soldier in the platoon. He'd get their affection, always cracking a joke, always liked to laugh. He was a down-to-earth digger who respected the principle, "You look after me and I'll look after you." That two-way business [is] like a family, a very tight family.'

That family closeness was something Jim experienced later in spades during his time in Borneo with the SAS. 'Now that's where we initially worked on the British four-man system patrol and eventually let it run out to five. That's an even tighter association, you are even more dependent because you're so far away from [support] — your aircraft can't get in to you often, and the other men can't even carry you out, probably. It's a much tighter family affair in the SAS but the same thing that is common throughout the whole infantry.' To him, bravery and responsibility go hand in hand.

Hughes was possibly the only Australian to serve as an officer in Korea, Malaya, Borneo and Vietnam. But of all those conflicts it was in Korea back in October 1951 when Jim Hughes believes he reached maturity, aged just 22.

'In October we really learned what it was all about,' he says. 'I grew up, in a great hurry. There was more to life than just playing around.'

VIETNAM: THE BITTER YEARS

Chapter 1

Too Busy to Die

Dave Sabben was determined that he would use his time as a national serviceman ('nasho') and junior officer in the Australian Army to learn as much as he could about managing men, in order to further his civilian career.

The glaring downside to his theory was the fact that he might be killed or disabled, but in 1965 going to war was no certainty and besides, for a 'ten-feet tall and bullet-proof' 20-year-old mortality is way down the list of concerns.

So when he was called up in 1965 he requested officer training and was accepted and sent to the newly established officer-training unit at Scheyville in the Hawkesbury Valley north-west of Sydney. He was part of the first intake of young nashos to graduate from there.

'I was toying with the CMF [Citizen Military Forces], my brother had been in CMF, but when nasho came up, and nasho basically said two years full time, and whilst you go onto reserve of officers if you become an officer, there is no further obligation and that suited me fine,' he says. 'It was two years and you get all the training and becoming an officer was a bonus because that was the man management and responsibility side I was looking for.'

Sabben was born in Fiji in 1945 to British Foreign Service parents and educated at Trinity Grammar School in Sydney where he served in the army cadets. He had been working for three years when he registered for national service in 1965. He had considered joining the regular army, but as a 19-year-old the six-year return of service obligation felt like a lifetime.

After graduating from Scheyville, he was posted as a second lieutenant to the newly raised 6th Battalion Royal Australian Regiment (6 RAR) based at Enoggera barracks in Brisbane.

'What you learn as an officer qualifies you for any managerial job in the future. You learn communication, the importance of communications, man management, setting goals and achieving them, reporting lines, all that sort of stuff,' he says. 'So after I spent a year in Vietnam as platoon commander, I came back and resumed my civil occupation and I just leapt ahead of my peers. Whilst they had two years of knowledge of their trade, I had had two years of very practical experience leading men and so when I came back, I leapfrogged over them and became a manager.'

His five years at boarding school had been sound preparation for the officer training unit, where the strict regimentation and 'constructive bastardisation' didn't bother him at all, unlike some of the other young men from less rigid backgrounds. Still, the training was intense because they were preparing men to lead others into battle after just six months' instruction.

'You understood that you were training for war so it's an extremely intense experience,' Sabben says. 'I looked around me at my fellow students and I felt inside that I had to pedal twice as fast just to keep up with them. Many years later I found out that they felt just the same way.'

When national service began in 1964 Vietnam was bubbling away, but the real fear in Australia was Indonesia, where opposition to the creation of Malaysia and sabre rattling by President Sukarno had grown to such an extent that all-out war between Indonesian and British and Australian forces — in support of Malaysia — appeared inevitable.

In May 1965 the Defence Act was amended to oblige nashos to serve overseas, and in March 1966 the government of Harold Holt announced that national servicemen would be sent to Vietnam. By late 1965, as his Scheyville course was winding down, it was clear to Dave Sabben that Vietnam was the main game and that he and his fellow nashos would most likely be sent there.

In early 1966 the 6th Battalion was undertaking regular infantry training, and Sabben was getting used to life as a junior infantry officer under the watchful eye of the no-nonsense commander of Delta Company, Major Harry Smith.

'By about March or April we knew that we were going to Vietnam and so we started to absorb what the 1st Battalion was telling us [about their experiences in South Vietnam], and the newsreel footages and so on and trying to do helicopter training,' he says. 'We trained specifically for Vietnam for three months or so, including going to Canungra [jungle training centre], which was manned to a large degree by World War II and Korea War warrant officers with the occasional warrant officer back from Vietnam.

'We knew pretty much what we were doing at our level as footsloggers — we knew our field craft, that doesn't change, and under Harry [Smith] every single fine detail was thrown into it.

He wasn't in any manner slack, nothing was left to chance, we trained for every damn thing, which made us really good.'

Little did the men know just how important their training, under the perfectionist taskmaster Major Smith, would prove to their survival.

The battalion arrived in Vietnam in June 1966 and, along with 5 RAR, formed half the infantry component of the 1st Australian Task Force based at Nui Dat. The base was built on a piece of high ground (Nui Dat means 'hill of earth'), surrounded by rubber plantations in Phuoc Tuy province.

The first 72 days were uneventful with some minor contacts as the battalion went about its job of patrolling, securing and ambushing. Securing the 13-kilometre perimeter of the task-force base was the most important job, so the work schedule was based around patrolling by day, defending the perimeter by night and planning and executing ambushes in the area around Nui Dat.

'The next day you put a half a day into field work, defending, digging pits and trenches and so on, and that afternoon you go out on a half-day patrol, then you put in an overnight ambush, which means being 100 per cent alert, and then patrol for the next half day and come back at lunchtime,' Sabben recalls. 'Then your platoon would be split up and you were sent to do battalion duties such as sorting stores or building facilities, and that night you would defend somebody else's perimeter.

'So each night you are either on ambush, defending your own perimeter or you are defending somebody else's perimeter.'

On June 21, 1966, the battalion was ordered to destroy the village of Long Phuoc as part of Operation Enoggera. It took a week to burn and blow up every dwelling and destroy the network of Vietcong tunnels in and around the village. The controversial 'scorched earth policy' adopted throughout South Vietnam by

America and her allies is widely blamed for turning many locals against the invading forces.

Sandwiched between the routine tasks was a special three-day company patrol where the infantry would range further afield to try and establish what the enemy was up to.

Delta Company was due out on August 18 to relieve Bravo Company. Early on the 17th, the task force base was attacked with rockets and mortars. Elements of B Company were sent out to find the source of the fire, but they did not have the manpower or the energy to follow the enemy.

Delta Company was supposed to go out and establish a minefield, but its orders changed following the mortar attack. After relieving Bravo Company and obtaining new maps, they went off in pursuit of the enemy force. By then it was 36 hours after the attack and, as the troops would discover, the enemy could cover a lot of ground in 36 hours.

Harry Smith looked at the tracks left by the enemy fighters and decided they were intended to lead his diggers into an ambush. Rather than follow the tracks, he decided instead to follow ruts made by heavily laden bullock carts heading off into the Long Tan rubber plantation.

It was obvious to Smith and the other officers, including Sabben, who was in command of Delta Company's 12 Platoon, that the carts were loaded with heavy weapons. They also concluded that the enemy was unlikely to mount an ambush in open country, or in a rubber plantation offering only limited cover.

Major Smith deployed 10 Platoon under Second Lieutenant Geoff Kendall to the forward left, 11 Platoon under Second Lieutenant Gordon Sharp to the forward right high ground and 12 Platoon under Sabben to the centre rear.

At about 3.40 pm a group of six enemy fighters stumbled into 11 Platoon, who engaged them, killing one and wounding several.

Sharp ordered his men forward and just after 4 pm a substantial enemy force attacked the platoon. At the same time, mortars began falling near the headquarters and the other two platoons, so Major Smith moved them north and ordered 11 Platoon to withdraw under artillery cover.

11 Platoon was being flanked and suffering heavy casualties — Gordon Sharp was fatally wounded. Platoon Sergeant Bob Buick took over as the men fought to survive and somehow link up with the rest of the company.

Delta Company had gone on patrol expecting to find some mortars and perhaps a platoon of enemy. What they had stumbled upon was a force of between 1500 and 2500 that had been preparing for a major assault on the task force base.

'There is nothing unusual about this — this is what we train for, this is what we are here for, let's get stuck into it,' Sabben says. 'So there is an element of enthusiasm, not dread or anything, not over-confidence, there wasn't anything to be over-confident about. We knew we had 108 men around us — it was going to be a sizable force to intimidate us — so we could just walk into the bush or plantation and be thoroughly confident in our ability, knowing that if push came to shove we had a number of artillery people in the background that could support us, the back-up support was all there. There was an APC [armoured personnel carrier] group in the base, there were American helicopters down in Vung Tau so with maybe ten to 15 minutes' notice we could call in air strikes. The monsoon wasn't due to start until about three o'clock so everything was on our side: numbers, it was open country, we could see for miles, there was nothing for us to fear at all.'

The men's confidence was also boosted by the fact that when they had patrolled through the Long Tan area a week earlier during a cordon and search mission called Operation Hobart there wasn't a skerrick of intelligence (available to them, at any rate) to indicate that a sizable enemy force was anywhere nearby.

'We knew there weren't any huge VC [Vietcong] installations, and the VC was the only thing on our mind. NVA [North Vietnamese Army] had not operated that far south up to that date,' Sabben says.

But that was about to change. The enemy force was made up of the 275VC Regiment, the D445 VC Provincial Battalion and the NVA's 274th Battalion. It soon became apparent to Smith and his officers that their 108 men would be sorely tested by what was coming at them literally in waves.

'It was like a target range and they just kept popping targets at us, they just kept throwing people at us,' Sabben recalls.

Training was the key, and he never doubted that the company would prevail — provided they could preserve their ammunition.

'You train for a level of expertise and when that expertise holds, irrespective of the circumstances, and then chuck surprises in, and Long Tan is a perfect example of that,' he says. 'You are talking about 108 men who were trained to meet enemy twos and threes, if you are lucky there will be six of them, and then you put them out in the field and howl down the rain and bring in the dark and then you have more targets than you've got rounds of ammo in your magazine. How did they adapt to that? Well, they adapted, one round, one enemy, bang and I don't have to worry about the fact there is 50 of them, because 20 of us can squeeze our fingers a few times in 50 seconds. We are OK, while we are not dead, we are OK.'

Thanks to the training, courage and leadership of the company, the professionalism of their artillery and air support, and the bravery of the RAAF chopper crews who resupplied them with ammunition at a critical moment, the Australian force not only survived but inflicted a major defeat on a vastly superior enemy force.

When the smoke cleared after several hours of intense fighting, 18 Australians lay dead, including 17 diggers from Delta Company, and 26 were wounded. Another man, from 3 Troop 1st APC Squadron, later died from his wounds.

Exact numbers of enemy dead may never be known, but a body count by the Australians revealed 254 killed, and subsequent information indicated that up to 850 might have fallen, with more than 500 wounded.

Dave Sabben witnessed numerous acts of extraordinary courage under fire by soldiers from Delta Company that day, but the one who stands out to him is his platoon medic, 'Doc' Davis. Private Graeme Davis was kneeling, tending to casualties as the platoon was taking withering enemy fire. He moved between the wounded, unarmed, exposing himself to the enemy as he treated his mates for almost an hour until the inevitable happened and he was shot and wounded. Even back at the Company Aid Post he was helping to treat others despite his own wounds.

'Now in any other engagement that would have warranted a VC,' Sabben says. 'But is that any braver than Gordon Sharp putting his head up to direct artillery and getting shot through the neck? They both knew the bullets were flying and they both knew in order to do their job they had to expose themselves.'

Another soldier who performed with great courage during the battle was Warrant Officer Class 2 John 'Jack' Kirby. He was awarded the Distinguished Conduct Medal for his efforts, but Harry Smith believes Kirby should be on the list for a retrospective Victoria Cross and has continued fighting for the popular professional soldier, who was killed by friendly artillery fire in Vietnam in 1967.

The entire Australian force was exposed to enemy fire because rubber trees offer virtually no cover, since bullets pass straight through them.

'Part of your training in the army, certainly in officers' course, says that if you can't do anything about a situation, well forget it, just deal with it and move on,' says Sabben. 'Change what you can to your benefit, but if you can't change it, you can't just blow the whistle and say, "Hey guys, let's move over to the bush because there is more cover." That is not an option, so after the initial, "Oh shit," we have to lie on the ground and do the best we can, well that's what you do.

'So there is a level of bravery and courage and valour and so on attached to that and it was displayed by every soldier. You take a person off the street and say in six months time you are going to be holding a loaded rifle, looking for another man with a loaded rifle and the only thing between you and him will be a cotton shirt, what sort of sensible man would say, "Oh great, terrific"? So each and every one of them has to display a degree of what we term valour.'

Dave Sabben says the fear of dying moved further and further down the priority list as the battle intensified and multiple command tasks took over.

'You are not particularly worried about how your girlfriend will receive the news of your death or anything, you are just too busy to die,' he says.

Australian Army officers are schooled in a routine known as 'appreciation'. 'Once you are trained, you do it forever and you think, has there been any change to my force? If nothing has changed forget it, leave it alone. What do we know about the enemy, has anything changed? Well, there are bloody more of the bastards, their aim is still to get to us ... Can't do anything about that, just defend. Weather, what's changed, is it getting darker ... and when you finish that you come back and ask, "Has anything changed for my forces?" That is "appreciation".'

In addition to those tasks, most of Dave Sabben's efforts were focused on calling in artillery and the tactical situation of the battle. After his platoon sergeant was wounded, he had the additional burden of ammunition resupply and casualties to worry about.

After the battle of Long Tan, Harry Smith made numerous recommendations for medals for his men. There were no unit citations in those days, so they had to be recommended on an individual basis.

The lack of unit awards has since been rectified and, in addition to a Vietnam Gallantry Cross with Palm Unit Citation and a US Presidential Unit Citation presented to Delta Company in 1968, an Australian Unit Citation for Gallantry was finally awarded in 2009.

In the same year, Harry Smith's Military Cross (MC), which had been downgraded from a Distinguished Service Order (DSO) due to the quota system, was upgraded to the Star of Gallantry. The quota system restricted the number of imperial awards that could be given to Australian troops during the Vietnam conflict.

The Star of Gallantry is the equivalent of the DSO under the new Australian honours and awards system and is the second-highest award after the Victoria Cross for Australia. It is given for 'great heroism' or 'conspicuous courage' on the battlefield.

Dave Sabben and Gordon Sharp had their Mentioned in Despatches (MIDs) upgraded to Medal for Gallantry, the equivalent of the MC, for which they had been recommended and should have received following the battle.

Like many Vietnam veterans, Dave Sabben is deeply disillusioned. He regards the treatment of Harry Smith and his men as obnoxious and a symptom of a deep malaise within the officer class and the British awards system under which they operated.

Sabben is under no illusions about the political element to military awards. He bristles when the discussion turns to the lack of a single Victoria Cross awarded to any soldier serving in an infantry battalion in Vietnam. The four VCs awarded during the war all went to members of the Australian Army Training Team Vietnam (AATTV).

'Anytime there is a VC, it's not because someone did something courageous, it's because the government needed to give a VC for PR [public relations] or to jazz the troops, so I'm not a great believer in the AATTV for VC awards,' he says bluntly. 'What they did, according to their citations, I saw dozens of people do at Long Tan, so not that they don't deserve it, but dozens if not hundreds of people deserve it.'

Sabben is also suspicious of the timing of the Vietnam VCs. 'Every time a VC was awarded in Vietnam to one of the Team [AATTV] it was immediately followed by something that was critically important that had a political ramification,' he says. 'One of them was just before we committed a second battalion and that was going to cause a political furore because it included national servicemen. The last one was just immediately before we withdrew and the government was preparing for casualties, so let's throw a VC into the mix. That sort of thing is why I disrespect them, not because of the valour of the men — they did an excellent job.'

Many other individual awards were either downgraded or removed from the Long Tan list, and Harry Smith has vowed to continue the fight for justice while he still has breath in his body.

'It became a matter of principle for us. They [senior officers and politicians] were wrong. What they needed to do was admit they got it wrong and right it, but it's not easy in Canberra,' Sabben says. 'I very much appreciate the fact that on the back of many doors in Canberra offices there were pictures of Harry and me on dartboards. I had a good relationship with a lot of people in Canberra who I have no relationship with at all now.'

The last straw for both men was when the government asked them to hand back their MC and MIDs when they received their upgraded Australian awards.

'Well, fuck off, Sunshine, if you want the MID, it's been gazetted by the Queen, or the Governor-General in those days. You get the Governor-General to rescind it and I'll hand it back. Oh no, that's too hard, so we'll just drop it, so no one now insists on these things.'

Sabben concedes that there is another crucial element to the awards dilemma and that is the 'fog of war'. Often commanders are so busy running the battle that they don't even recognise an outstanding act of bravery right in front of their eyes.

'One of my diggers was killed right at the end of the battle and all I could see was that he was slumped over his weapon,' he says. 'Two diggers got up and pulled him back; now I didn't watch them pull him back, I didn't know who they were. Two riflemen picked up this third rifleman and dragged him back to the CAP [company aid post]. My interest was that there were now three men missing on my perimeter, I better get three men over there.'

Meanwhile, the two men who had saved their comrade had returned to their positions on the perimeter. They had left their weapons out there so had been unarmed as they dragged their mate to safety.

'I didn't know until the next day who those [men] were. Yes, it's a bit of a fog of war, but the platoon is operating, the machine is happening, the cog is grinding.'

Dave Sabben does not believe that gallantry is serendipitous, it doesn't just happen; an individual is on the battlefield and must make a conscious decision, regardless of the risk to their own safety, to do something brave.

'Everyone on the battlefield is prepared for it and a few will take the risk, take the extra risk. We are already in a risky situation; a few of them will say, "This is suicide but I'll do it," and they do it, and whether they live or die, if it had a beneficial outcome, then they are up for an award.'

Chapter 2

The Nick of Time

Bob Buick was never going to win a popularity contest in the ranks of the 6th Battalion, Royal Australian Regiment (6 RAR). However, the ill-tempered, South African–born platoon sergeant was exactly the type of senior non-commissioned officer that Harry Smith wanted in Delta Company.

Even now, 40 years after the end of the Vietnam War, this gruff bear of a man evokes mixed emotions from those who served with him and a seemingly larger number who didn't.

The son of Irish and English parents, Buick moved with his family to Perth in 1954 and joined the Australian Army in 1959. After six years as a grunt, including a tour of Malaya with the 2nd Battalion, he transferred to the RAAF to learn a trade.

The move didn't work out, so in 1964 he was back in the army. In September 1965 he was posted to 6 RAR and to Harry Smith's company. It was the first fresh battalion raised in Queensland since

World War II and it celebrated its first birthday on the back beach at Vung Tau in 1966.

Buick is well aware that his character and bluntness often rubs people the wrong way, but he also understands that the job of platoon sergeant is not a popularity contest.

'As the platoon sergeant you tend to be a big brother and a father and you know what needs to be done. If my character was very abrasive towards other people and they didn't like the way I was, well I'm sorry about that, but that's the position I was in, and that's the position I took,' he says.

Bob Buick has been through the mill since his Vietnam service and the publication of his memoir, *All Guts and No Glory*. In the brutally honest book he tells the story of how he put a gravely wounded enemy soldier out of his misery with two shots to the heart.

That stirred up a hornet's nest and sparked a debate that still rages as some of his detractors are determined to pursue the issue and to even bring the matter before a court. In typical Buick fashion he shrugs off the criticism and explains the incident is part of the brutal business of infantry warfare and an honest telling of military history.

'The platoon sergeant in fact is recognised as the bloke that's got the most experience in the platoon. One of his jobs is to make sure that the platoon does the right thing according to training, and we train infantry blokes to survive, but also to kill other people. That's the whole job of infantry,' he says. 'Consequently I adopted a position where if I had to be a real mongrel and be a mongrel to other people to get the job done, I'd do that. That's always been my philosophy in life, even before I was in the army.'

There is a fair bit of mongrel in most successful warriors, and Harry Smith regards Bob Buick as one of the finest soldiers he has had the privilege to serve with.

By the time August 18, 1966, came around, Bob Buick, like all the soldiers in 6 RAR, was still trying to figure out what fighting in Vietnam was all about. Before they deployed they had been told that it would be like Malaya, but it wasn't. The Vietcong was an extremely different beast from the Indonesian Army.

In the lead-up to Long Tan, during Operations Enoggera and Hobart, the troops uncovered large caches of rice and fish heads, but no one put two and two together to conclude that these food stores had been established to sustain a much larger force later on. Only after the battle did Buick understand the significance of what they had been uncovering.

Along with Harry Smith, Dave Sabben, Gordon Sharp and all other members of Delta Company, Bob Buick had no idea that a large enemy force was lurking just to the east of the task force base at Nui Dat preparing to strike at the heart of Australia's commitment to Vietnam.

Up to 2500 enemy troops were just an overnight walk from the brand-new Australian task force base, which represented a very juicy target for the Vietcong and their North Vietnamese masters. This formidable foe had, as recently as April 1966, knocked over an armoured South Vietnamese marine battalion and captured all their American advisers just 25 kilometres north of Nui Dat.

But the diggers were kept in blissful ignorance of their presence.

'There was intelligence information that was never passed down to platoon commanders or platoon sergeants, let alone to the soldiers,' Buick says. 'We went out on the 18th of August absolutely blinded by what happened. We didn't have any bloody idea what was out there.'

About two weeks earlier Smith had ordered Buick to move to 11 Platoon to 'sort out' a few issues in the ranks. When the company moved into the rubber on August 18, Buick's platoon, under the command of Lieutenant Gordon Sharp, patrolled in arrowhead formation at the head of Delta Company.

As he came to a track that had been crossed by lead elements of the platoon, Buick saw half a dozen enemy fighters moving from south to north along the track utterly oblivious to the presence of the Australian patrol.

'They were just strolling down the road covering about 500 metres every few minutes, taking a casual stroll,' he says. 'I couldn't allow them to proceed any further into the company because that would have then started to get into where the headquarters was, which was to my left, so I fired two rounds and knocked this bloke arse over.'

The enemy fighters fled, dragging their wounded comrade, who had dropped his AK-47 assault rifle when he was hit. By the time the Australians began to move again the enemy were long gone to the east, past the forward elements of 11 Platoon. Sharp got the OK from Harry Smith to pursue them, so 11 Platoon moved off due west to chase the men who had stumbled into their patrol. As they approached a clearing the enemy opened up and Buick's immediate thought was that they had run into a platoon or possibly a company-sized force. He estimates that within the first 15 minutes of the battle the entire lefthand section of 11 Platoon had been either killed or wounded.

Lieutenant Sharp initially called in artillery fire onto the southern slopes of the Nui Dat feature about 400 metres away. After an earlier friendly-fire incident the commanders had added 1000 metres to any fire mission with the shells to be 'walked' onto the target to prevent 'own goals'.

'The problem is when you've got 80 to 100 VC attacking you from 50, 60, 70 metres away you need to get fire into that area very, very quickly to neutralise it, and this wasn't happening,' Buick says. 'Sharp was on his hands and knees looking to where the gun fire was, I yelled out, "You're going to get yourself fucking killed", and he turned to me and said "Ah, they're not good enough."'

Sadly they were. Within a minute or two Lieutenant Gordon Sharp was shot through the throat and killed.

Buick immediately assumed command of the platoon. Satisfied that his section commanders and machine gunners were doing a terrific job of supressing the enemy infantry without wasting ammunition (after 20 minutes just ten per cent of rounds had been spent) he turned his attention to the artillery. By then a monsoon deluge had mercifully descended upon the scene, reducing visibility to about 50 metres.

Buick was radioing grid references to Kiwi artillery forward observer Morrie Stanley to walk the shells in from 150 metres to 100 metres. Finally, out of sheer desperation, he gave his own position to the guns.

The platoon was down to about a dozen men who could still fight and, despite the brutal toll inflicted by the 105 mm and 155 mm guns, there was no sign of weakness in the enemy's resolve. After six rounds of fire (six rounds from each gun, or 36 rounds) landing between 25 and 50 metres from Buick's position, there was a lull in enemy activity.

'That's exactly where Charlie [the enemy] was and that was where there were about 120 odd bodies the next morning,' Buick says.

This was the turning point in the battle for the remnants of his platoon. 'I could not move prior to that, I could not order any withdrawal, I couldn't even move 20 metres without getting a hail of shots,' he says.

Without the artillery there is little doubt that 11 Platoon would have been wiped out, providing the enemy with a clear path into Delta Company's headquarters.

After considering his options Buick decided the best plan was to withdraw about 150 metres to the west, consolidate and then make his way back to Suoi Da Bang creek where he could hole up for the night before returning to Nui Dat at first light.

'I can honestly say, even nearly 50 years onwards, that I had to idea where the rest of the company was and I thought, "Well there is no one behind me." I didn't know who I was talking to, I didn't hear any orders, I was too busy trying to do what I had to do,' he says.

Finally, Sergeant Buick was forced to give the order to his surviving men to withdraw, and on his command of 'Go-Go-Go!' they got to their feet and ran like hell.

Fortunately Dave Sabben's 12 Platoon had moved up behind 11 Platoon and Sabben let off yellow smoke to guide the survivors back to relative safety.

Bob Buick had four holes shot in his bush hat and, like most of the survivors, his shirt was shredded by enemy fire and he had multiple shrapnel wounds. But by some miracle he had not been killed.

He had also been part of a mighty victory against incredible odds, whereby 105 Australians from D Company and three New Zealand artillerymen, with great support from artillery and RAAF helicopters, had defeated up to 2500 enemy.

Bob Buick is quick to acknowledge the role of the big guns in saving the day at Long Tan, but he lays the credit for the ultimate victory squarely at the feet of Harry Smith and the Delta Company diggers.

'Our philosophy of fighting, where we only shot when we knew we would hit someone, allowed 11 Platoon to survive for nearly two hours with 120 rounds of ammunition per rifle, and 600 to 700 rounds per machine gun,' he says.

Buick received the Military Medal for his courage and leadership on the battlefield that day, and he recommended Bluey Moore and Ron Eglinton for the same award for their efforts in securing the platoon's southern flank. Eglinton kept his machine gun operating throughout the battle despite his rounds being caked with mud. Apart from those two men, Bob Buick cannot separate the efforts of the remainder of his platoon.

That is why he was so pleased in 2009 when Delta Company was awarded the Unit Citation for Gallantry after earlier receiving the US Presidential Unit Citation and the South Vietnamese Gallantry Cross with Unit Citation.

'It hasn't got to be an individual to do anything, the main game is to survive, to protect yourself and your mates and if you all go down, well that's the way it is.'

Final proof of the impact of the battle on the enemy came in 2006 when Bob Buick and Dave Sabben returned to Vietnam with a television crew. Discussing the battle with former enemy commanders, Buick says they were still flabbergasted that just 108 soldiers had prevailed. 'I think D Company put up such a resistance to these fellows that they must have thought there were 300 of us.'

Just like Harry Smith and Dave Sabben, Bob Buick is disgusted by the imperial awards system that protected the interests of the brass ahead of the brave men who fought the battle. Medals were awarded from the top down, which meant that under the quota system, Australian senior officers, who were well away from the battlefield, were given high-level awards while soldiers in the thick of the action often missed out.

'The Americans have a separate system where they have a highly specialised, trained group of people, who after an action sit down and talk to anyone in that unit to determine who did what and how,' he says. 'They then go back and write up people for the citations, and that to me is the only honest way of doing it.'

Like many Vietnam veterans, Buick has had to deal with his fair share of demons since returning from the war. The day after Long Tan he was back on the battlefield sifting through the detritus of war and the remains of hundreds of young men blown to bits by the big guns.

'I saw one guy that had no arms, legs, a head, there is his torso, not a mark on his torso, no clothes, stark bollocky naked, no legs, arms or head. Another half a guy, I didn't see his hips or his legs, but his guts are all hanging out,' he says.

Suddenly there was a movement. A body with half its skull missing and its insides hanging out had twitched; the VC soldier appeared to be still alive.

'I thought, "you poor fucking bastard," and I instinctively put two rounds in his heart to put him out of his misery. He had half a metre of his guts lying out, you could see where he had his rice, his gut had been cut open with probably a bit of splinter from an artillery round, and the rice was just falling out of it.

'We treated all the wounded with respect, we treated the dead with respect, we buried them properly as much as we could. I think if I had to do it again, I most probably would, simply because it is so distressing to see some bloke like that.'

Chapter 3

Live Aid

As Bob Buick and his men were fighting for their lives in the Long Tan rubber plantation, Bob Grandin was back at Nui Dat trying to convince his fellow RAAF Iroquois (Huey) chopper pilot Frank Riley not to risk his skin on a suicide mission.

August 18 had begun quietly enough at the helicopter base at the port town of Vung Tau as co-pilot Grandin and his captain Frank Riley prepared their Huey for a 15-minute dash to deliver entertainers Little Pattie, Col Joye and the Joy Boys and all their gear up to Nui Dat for a concert. It would be a two-ship flight — the second Huey would be flown by Cliff Dohle and Bruce Lane.

Air force choppers operated under RAAF operational command in Vietnam and, despite loud protests from the army, the safety of the machine took precedence over any other considerations. As Bob Grandin discovered, that included the safety of the task force commander, Brigadier Oliver Jackson.

'Bruce and I flew over to Nui Dat one day to take the brigadier out to check how everything was going,' he says. 'We asked if the landing area was a secure area and the brigadier said to us, "Wherever the brigadier goes it's secure."

'So we landed, we re-cocked the aeroplane to take straight off again, which means you've only got to press the starter and she winds up and away we go. We'd only been there a couple of minutes when suddenly there was small arms fire around the perimeter of the paddock. So we just took off, swoosh, up we went, he came running back out looking for his aeroplane to get him out of there and we were gone. We told him he would have to secure the pad before we could come back and get him.'

All pilots were briefed that they worked for the RAAF and not the army and would operate under air force orders. This meant that they would not take direct orders from the army and that the security of one of the six precious RAAF Hueys deployed to Vietnam was more important than the security of a pesky brigadier.

The tension between the army and the air force in Vietnam left a deep scar in relations between the two services. The generals never forgot, and after years of lobbying the army finally won control of the rotary wing fleet in 1986. No brigadier would ever be abandoned again.

After delivering their cargo to Nui Dat at around 10 am the crews of the two choppers were told to hang around the base and be ready to fly the entertainers back to Vung Tau after the concert. Just before 4 pm the artillery battery to the west of the helipad opened up. Grandin and his fellow flyers knew something serious was going down.

Bob Grandin is a thoughtful man who freely admits that he joined the air force to go flying and see some action. At first he flew Neptune bombers.

On a mission out of Laos to escort the aircraft carrier HMAS *Sydney* — known as the 'Vung Tau ferry' for all the men and supplies she carried to Vietnam — his aircraft's crew thought they had detected an enemy submarine. Grandin's plane carried 44 torpedoes and had a full load of fuel.

'It happened to be one of our other aeroplanes that turned their attack radar on us and they went over the top, but you get that sense of action,' he recalls. 'We were all talking about the Third World War and what would happen if a Russian submarine popped up. I did join the service for action. I'd come out of the Second World War, Biggles and all that sort of stuff, so you have that sense that you would like to be where the action is.'

In 1965 it was obvious to even a junior officer like Bob Grandin that Vietnam was where the action was going to be and rotary wing aircraft would be right in the thick of it. So he transferred to choppers in January 1966 and moved to RAAF Fairbairn at Canberra airport to train as a rotary wing pilot.

Taking off from Vung Tau on August 18, 1966, with Aussie entertainers in the back of his 9 Squadron Huey, Bob Grandin had not a care in the world.

The helipad at Vung Tau was located on the end of a narrow peninsula with a back beach on one side and an ocean beach on the other. In between was an airfield supply area. Heading north there were mangroves to the west and ocean to the east with the Long Hai hills in the distance. The hills were a VC stronghold and supply area along the Ho Chi Minh Trail.

Flying inland the mangroves were soon replaced by dense jungle broken by clearings where local people eked out a subsistence living. The clearings were linked by narrow walking tracks, and a single dirt road ran up the middle to Nui Dat.

The area was regarded as hostile, so the Huey crews flew at 700 metres to reduce the chances of a stray small arms hit to about 20 per cent.

In the first weeks of their deployment, 9 Squadron was tasked with the odd medevac flight to the field hospital and 'hash and trash' missions, delivering supplies to bases around the province and flying officers around. Before August 18 the squadron had not seen any serious action.

As the concert began and the artillery fire grew in intensity, Grandin and his mates suspected that something very serious was happening.

'I seem to recall saying things like, "Shit, what are they doing that for? I wonder if that is just daily interdiction or somebody has found a target," because every day the artillery fired this random [speculative] fire.'

The concert finally finished and Little Pattie was on a joyride in an armoured personnel carrier, while Col Joye had been 'kidnapped' by his fans and was being held somewhere in the lines. 'There was no big panic to go home. Nobody had gone to war yet, there had been some clearing exercises and a tiny bit of this, that and the other thing, but nothing major.'

As the firing dragged on Frank Riley decided to go to the command post to find out what was happening. 'I said, "I'll come too," because I never let Frank out of my sight as I never knew what he was going to get up to, but I was intrigued,' Grandin says.

They arrived at the command post to a scene of utter chaos. Radios were blaring, people were yelling and no one took the slightest bit of notice of the flyboys in their midst.

'I heard things like, "There are thousands of them, they are everywhere, we need to do this, need to do that," and people arguing over what they were going to do and what they weren't going to do,' he says. 'There was just a lot of commands and actions and then they were saying somebody had been killed, things like that.'

By this time every gun on the base was firing into the rubber plantation in front of D Company, generating a tremendous amount of noise. Through the hubbub came the unmistakable message that without ammunition resupply Delta Company was in grave danger of being overrun.

Brigadier Jackson and the senior RAAF officer, Group Captain Peter Raw, were arguing about using the RAAF Hueys to get the ammo out to Smith and his men. Raw even suggested he might need to call Canberra to clear the matter up.

Jackson, who just the week before had watched his own RAAF Huey flee from a hot landing zone, was so disgusted he requested US helicopter support to do the job, but was dismayed when told the US machines were at least an hour away.

Finally, Frank Riley could stay silent no longer and broke the impasse by volunteering to fly the ammo out immediately. Riley said he would go alone if necessary, thus shaming Raw and the RAAF hierarchy into action.

'I thought, "Shit, this is madness, this is just suicide, going out there with all these guys." That was my rational brain starting to think too quickly,' Grandin says. 'I said, "You know we are not meant to go into an unsafe area," and Frank just said, "Look I'm in charge of this aeroplane, I'm detachment commander, I'll decide what's the go."'

When Raw suggested calling the boss in Canberra, Riley said, 'He can only say no!' So the call was never made and Riley told Jackson he was ready to go. They raced back to the aircraft and started loading the machines with ammunition boxes for the desperate diggers. 'I'm saying to Frank, "This is bloody madness, how are we going to do this? This is just a bloody suicide mission." He said, "I don't give a stuff, we are going." Frank was a good heavy drinker and a wild man, and he said, "That's what you come to war for, Bob," and I was trying to be rational.'

They finally decided on a tactic they had practised with the SAS whereby one machine would fly in at 2000 feet, check everything out, find the pad and guide the other guy in at treetop level. The second machine would dive in and deliver the ammo before the enemy knew what was happening.

'I was comfortable with that. I thought, "That's all right, we'll be up there out of the road,"' Grandin says.

Riley told him he did not have to undertake the mission if he didn't want to.

'"Of course I'm going to fucking come!" So it was a fascinating thing to reflect on, how much I realised this was madness, yet I had no desire to pull out. I was madly trying to work out, if I am going to do something insane, how am I going to get away with it?'

As the boxes of ammunition were unstrapped and loaded into the two choppers Bob Grandin prepared himself for the most dangerous flight of his short career. Major Owen O'Brien and Warrant Officer George Chinn joined the crews to make sure the ammo, wrapped in blankets, was delivered.

'I got myself right back into the seat, made sure the front bit was between my legs so if anything came flying up through the bottom it didn't get me in the private parts,' he says. 'I had the maps and things out and was ticking over in my mind all the things I had to do, the callsigns, and I was going through all this step by step.

'When I have a crisis I will become very cool, calculating; I don't panic or run away. I was frightened, the adrenaline was pumping around my body, I was scared. I didn't like this at all. I thought, "I can't see how we are going to get away with this."'

As the guns fell silent, the choppers lifted off and turned towards Long Tan. They were greeted by the ominous sight of a pitch-black monsoonal storm cloud bearing down on them at a rapid rate of knots.

The diggers were only about four kilometres away from the main base but the jungle had disappeared into this massive cloud formation and sheets of torrential rain. Normally such extreme weather is the mortal enemy of a helicopter pilot, but in this case the rain would assist their mission by masking their flight above enemy forces.

Riley was flying and Grandin was map-reading and watching the treetops between his legs. Suddenly he saw where the road at Long Tan turned 90 degrees and he realised they had gone too far and were now over enemy territory, so they turned 180 degrees and called on Delta Company for smoke. Orange smoke appeared through the jungle canopy; the smoke was supposed to be red, so they waited until they saw red smoke and moved into position. Torrential rain was battering the aircraft and jungle below, making it impossible for the enemy to identify the chopper's location.

Cliff Dohle and Bruce Lane were airborne at Nui Dat with a cabin full of ammo boxes waiting for the word to go. 'We asked Cliffy to turn on his anti-collision light, which is a red one on top, and we said "We've got you," and we directed him at treetop level, straight to the spot. Frank was guiding, "Left, left, right, right, roll out." All he did was a 180-degree roll and all the ammunition fell out right on top of them. Then we dived in behind him and rolled on our side and out it went.'

Having saved the day, and after less than ten minutes over the battlefield, the two Hueys were back on the helipad at Nui Dat.

The boxes had landed directly on company headquarters. Jack Kirby distributed the life-saving rounds to his men just as the next wave of enemy attacks began.

Frank Riley received the Distinguished Flying Cross for his courage that day, while Cliff Dohle's Mentioned in Despatches was later upgraded to a Distinguished Service Medal that was presented to his widow Joan by Governor-General Quentin Bryce in August 2010.

Chapter 4

A 40-Year Campaign

Tears welled up in Harry Smith's eyes as he stood before the Long Tan Cross at the Australian War Memorial in July 2012.

More than 46 years after the battle of Long Tan in Vietnam, he could see in the cross the faces of the 18 Australian soldiers, aged between 19 and 22, who were killed in action on August 18, 1966. Seventeen of the dead and 23 wounded diggers came from Major Smith's Delta Company of the 6th Battalion Royal Australian Regiment (6 RAR).

The original cross, erected at Long Tan in 1969, was on loan to the Australian War Memorial from a museum in Vietnam. 'It brought tears to my eyes … because there on the wall is the cross and it says 17 in Delta Company and one Armoured Corps fellow, who was mortally wounded and didn't die for another nine days, so there are 18 lost in the day and I can see faces on that cross. That cross enshrines the spirit of the 18 men we lost that day.

Looking back it's very sad, the battle shouldn't have happened of course, and it was a war that we couldn't win.'

The Delta Company troops, who were about 50 per cent national servicemen, carried the day during the four-hour pitched battle against the vastly bigger enemy force.

'I believe if it hadn't been for them being such a good team, that maybe none of us would have survived,' Smith says. 'It was up to the frontline soldiers to stop the enemy, and if they couldn't stop the enemy running over them, we would have all been overrun. They didn't let the enemy get through. They mowed them down, if I can use that expression, and not one enemy soldier got inside our forward line.'

The Hervey Bay area of the Queensland coast houses more retired military folk than any other part of the nation. The sub-tropical climate and calm seas make it an ideal location for old soldiers to spend their sunset years, especially if they are keen sailors.

Smith is a very keen sailor and, as he sits today in his home enjoying a light lunch, there are images all around of Harry, his wife Felicia and their various boats. The Smiths spend as much time as they can each year cruising the waters of the Great Barrier Reef on the current family vessel, a beautiful motor launch called MV *Melaleuca*, moored just down the road at Hervey Bay marina.

Close to the marina in Dayman Point Park there is a black granite memorial cairn built to honour the men from 'Z' Special Unit who undertook the Operation Jaywick raid on Singapore Harbour during World War II. Many 'Z' Special operatives trained on Fraser Island, just across the clear blue waters of Great Sandy Strait.

The peaceful surrounds of the Queensland retirement coast are far removed from the blood and sweat of the South Vietnamese jungle in 1966, when, as Major Smith, Harry led his men into the Long Tan rubber plantation with absolutely no idea that the very large mixed enemy force of North Vietnamese regulars and Vietcong had been moving south towards the task force base.

'The mindset was guerrilla warfare, yet we should have been given more information about what the enemy could do,' he says. 'We weren't told that an American company was wiped out about 25 kilometres north of Nui Dat the previous December. We were not told about the Americans losing something like 19 killed and 90 wounded at Long Phuoc, which was only about three kilometres east of where we were.'

Much has been written about exactly how much information task force headquarters, under Brigadier Oliver Jackson, knew about the movement of the large enemy force. What is without question is that when Harry Smith and Delta Company entered the Long Tan rubber plantation they had no idea there was even a remote possibility of encountering such a large force so close to home.

'There was very little information given to us and it's a tragedy because the information was available to task force headquarters, but was held within the ranks of three or four officers: Brigadier Jackson, the intelligence officer, signals intelligence officer and maybe Jackson's PA,' Smith says.

According to Harry Smith, Jackson was also advised that mercenary troops at the village of Binh Ba had deserted because they knew the enemy was coming. 'We weren't told that, we weren't told the enemy was tracked coming in along the east of the Long Tan rubber plantation by radio intercept; it was all kept secret.'

Smith also says that in 1967 at Canungra jungle training centre, Jackson admitted that he had known the enemy was out there and had sent Smith's company out to lure them into artillery range.

Being a professional soldier and a qualified commando, Harry Smith was a hard taskmaster and a stickler for going above and beyond when it came to preparing his men for war.

He grew up in Tasmania and joined the army cadets at Hobart High School, where he loved firing weapons on the range. His father had been a sergeant during World War II, serving with the 2/9th Armoured Regiment in General Grant tanks.

One of Harry's favourite pastimes was shooting rabbits with a .303 rifle, but when caught with a pocket full of .303 rounds belonging to the army he was discharged from cadets. Six months later he was back as a corporal.

After starting work as a cadet metallurgist, young Harry joined the CMF (Citizen Military Forces), the forerunner of the Army Reserves. In 1952 he was drafted into the 90-day national service scheme and became a corporal. Returning to his job in Hobart, he found it no longer existed, so he decided to join the regular army. Acting on his father's advice, he elected to train as an officer, and was accepted at Portsea officer training school in July 1952, graduating as a second lieutenant in December of that year.

He requested the armoured corps to follow in his father's footsteps, so naturally the army disagreed and sent him to the infantry at Puckapunyal in Victoria before posting him as a platoon commander for national service. After passing his parachute course he was posted to the 2nd Battalion and spent two years in Malaya.

'I did see the odd angry shot fired,' he says. 'The first one was when my platoon set an ambush in a track outside the village. At about nine o'clock at night all hell broke loose, flares went off and my machine gun was ordered up, so we opened fire and killed what we thought was a communist terrorist.

'It turned out to be a 70-year-old village chief, who unfortunately had been to another village, got pissed and was on his way home, but anyone outside curfew from 7 pm to 7 am they hit no questions asked.'

On another occasion the local trackers had spotted a terrorist going into the jungle. Harry's patrol followed and soon had the man cornered.

'I used to carry an American M1 carbine, which was handy to put under your arm to read maps and compasses,' he recalls. 'And I went forward and they pointed into the bush and you could see the terrorist. He appeared to be going to throw a grenade so I shot him, and I shot him several times, probably more than was necessary, and he was taken back to the local police station and hung up on the wall as a warning to everybody else that wanted to become a terrorist.'

His jungle experience would prove to be invaluable in Vietnam. After completing his commando training, Smith was posted to 6 RAR on promotion to major in October 1965. Now commander of Delta Company, Major Smith did not endear himself to his fellow officers by opting to train his men along commando lines, including eight-kilometre runs every morning. His commanding officer, Lieutenant Colonel Colin Townsend, even pulled him aside and chipped him for training his men beyond normal battalion limits.

'I said, "Well as company commander, it's my company, that's the way I want to go." It was obvious then that fellows who couldn't run five miles I moved out, and I finished up with a wonderful team,' he says.

The team included the experienced warrior and Company Sergeant Major Jack Kirby, whom Smith describes as a great man.

Despite the pressures, Harry Smith was not about to ease up on his men. He had great respect for the training regimes of special forces units such as the SAS and Commandos, whose training is so arduous and mimics combat conditions so closely that several soldiers have died undertaking it.

'You've got to engender a spirit of teamwork and confidence in people so when the chips are down they will perform and they know they can perform,' Smith says.

By the time they arrived in Vietnam in June 1966, Delta Company was a well-oiled machine and a tight-knit infantry unit.

'The company was a wonderful group of soldiers and corporals and sergeants and CSMs [company sergeant majors] and young officers,' Smith says. 'I was only 33; they were younger than me. Dave Sabben and Gordon Sharp were only 21, but the company itself was a well-trained team; they knew what was expected.'

Harry Smith had his own set of patrol rules or standing orders that all of his soldiers were expected to follow. 'You will always have your sleeves rolled down, you'll always have your collars done up, you will always have your hat on, you will wear camouflage … This wasn't the normal thing, but I maintained a high standard. I'd been in Malaya, I knew what was required for this sort of jungle type warfare. I instituted rules and regulations that didn't necessarily please everybody, [but] my men respected them and knew that if they followed the rules and regulations they had a better chance of winning and surviving any battle we might come across.'

Even inside the task force base, when others might be relaxing and enjoying a few beers, Delta Company worked from dawn till dusk, building paths, digging drains, even planting banana trees to brighten the place up, anything to keep busy.

'We even put wire all around our own company position, because if the enemy were going to come into that bloody base, they might as well come through another company or battalion headquarters,' he says. 'The CO came in one day and said, "Why have you got barbed wire behind your company, Smith?" I said, "Sir, because I don't trust another company or battalion headquarters to protect that sector."'

Team spirit was strong. One of the diggers suggested they adopt as their theme song the Nancy Sinatra hit of the time, 'These Boots Are Made for Walking'. 'We could outmarch any other bloody company,' Smith recalls with pride.

Following a mortar attack on the base on the morning of August 17, Major Smith was ordered to take his men out fully equipped to search for maybe 30 or 40 enemy who had probably already left the area. 'We now know that on the 15th of August there was an [enemy] regiment about another kilometre and a half to the east, but they didn't want to show their hand because they were waiting to attack the base on the night of the concert,' he says.

The concert, featuring Little Pattie and Col Joye, was well underway when Delta Company left the base at 11 am to rendezvous with Bravo Company, who were due out on leave. The operation was codenamed Vendetta. They could hear the music all the way out to the western edge of the Long Tan rubber plantation where the two companies married up.

'People deny that the base was the target, but that's the fact because I was there when two North Vietnamese prisoners said to Brian Wickham, who was the intelligence officer, through an interpreter, "We were on the way to attack the Nui Dat base." That's good enough for me.'

The evidence is supported by the official history of the Vietcong's D445 Battalion — one of the enemy units that took part in the Long Tan battle — which refers to the planned 'annihilation' of the Australian force. For his seminal book

Vietnam: The Australian War, author Paul Ham interviewed the commander of the North Vietnamese Army's 274th Battalion, Nguyen Nam Hung, who told him that the enemy's intention was to destroy the Australians.

As Harry Smith led his men through head-high elephant grass towards the Long Tan rubber plantation, he was secure in the knowledge that his 108 diggers, supported by artillery and air power if required, would be more than a match for a mere 30 or 40 enemy fighters.

Once the battle started and he realised what he was up against he wasn't so sure. Between arguments with headquarters about ammunition and air support, and managing the battle, Harry Smith says he never had time to become frightened.

Despite the gravity of the situation and the possibility of being overrun, Smith is convinced that task force headquarters remained blissfully unaware for most of the battle of just how dire the situation was for Delta Company.

'At about 6.30 the enemy had obviously pinpointed us and had brought in reserve troops, fresh troops who were climbing over each other and the bodies to get to us,' he says.

The guns had been silent for some time while the helicopters had resupplied them with ammunition and the enemy was advancing fast. Smith ordered his forward artillery observer, New Zealander Captain Morrie Stanley, to radio the gun line to 'drop 50'. In other words, bring the artillery rounds 50 yards closer to the Australian position, from 150 to 100.

There was a debate about the safety of such close artillery, forcing Harry to send out a very clear message. 'I picked up the bloody radio and I said, "Just tell them to fire the bloody guns where we want them to fire, otherwise you will lose the whole bloody lot of us," and then Morrie said to me about ten seconds later, "Okay, they got dropped 50, they dropped 50." The artillery fire was coming over the top of us; it was exceptionally accurate. All the burst of the shells went forward into the enemy. It was wonderful support and without the artillery we certainly wouldn't have survived,' Smith says.

Apart from just before his call to 'drop 50', he says at no stage during the battle, especially while the artillery rained down, did he fear his men would be overrun and wiped out. 'I was so confident in my soldiers and the way they were performing. We had plenty of ammunition after the helicopters had been in; I was prepared to fight through the night if we had to.'

Retreating was never an option due to the large number of casualties left on the battlefield. 10 Platoon alone had lost 15 of its 29 men within 200 metres of the company headquarters.

'I didn't want to leave and I still recall thinking — because I'd heard about the enemy up north cutting soldiers' testicles off and shoving them in their mouths and these sorts of atrocities — I said "I do not want to withdraw, I am staying here",' he says. 'You are better off sitting where you've got an all-round defensive position, all this wall of fire around you, than trying to get up and move. That's the last thing you'd want to do because it's also possible that they might have got behind you and would ambush you on the way out.'

Harry Smith says the gallantry displayed by his men at Long Tan was absolutely outstanding. 'They supported each other, they went out and pulled back wounded under fire, and it's criminal that some of these fellows who performed acts of gallantry as good as the first VC in Afghanistan were never recognised,' he says.

He has waged a 46-year battle against the top brass and the Canberra bureaucracy for proper recognition for his men. Some injustices have been corrected with individual awards and unit citations, but Smith maintains several matters remain outstanding.

These include a possible posthumous Victoria Cross for Company Sergeant Major Jack Kirby, who was awarded the Distinguished Conduct Medal following the battle.

'He [Jack] disregarded enemy fire, he moved around, he took ammunition around and before he got the helicopters in, Jack was coming back to the company headquarters taking ammunition off wounded and taking it forward, disregarding the fire,' Smith says. 'He'd give words of encouragement to soldiers, telling them, "Anybody you don't know, shoot him."

'Jack went forward and shot a machine-gun crew as they set up their weapon right in front of him. [He] chose to go out there and do that, and that is exceptional gallantry; it's an instinct, shall we say, of what you can do to protect your mates, to kill the enemy so they won't kill any more of us.'

Then there was radio operator Bill Akell, who without hesitation ran forward into the maelstrom with a spare radio when communications with 10 Platoon were lost. He reestablished comms and returned to the headquarters after killing a couple of enemy along the way. Akell was nominated for the Military Medal, but this was downgraded to a Mentioned in Despatches.

The full impact of what he had lived through didn't strike Harry Smith until later that night, after the wounded and some bodies had been flown out. 'I suddenly felt frightened, yet unbelievably surprised that I was still there,' he says.

The men sat up for the rest of the night before going back in to retrieve bodies after first light. 'I wondered whether they'd taken all their bodies and whether they'd mutilated our bodies and pinched all the weapons they had. I was very relieved when we went back in and our fellows were still there. They hadn't been touched, there were still two alive [Private Jim Richardson, who had been shot in the chest, and Private Barry Meller, shot in the mouth and leg]. Bob [Buick] and his men obviously thought they were dead, they wouldn't have left them otherwise.'

Meller spent the night propped up against a tree where he was found the next morning. 'All the dead soldiers still had their rifles in their hands, still pointing at the enemy direction, and there were enemy bodies everywhere, unbelievable carnage. I suddenly realised we had won the battle over the enemy, unbelievably, due to the gallantry and courage and dedication of my soldiers and the support from the artillery.'

Harry Smith believes the survival of Delta Company had a lot to do with the spirit of his soldiers, the spirit of looking after their mates, firing in support of their mates and the knowledge that they could do it.

'We were there to kill the enemy and we'll bloody well do it. I mean the role of the infantry soldier is to kill the enemy, that's the bottom line and that's what we trained for,' he says. 'I had the highest regard for all my soldiers, as I often said I owe my life to those guys and they fought over and above what you would normally expect from an infantry company, just to be, to face waves of suicidal enemy, under artillery fire, and they were able to knock them down or blow them away.'

Gunner Bayne 'Gus' Kelly (centre) dressed for action during the Vietnam War.
Bayne Kelly

Bayne Kelly proudly wears his medals after receiving the US Commendation Medal for Valour more than 40 years after he was awarded the gong during the Battle of Long Khanh in Vietnam in 1971. With him are his brothers Lincoln and Hayden, wife Margaret and sons James, Dominic and Nicholas. Bayne Kelly

Former Army Brigadier, Military Cross winner and novelist Adrian D'Hagé. After his commanding officer was shot, D'Hage showed courage and leadership under fire during a pitched battle in Vietnam. Adrian D'Hagé

Vietnam veteran and former navy helicopter pilot Andy Perry, who was awarded the United States Silver Star for gallantry in action, on board his boat, *Bill Bailey*, in Port Huon marina, Tasmania. Ian McPhedran

Andy Perry at the controls of an Iroquois 'Huey' helicopter during the Vietnam War. Andy Perry

THE UNITED STATES OF AMERICA

TO ALL WHO SHALL SEE THESE PRESENTS, GREETING:

THIS IS TO CERTIFY THAT
THE PRESIDENT OF THE UNITED STATES OF AMERICA
AUTHORIZED BY ACT OF CONGRESS JULY 9, 1918
HAS AWARDED

THE SILVER STAR

TO

SUB-LIEUTENANT ANDREW C. PERRY, 02877, ROYAL AUSTRALIAN NAVY

FOR
GALLANTRY IN ACTION

IN THE REPUBLIC OF VIETNAM ON 18 MAY 1970
GIVEN UNDER MY HAND IN THE CITY OF WASHINGTON
THIS 28th DAY OF FEBRUARY 1973

CREIGHTON W. ABRAMS
General, United States Army

SECRETARY OF THE ARMY

Andy Perry's Silver Star certificate, dated 28 February 1973, was finally presented to him in April 1995.

Governor-General Quentin Bryce pins the Medal for Gallantry onto Dave Sabben's chest on 6 August 2011, 45 years after he earned it as a young lieutenant at the Battle of Long Tan in Vietnam.
Dave Sabben

Platoon commander Lieutenant Dave Sabben (left) with platoon sergeants Lance Larcombe (centre) and Bob Buick (right) in Vietnam in 1967. Dave Sabben

Australian Task Force commander Brigadier Oliver Jackson pins the Military Medal to the chest of Sergeant Bob Buick at Nui Dat following the Battle of Long Tan in August 1966. Bob Buick

Lieutenant Jim Hughes (left), fresh from Duntroon, had his baptism of fire at the brutal battle of Maryang San during the Korean War. Hughes family
(right) Now retired, Major General Hughes reads about the Korean campaign from his Melbourne home. Ian McPhedran

Former SAS officer and Star of Courage winner Andy Harris. Despite suffering from horrendous injuries, Harris saved his passenger's life following a horrific crash in an Aero Commander. Ian McPhedran

Boatswain or 'Buffer' Matt Keogh alongside the Armidale Class Patrol Boat HMAS *Wollongong* prior to a border protection patrol under Operation Resolute. He was awarded the Medal for Gallantry for his courage after an illegal entry vessel blew up. Ian McPhedran

Petty Officer Ben Sime jumped from his Seahawk helicopter into the Persian Gulf in a daring bid to rescue a badly injured sailor in the aftermath of a terrorist attack. He was awarded the Medal for Gallantry. (below) Iraq's Abot offshore oil terminal where the incident took place. Ben Sime

Ex-navy clearance diver Justin Brown (above) received the Commendation for Gallantry (the orange ribbon) for his late-night swim off a militia-held beach during the 1999 East Timor conflict. He remained in the water despite enemy headlights beaming on him as he kept guard over his mates operating below the surface. Ian McPhedran (left) Queen Elizabeth II congratulates him on the honour.
Justin Brown

Chapter 5

A Kaleidoscope of Ugliness

Adrian Stuart d'Hagé is one of the most unusual characters ever to have donned the khaki uniform and rising sun badge of the Australian Army. The former infantry officer, bookie's clerk, military pubic relations chief and now best-selling author also knows his way around a good red wine and is possibly the most accomplished person to have occupied the controversial post of head of military public affairs.

'Darj', as he is known to his legion of mates and his many enemies, rose to the dizzy heights of brigadier many years after he was awarded the Military Cross for 'exemplary gallantry during active operations on land' during Operation Lavarack with the 6th Battalion in South Vietnam in June 1969 as a newly minted captain.

The battle lasted for four hours, during which time Darj assumed the role of company commander when that officer was wounded.

'Throughout the heavy contact, which lasted for four hours, Captain d'Hagé's leadership was exemplary and his gallantry a great inspiration to all ranks of the company,' his citation reads. Like most war heroes Darj dismisses his courage as the actions of a frightened, desperate but well-trained soldier.

The cosy living room of his writer's nook at Wentworth Falls in the Blue Mountains is about as far removed from the deadly jungles of South Vietnam as you could imagine. As the wood stove crackles, the former soldier and renowned 'shit stirrer' reflects on his act of bravery 43 years before.

Born and raised in Mosman ('the battler end, not leafy Balmoral') on Sydney's north shore, he was brought up in a conservative God-fearing household with a violent father, who his son now understands must have suffered from post-traumatic stress disorder from his service with an artillery unit in North Africa during World War II.

A regular at Sunday school, young Adrian tossed up between careers in the priesthood and the army. Finally settling on the army, he applied for a place at the Royal Military College, Duntroon (RMC). 'The military's brochures were a little more glossy,' he explains.

An avid army cadet, he played first trombone in the North Sydney Boys High School cadet unit band, but just before the 1963 passing-out parade he had been busted from sergeant to private for drinking and smoking. The commandant of Duntroon was to be the reviewing officer at the school parade, so d'Hagé thought he should draw the attention of his command chain to his low status within the unit.

He went in to see the cadet major and said, 'Listen, sir, it's not going to look too flash because [the reviewing officer] is going to ask, "Is anybody going to Duntroon next year?" "Yes, Cadet d'Hagé who is playing trombone in the band." It's not going to look too flash.

'So they gave me my three stripes back for the parade,' d'Hagé recalls. His disdain for authority would always make his career choice a challenging one. Despite his run-in with the Cadet Corps hierarchy, young Adrian was duly accepted into RMC as a trainee army officer.

When the big day arrived he and his father had to manhandle the huge shipping trunk, complete with bamboo reinforcing batons, which his mother had purchased as a going away gift. She included a winter dressing gown for the cold Canberra nights, an ironing board and pink rubber gloves to protect his fingernails from boot polish. His aunt had packed a valve radio so he could keep in touch with the outside world.

His father helped him to carry the huge trunk onto the platform at Central Station. When the wide-eyed, fresh-faced cadets arrived at Canberra Station, the legendary Duntroon Regimental Sergeant Major Tom Muggleton, and his merry band of drill sergeants, were waiting to greet their new charges.

'Our luggage arrived in a truck and we were ordered to get it out of the Studebaker truck and line up. Well, everybody lined up but I couldn't actually lift mine out of the truck,' d'Hagé says. 'So I said to the nearest friendly drill sergeant, "Would you mind giving me a hand?"

'That seemed to prompt an involuntary bowel movement and I was rather grateful that I'd convinced my mother that Duntroon probably had ironing boards, because an ironing board might have been an unnecessary complication.'

Bastardisation has become a controversial topic for the military in recent years, but in the 1960s the term had an entirely different meaning and was part of the process for new cadets.

Woofering (the sucking of genitals into the nozzle of a vacuum cleaner), corporal punishment and bizarre rituals such as cleaning toilets with toothbrushes and pushing peas around the parade ground with your nose were standard procedure for decades at the army officers' elite nursery.

Another classic ordeal for new cadets was the 'screed test', in which a cadet would be required to recite the inscription on the gravestone of the college's first commandant, General William Bridges, located on a hill high above the college. If they could not manage it they were sent up the hill at mealtime to memorise the words.

Then there were the sinker races where cadets were required to scoff their sponge cake and custard and turn the empty bowl onto their heads. Few could escape the slimy goo running down their face.

By far the most common form of bullying involved the cadet rank structure whereby second- and third-year cadets could lord it over the first years at will. 'On the first day they come into your room and surround you asking, "Who am I? Don't know? Then bog off and find out."

'You would go to leave and they'd say, "Don't you excuse yourself?" "Excuse me", "Excuse me who?" "Don't know." It was that sort of constant mental bullshit,' d'Hagé says.

Later on his first night he hadn't had a chance to polish anything, so he put on his pink rubber gloves (courtesy of his mum), put a blanket over the window, lit a candle and got under the bed and started polishing.

'The door was flung open by a second-class cadet and the light was snapped on and all you could see was my bum sticking out from under the bed,' he recalls. '"What are you doing under there?" So I got out in my pink rubber gloves holding a candle like Wee Willy Winky and he said, "Hey fellas, come and have a look at this dickhead." So my career at Duntroon got off to a fairly shaky start, but I enjoyed it.

'There was lots of sport. The food was crap; it's improved a lot these days. We got Brussels sprouts every night. I've never eaten Brussels sprouts since I left Duntroon.'

Cadets weren't allowed to leave the campus for the first ten weeks. D'Hagé was going out with Margaret Waterhouse of the bookmaking clan at the time. On Friday nights he would hitch a ride up the Hume to Sydney to see her, and he would coax one of his mates to call him present at the Saturday roll call.

He was also working on the bag for her dad, Jack Waterhouse. Once Jack discovered that young Adrian was hitchhiking up from Canberra he insisted that his young employee and possible future son-in-law fly between the capitals.

Duntroon cadets were paid the princely sum of ten shillings a week at the time, and he tried to explain to Mr Waterhouse that an airfare was beyond his means.

'He said, "You'll either fly on the company account or you don't see my daughter. What's it going to be?"'

'I said, "I guess I'll fly." So I used to go out to Canberra airport and sometimes there would be officers from Duntroon on the old Vickers Viscount, so I'd wait until the last moment and duck on board and I'd always get a seat down the back and fly up to Sydney to see his daughter,' he says.

It was a lifestyle that a young army officer might have become used to, with cars and hotel rooms at Coogee, Bronte and Chatswood all laid on.

At his graduation from RMC, d'Hagé's father asked one of the senior officers how his son had performed. 'If your son had been a bit better than a day boy, Mr d'Hagé, he would have done a lot better,' the officer said.

'They were onto me, they just couldn't catch me,' d'Hagé says.

Rat cunning is a key ingredient for a successful soldier, particularly in war, so young d'Hagé had all the ingredients to be a leader of men and to keep himself, and them, alive.

He was posted to the Brisbane-based 6th Battalion as a second lieutenant, and 18 months later he arrived at Vung Tau in Vietnam on board the converted light aircraft carrier HMAS *Sydney*.

'All of a sudden you realise you are in a war zone — they had speed boats towing lengths of barbed wire around the aircraft carrier to prevent divers putting mines on it,' he says. 'You realise, "Jesus Christ this is serious," and then I got the news that John Lee, one of my best mates at Duntroon, had been killed four days before in an ambush and had bled to death. Suddenly the war got personal, not that I think that clouded my judgement — you could never let that happen, but it hit home that this was ugly.'

It was late May 1969 and d'Hagé's unit, 5 Platoon, Bravo Company 6 RAR, missed out on the normal luxury of doing some shorter week-long patrols to become acclimatised and was almost immediately sent out for a month-long mission codenamed Operation Lavarack.

The object of the operation was to support the Army of the Republic of Vietnam through securing larger areas of countryside to the north of Nui Dat by establishing fire support and patrol bases. The diggers' main job was to patrol the jungle and root out the enemy so that the area was secure.

The Vietcong and North Vietnamese Army were not the only threats to the Aussie troops. D'Hagé recalls one occasion where the company was late arriving at an ambush site. He and one of his corporals had placed claymore mines in the kill zone and were walking back when — boom! One of the mines detonated, covering the men in blast debris but fortunately doing nothing more serious.

'War is not only ugly, it is full of fuck-ups,' he says. 'The rule was with claymores that you weren't allowed to site them with the detonators in. You sited them, made sure everything was right then you primed them with the detonators. A brown cord ran from the detonator to the "clacker" or trigger that you squeezed and it generated an electric pulse and it set the detonator off.'

It got dark early under the dense jungle canopy. D'Hagé set the mines with the detonators in and ready to go. 'I hated to get into an ambush after about four o'clock,' he says.

He left one of his less capable diggers in charge of the clackers. As they walked back towards him, there was an enormous back blast. The soldier had sat on one of the clackers. 'You get accidents with the best trained diggers in the world, but I am fortunate to be here telling the story. I could easily have been one of the 500 [Australians killed in the Vietnam War].'

The company commander was quickly on the radio demanding to know the body count, only to be informed that there were two very shaken but alive Australians.

Body count was an important indicator during the Vietnam War, and many a senior officer's Distinguished Service Order would hinge on how many enemy his troops had killed. 'There was this enormous concentration on body count because that was the way the battalion was judged,' d'Hagé says.

In the lead-up to the big battle of Operation Lavarack in the north of Phuoc Tuy province on June 11, Bravo Company was ordered to concentrate its force after intelligence had picked up a large enemy presence in the area. On June 11, as Bravo Company patrolled, the thumbs-down sign indicating the enemy's presence came down the line; d'Hagé recalls a chill running down his spine.

In the lead was 6 Platoon, followed by 5 and then 4. The lead element had detected a small number of enemy sheltering from the rain, so 6 Platoon decided to mount an attack — but no one realised that the enemy force was merely an outpost of a much larger group. The company had stumbled upon a meeting of senior North Vietnamese Army officers, who were protected by a force of more than 200 fighters.

'When the attack began on the outpost it was soon apparent that the rest of them were not pleased to see us and all of a sudden the jungle just sort of erupted,' d'Hagé recalls.

He was ordered to send in a section to reinforce 6 Platoon, but as the intensity of the enemy attack grew he was told to take his platoon and extricate his mates, who by this stage were in deep trouble.

'For some inexplicable reason, and I can't explain this, but something kicks in. There were bullets and shit going everywhere. I said to one of the corporals, "I need to have a leak first," so I had a wee behind one of these buttressed bloody trees,' he says. 'I don't know what made me do that, it wasn't a nervous leak, and I just needed a wee.'

He got his men into a position where they could assault the enemy. The jungle was alive with noise and rounds. 'Normally you would do a reconnaissance to the left, to the right, suss out what is there, but any surprise was blown so I put in a frontal assault.'

He moved no more than five metres when the radio handset he was carrying was shot out of his hand. The noise was horrendous, but as soon as the attack started it reached a new pitch.

140

'It was like a World Cup soccer match where the crowd is yelling and all of a sudden it looks as if the other side is going to score a goal or something and the crescendo goes up 49 runcheons.'

To his dismay d'Hagé realised that the enemy even had heavy machine guns placed up in the trees. 'That was the first time I'd come across that; mind you, I'd only been there three weeks.'

Ammunition is a life or death obsession for infantry soldiers and d'Hagé soon found himself worrying about his platoon's supply of rounds. 'Ammunition for the infantry in a prolonged firefight is critical and when there is this much shit coming at you, it gets doubly critical,' he says. 'The volume of fire was just extraordinary, so I found another very large bloody buttress tree to set up my headquarters.'

For a fairly green 22-year-old lieutenant the battle was rapidly developing into a baptism of fire. A second concern soon arose as the number of wounded, including one or two who were very seriously hurt, began to mount up. The company commander joined him behind the HQ tree, so there were now two large radio aerials sticking out from behind the buttresses of the rainforest tree.

A key role for an infantry commander during a heavy contact is coordinating fire support. As the battle raged d'Hagé found himself spending a long time on the radio talking to the gunners and calling in artillery.

'There is a procedure known as "danger close", and that means firstly to those on the gun line, God bless them, that these guys are in the shit, they are calling it in as close as they can get it without putting it in amongst themselves,' he says. 'So we'd gone to danger close and that means the gun lines double- and triple-check all their coordinates as I called in the artillery to the point where the shrapnel was coming back at me.'

There is only a limited margin for error with 105 mm howitzer shells, so when he got them as close as he thought safe he added another 25 metres just to be sure.

Just as the tide was turning in the Aussies' favour, the artillery's guns ran out of ammunition. 'I wasn't there, but I was told the gun barrels were starting to glow, 105 mm howitzers, and they ran out of ammunition and the Chinooks [helicopters] swooped in with ammunition in wooden crates suspended underneath and were dropping it beside the guns while they were firing.'

As the guns glowed red-hot, any able-bodied man was called upon to open ammo boxes and carry shells to the guns while they maintained constant fire support.

Like many Australian soldiers in Vietnam, d'Hagé probably owes his life to the artillery units that kept the enemy at bay during most of the big battles of the war.

'As a rule you wouldn't patrol outside artillery range, but on occasions we did and you felt damn uncomfortable when you were outside; that really was your prime support and that was the advantage we had over the other side,' he says. 'Looking back I have nothing but the greatest respect for those North Vietnamese and Vietcong as soldiers, because they didn't have that support.'

He also called in air support in the form of American Phantom jet fighters to land some 125-kilogram bombs on the enemy force for good measure.

The momentum was turning but the enemy was determined and d'Hagé noticed hostile fighters sneaking through the jungle carrying garbage-tin lids full of explosives pilfered from Aussie claymore mines and covered with nuts and bolts; the makeshift mines went off with a huge bang, creating a wave of deadly shrapnel. His headquarters tree was partly shredded by one of the mines at about the same time as his company commander was shot and wounded.

The final challenge for the raw platoon commander was the fact that darkness was falling and that meant no more heavy air support. It also meant guiding in the medevac choppers in the darkness to evacuate the half dozen or so wounded men.

'I can still recall this conversation: the Phantoms had to go because they can't deliver bombs in the dark, so they sent me [callsign] Spooky 77,' he says. 'Spooky 77 was a DC3 with Gatling-style machine guns in either door, full of ammunition. These days they are a lot more technical and they've got machine guns that will fire 6000 rounds a minute, but this was the forerunner to that. Now this must have been the dumbest question in a military conflict. My callsign was 22, we were using flares to direct him and you could see the one in five, one in seven tracer [ammunition with a pyrotechnic charge that makes the projectile visible] spiralling down, quite sort of extraordinary. And after a while, I said, "Spooky 77, this is 22, what's your ammunition state, over."

'I can only imagine this big American pilot; he said, "22, this is Spooky 77, we still got about a million rounds up here," which compared to our 140. I said, "Oh great!"'

D'Hagé describes his situation as a 'kaleidoscope of ugliness'. No one was dead but several troops were badly wounded, it was dark, the enemy was regrouping and his ammo supply was dangerously low.

After four hours of intense fighting the company was ordered to break contact with the enemy and d'Hagé directed the successful withdrawal of his troops.

'Medics were trying to stem blood flow; we all carried a bandage, but we were desperately short of bandages, getting these guys out under fire … I think the medic did get a Mention in Despatches and probably should have got more because he certainly was moving in the areas of heaviest fire.'

The worst of the wounded was a digger called Mick Dunn, who had taken numerous rounds. He was rescued from the contact by several of his mates under withering fire.

One of the greatest morale boosters in Vietnam was the knowledge every digger carried that regardless of where they were fighting they were never more than about 30 minutes away from a field hospital by helicopter. The 'dust-off' chopper crews did remarkable work, as did the medical teams at the field hospitals.

'My cousin was a nursing sister down there,' says d'Hagé. 'Some things have been written on these guys, but it's not unlike MASH, the television series; it's pretty true what happened down there. The triage is like, "This bloke is not going to make it," those life and death decisions that doctors made. But at least the diggers knew way back behind this contact, the dust-off choppers were coming in and taking the wounded out, and you know those guys, a lot of bullets flying, those guys are doing a great job.'

During one night battle an American helicopter flew in to a tiny landing area. 'The pilot said, "Fuck it's tight but I'm coming in," and the tips of the blades were cutting foliage as he landed.'

Courage was on display all around during the six-hour-long battle. 'You don't really have a choice but you have to dig deep,' d'Hagé says. 'Often that is on the spur of the moment, unlike those who are awarded a George Cross [for acts of the greatest heroism or most conspicuous courage in circumstances of extreme danger] who are told to go and defuse a 500-pound bomb and have got time to think about it — that to me is valour. When you are being shot at and it's kill or be killed, a lot of it is instinctive, you train for it, but nevertheless you have to have the guts to take it on.'

What surprised him more than anything during the intense fighting was the calmness that descended upon him. 'I think that we are trained hopefully to slow down, the tougher it gets the more you slow down, if you like, and the more deliberate you get, because you have to be.'

D'Hagé was awarded the Military Cross for his calm leadership that day, but he says the medal is not just his — it belongs to the entire platoon. 'I was probably the rock around which things revolved but it's as much for the diggers as it is for me. It's not as if I've stormed a machine-gun post on my own. I stormed more than a machine-gun post, but I had a lot of guys with me.' The medal was presented in country which was unusual at the time.

D'Hagé says his senior non-commissioned soldiers were the most important and influential people that he worked with. 'The theory at Duntroon was fine, but my senior NCOs taught me far more,' he says.

As he whiles away the hours and days in his writer's shed deep in the Blue Mountains, d'Hage acknowledges that Vietnam was his opportunity to earn his stripes and to prove he had what it takes. The medals he occasionally wears prove it, but these days he advocates for a better way to solve problems than sending young men off to kill other young men and to be scarred for life by the process.

'It is just ugly and brutal and there are better ways. I couldn't espouse it in those terms when I was collecting the Queen's shilling, but it's pretty well been my philosophy since Vietnam, in a sense,' he says. 'I think many servicemen came back and realised there are better ways to solve problems. In those days it was the old domino theory: the communists were going to come down from the north and take South Vietnam, Thailand and Malaysia and Singapore — absolute bloody claptrap — but that was the theory of the day.

'Looking back on it, my main mission in life in Vietnam, and I say this unashamedly, was to get all the troops back. I couldn't have given a rat's arse about the bloody strategic domino theory; my mission was to get the diggers back in one piece. I got them all back, but a lot of them were not in one piece.'

Like most veterans, d'Hagé was appalled by the attitude of the Australian public towards the diggers. Because of the public outcry over Australia's involvement in the Vietnam War that included verbal abuse and even buckets of red paint thrown at returning soldiers, troops were often spirited back into the country under the cover of darkness and their service was not properly acknowledged until decades later.

'Years later when I ran Defence public relations and the opportunity presented itself and the public was up in arms over whatever we might have been doing, I would say to the Australian public, "Look, take your frustrations out on the government because this is government policy, but don't take it out on the diggers in the street because they don't have any say in this."

'I think that is a shameful period in Australia's history and while it didn't worry me, I couldn't give a rat's arse quite frankly, I know a lot of the diggers felt it deeply.'

The RSL was another problem for the Vietnam vets. 'The incidences of guys walking in with their medals and an old codger coming up and saying to them, "Listen, when you've been to a real war you can come and be a member here," so a lot of the diggers said, "Bash it up your arse, RSL," and I was one of them.'

The RSL's attitude softened over the years when the World War II diggers realised what a 12-month tour of the jungle had involved. 'The average battalion in World War II saw six weeks of action over five years,' d'Hagé says. 'That doesn't mean they weren't under the bloody hammer the whole time, they were, but jungle fighting is even more intense.'

Darj's last official appointment was as head of Defence planning for security for the Sydney Olympic Games, and he left the army in October 2000. The Australian taxpayer kindly paid for him to retrain as a ski instructor, but his fledgling career on the slopes was cut short when he smashed his leg. Now armed with an honours degree in theology, he continues to write thrillers involving Byzantine Vatican-tinged plots and dire prophecies. He uses his knowledge of the security area but keeps away from the thing he knows best.

'After ten years of dealing with politicians in Canberra and some grubby people in the Olympic Games movement I had just had enough,' he says. 'I had done my bit after 37 years and it was time for a clean break.'

While he does not write directly about military affairs, d'Hagé is a regular media commentator and he uses his military insights, particularly his intimate knowledge of intelligence agencies and their activities, in his novels.

'It is nice to be able to occasionally provide a window into what goes on behind the scenes.'

Chapter 6

Emus Do Fly

Australian Navy pilot Andy Perry was flying low and fast against a hail of enemy fire as he manoeuvred his Iroquois 'Huey' helicopter into a hot jungle landing zone in South Vietnam on May 18, 1970, when he felt a bullet slam into his right boot.

Unsure whether he had been seriously wounded, Perry kept flying into the maelstrom to deposit a dozen or so South Vietnamese, or Army of the Republic of Vietnam (ARVN), troops onto the battlefield. The enemy fire was so intense that as the men piled out of the machine most of them were hit.

In the darkness Perry had landed right in front of an enemy bunker during a combat assault mission with the US Army.

'They [the enemy] were dug in, they had trenches, they had bunkers, they had lots of automatic weapons and they had a big force,' he recalls. 'As I'm flying in there are tracer coming up, and I could hear [pilot] Dave Farley telling me that he was taking 50 cal [calibre] fire, so he just kept on climbing. I think he was at 5000 feet in the end to stay away from the 50s. Usually you are already in the flare before they open fire and sometimes they even wait until the skids hit and you are most vulnerable, you are stopped, but I started taking fire at like 1000 feet. I was still miles away.

'It was all coming at me … the whole flight was yelling about taking fire from everywhere. Anyway we went in, and we put it down and I put the machine down, but the biggest problem I had was that one of the pilots down the back turned his landing light on.

'They were air cavalry and they weren't used to [combat assault] so they pulled out. "We're not up for this, fuck off, we're going home," and they did. That was after the first assault and, yeah, we took a lot of fire. I landed, there was a bunker in front of me, troops got off, most of them were hit, the machine was hit all over the place.'

As he bent down to check the damage to his right foot, a burst of automatic fire peppered the Plexiglas windscreen and tore through exactly where his head had just been.

'I thought I'd taken a round through my foot, but it was just where it struck the pedal and my foot is on the pedal. That sort of made me bend down and when I came up there were all these holes right across the windscreen … so I think that was lucky. Nothing was damaged and I was still flying, so that's all you care about.'

A 30-calibre round had hit the rudder pedal, creased his boot and lodged in his seat. Miraculously the bullets that penetrated the windscreen missed any vital equipment and Perry and his crew made two more sorties into the hot landing zone that night.

Acting Sub-Lieutenant Perry of the Royal Australian Navy was seconded to the 135th Assault Helicopter Company of the US Army's First Aviation Brigade, known as 'The EMUs', short for Experimental Military Unit. Their motto was 'Get the bloody job done'. And that usually meant flying hard and fast under fire into hot landing zones, dumping troops and getting out as rapidly as possible. The EMUs were the only fully integrated multi-national helicopter company fighting in Vietnam. Perry was based initially at Camp Martin Cox at Bear Cat in Bien Hoa province east of Saigon, and later at Dong Tam in the Mekong Delta south of the capital.

More than 200 Australian navy pilots, plus observers and maintainers, were posted to the US unit on 12-month cycles between 1967 and 1971.

'For an adrenaline junkie it is the ultimate, because every single time you are doing it, you are betting with the highest of stakes — your own life — and when you come off, when you come out of there and go "Phew!", and you look at your mate, you've got this fucking shit-eating grin on your face. "Wow, far out, we are all alive, everybody OK?" "Yeah, we took a few rounds today, is anything dripping or anything like that?" "No, no, we are good sir." "OK, we'll go back and do that again."'

For his efforts on the night of 18 January, Perry was recommended for the US military's Silver Star. This is the highest American award that can be given to non-Americans and the third highest award for bravery in combat behind the Medal of Honour, the American equivalent of the Victoria Cross, and the Distinguished Service Cross. By contrast, the Australian Government presented him with a Mentioned in Despatches — the same award given to the postal clerk at Vung Tau for good service.

But thanks to politics, quotas and bureaucratic incompetence it would be a quarter of a century before the Silver Star would be pinned to Perry's chest.

In mid–1970 a senior US officer arrived at the EMUs' base in Vietnam for a medal presentation ceremony. 'The whole company stood down for the day and they were going to have an American medal ceremony,' Perry recalls. 'A bunch of guys were going to get air medals, and purple hearts and everything. I don't know who the general was. It might have been the boss who flew in to shake everybody's hand.'

But during the Vietnam War, no Australian serviceman was permitted to accept and wear an individual military decoration from a foreign country. When the American general was told that he wouldn't be able to pin the Silver Star on the young Australian pilot, he called the whole thing off so there was no medal ceremony at all.

'He said, "If we can't do the big one we are not doing any of it,"' Perry recalls. 'He came over and we had our cucumber sandwiches with the rinds cut off and we stood around and he shook me by the hand and said, "Bloody good job, son," and "Piss poor on your government's behalf, it's a bloody shame and one day we might get over it, and get it sorted, but right now I can't do anything. That's what the politicians have told me; it's come down from even higher than me."'

Andy Perry was unhappy that his medal could not be presented but the war went on and the next day it was back to flying and 'getting the bloody job done'.

That job included clandestine and highly illegal flights into neighbouring Cambodia carrying a variety of American passengers, many of them dressed in civilian clothing.

The government had ordered Australian personnel not to enter Cambodia or Laos, or even go within a certain distance of the border, under any circumstances. The Australian Embassy in Saigon had reinforced the point just before the EMUs began operations into Cambodia, but Perry says he and other RAN pilots working with the 135th regularly flew across the frontier on secret missions for the US 5th Special Forces or Navy SEALs who were infiltrating the southern end of the Ho Chi Minh Trail that ran from North Vietnam into Laos and Cambodia and then back into South Vietnam. US forces ran an undeclared secret war in both countries in a bid to stem the flow of supplies along the trail.

'They even gave me the uniform, bits of which I've still got. They were marines mostly, but they did all kinds of stuff. Their callsign was Cheap Tricks. We also worked with the SEALs, and the SEALs had the odd Australian with them as well,' he recalls. 'They did phoenix jobs and stuff like that, all single ship work, people dressed in civilian clothes, and they'd want to go somewhere — "We'll tell you when we get there."'

The special forces boys would often request pilots by name and Perry was popular because he was willing to have a go at most things, regardless of what the government said.

Fortunately Acting Sub-Lieutenant Perry, who celebrated his 21st birthday in Vietnam, survived the cross-border missions physically unscathed. So after an eventful ten-month deployment he was back at HMAS *Albatross*, at Nowra on the NSW south coast, trying his best to transfer out of the training base.

His US Silver Star citation sat in a safe at Defence Headquarters in Canberra for years during one of the most shameful periods in Australian political history, when Vietnam veterans were being vilified and treated as pariahs.

In January 1985 the Defence Minister, Kim Beazley, responded to one of Perry's many representations through his local member of parliament, Peter White, with a flat denial that the award had ever been given. 'Mr Perry's service records contain no evidence of a Silver Star being awarded to him,' Beazley's letter said. 'Enquiries have revealed that it is now difficult, and in many cases impossible to validate claims by individual Australians for United States awards which were made in the field. In these circumstances I regret that it is not possible to establish whether the Silver Star was awarded to Mr Perry.'

By mid-June the following year the American citation had been discovered in a separate honours and awards file. But the Minister for Sport, Recreation and Tourism, John Brown, in another letter to Peter White, stood firm about the government's policy.

'Given that the traditional British awards were available to our servicemen, there is no justification for granting permission to formally accept and wear these foreign awards,' his letter said.

Three Australians serving with the EMUs were granted Member of the Order of the British Empire, eight received the Distinguished Service Cross, five the Distinguished Flying Cross, one the British Empire Medal and 25 were Mentioned in Despatches. This was more than half the honours awarded to navy personnel during the entire conflict.

Today, as he enjoys a very large cup of tea aboard his 16-metre converted Tasmanian timber fishing boat *Bill Bailey* in the beautiful Port Huon Marina, about 60 kilometres south of Hobart, Perry says he doesn't regard what he did in Vietnam that night in 1970 as anything special.

'Every time we went in we'd take more rounds, have more holes punched in your machine. The thing is, you look at your instruments. As long as it is turning and burning it's good; that's all you worry about.'

But he makes no secret of his pride in the professionalism of the EMUs. 'If they wanted the best people for the job, the EMUs got the job because we could do more with less and we could fly faster, harder, whatever it took, because we were into it. You are there to do the mission, to "get the bloody job done" and we were really imbued with that philosophy.' He says that he was just a 20-year-old kid from Tassie doing his job and having the time of his life.

As a lad sitting on his horse watching over 500 'woolly-arsed sheep' on the family property near Ouse in central Tasmania, Andy Perry had dreamed of flying one of the DC3 transport planes that would swoop down the valley and overhead as he tended his flock.

The second of four children of soldier-settler and former World War II 'Z' Special Unit operative Dick Perry, young Andy would watch the aircraft and think, 'Fancy being up there doing that instead of down here doing this.'

The would-be pilot was also attracted to the military life after hearing some of his dad's war stories. Dick Perry had fought with the 6th Division in Egypt and was involved in the fighting in Greece and Crete before he returned to Australia where he was recruited into the 'Z' Special Unit.

Perry senior took part in Operation Semut 1, parachuting into Japanese-occupied North Borneo in 1945 to recruit and train local native fighters and to gather intelligence for the high command.

'These guys were given a mission to wander off into the bush, get as many people as you can together, teach them how to attack the Japanese and go for it,' Andy says. 'They had little pedal radios and Dad talked about missions going wrong and he'd be on the run, and they'd hide the radio and then him and his mate, they would just keep running.

'He said you just kept moving because there were lots of Japs and they were after you. He said that the local Dayak people really looked after him in Sulawesi, and he told stories about living with the Sun Dayaks and being fed and being housed. They'd have no clothes left and he said often all he had were his boots and sometimes he'd run out of them too. The biscuit bombers, C-47 Dakotas, would come across and drop a bit of stuff in the bush and the natives would go and pick it up.'

His dad's war tales intrigued young Andy as he enjoyed the simple life, far from the world's trouble spots, on a farm in peaceful Tasmania. 'He told me stories of creeping into installations because the whole idea was not to take anybody on, was to go in, put the mines and demolition things around their fuel and vehicles, and boats in one case, and run off into the bush.

'Another time he rescued prisoners of war out of a camp and put them on a Catalina flying boat. There were women and kids amongst them and he said, "We just kept putting them on and even when they said we can't take any more we just put them on." Even in the dark it went out past the end of the bay and it was still on the water, still going flat chat trying to get enough air speed to get airborne, and he said eventually it got airborne, but it went for miles on the water, it was that overloaded.'

As Andy's questions became more detailed, his dad would clam up and order his son back to work. 'You got no names, no pack drills, you just got this little taste,' he recalls.

Andy and his three siblings enjoyed a tough but idyllic Tasmanian bush childhood minus mod cons such as telephones and electric power. They caught rabbits and chopped wood and at the age of four Andy and his younger brother were riding a horse by sharing an old cavalry saddle.

The idyll came to an abrupt end at the age of seven when he was enrolled as a boarder at The Friends' School in North Hobart. The largest Quaker-run school in the world, The Friends' includes among its alumni the Hollywood actor and hell-raiser Errol Flynn and Australian cricketer Max Walker. For Andy Perry it was a rude shock after the freedom of his distance education course supervised by his mother.

'She rang the bell and if we weren't within hearing of that bell, then the bell hadn't rung.'

More often than not, Andy would be off in the bush on his horse well out of earshot. At The Friends' there was no such escape and the school was run along strict English public school lines.

Four years later the family moved into Hobart after Dick Perry became too ill to run the farm. Andy lasted at The Friends' until the age of 15 when he and the hierarchy had a difference of opinion and it was suggested that he might be better served attending another institution. He had applied to join the RAN and the RAAF, but they only took students who had matriculated.

So he completed his schooling at the Hobart Matriculation College, although further distractions in the form of girls and his first motorcycle, a sparkling Triumph Tiger 650 'covered in chrome', intervened.

Despite the dual distractions he managed to matriculate. After years of reading about World War II flying ace Douglas 'Tin Legs' Bader and other Battle of Britain heroes, he was more determined than ever to pursue his dream of flying.

Andy joined the navy and went to the recruit training school at HMAS *Cerberus* in Victoria. After that, still in the navy, it was off to the RAAF flying training school at Point Cook near Melbourne to learn to fly on Winjeel training aircraft. From there he went to the fast jet school at RAAF Base Pearce in Western Australia and graduated to Vampire jets.

Then it was on to the navy's Fleet Air Arm at HMAS *Albatross* where he was posted to 723 Squadron, flying Bravo model Iroquois (Huey) helicopters whose distinctive rotor sound became an abiding symbol of the Vietnam War.

In 1968 he was posted to the RAN Helicopter Flight Vietnam (RANHFV), specifically formed for service in Vietnam, and spent most of that year working up for a possible active deployment.

During this period Perry began to clash with the navy hierarchy, mainly over his lifestyle choices — including the fact that he rode a motorcycle and wore leather jackets when he was off-duty. One senior officer had even questioned his suitability to be a navy officer.

'I had been seen in the main street of Nowra talking with other people who were riding motorbikes. I was a naval officer. I was told, "You are mixing with the wrong kind of people, don't talk to lower deck, don't talk to bike riders."'

Laughing, he recalls, 'When I got back from Vietnam do you know what the cool thing was on the squadron? The cool thing was to have a bloody motorbike! Not one like mine of course, but one you could get on at the squadron and go up to the wardroom for lunch and then get on again and go back to the squadron and then get on again and go out to the married patch. There were lots of motorbikes.'

When he returned from Vietnam in 1971 Perry was stuck in Nowra. Because he had gone straight from a training squadron to the war he lacked so-called 'frontline' flying experience. Active duty under fire in a war zone didn't cut it — nor did the fact that he had embarked on a solo crusade to obtain an American medal that he had earned with blood, sweat and fear.

'All the things I wanted to do when I got back to the navy from the army required frontline flying experience. I wanted to be an instructor, I wanted to go on the Moresby flight, anything but hanging around in Nowra,' he says. 'The year I spent in Nowra was the absolute end of me, and I finished up having a fight, having a disagreement, and I was grounded and they wouldn't let me out of the navy — "You're going to be an embarrassment, one day we will all be able to get this medals business sorted out."'

Little did he know that 'one day' meant 25 years. 'The number of times I heard "loose cannon" and "embarrassment"!'

The mental scars from the war remained, but after two attempts he was able to conquer the self-medicating lure of the demon drink that had been with him right through his Vietnam tour. 'I was drinking too much before I went, I was certainly drinking too much when I came back,' he says.

In between there had been the company bar and an endless supply of cheap alcohol.

'There were mornings I'd get up and I'd have that much [several fingers] of Chivas Regal in like a Vegemite glass, before I'd go flying. We didn't talk about it because you are not supposed to, but fuck, there was that much stuff that went on up there. You talk about war crimes, you talk about all of this shit that goes down, you know, you can see it every day, your whole day is a war crime. You know, the most amazing stuff going on right in front of your eyes and for a young bloke, I was 20 years old, I turned 21 up there, I couldn't even vote for Christ's sake and I'm up there killing people.'

He left the navy in late 1971 and the following year was flying choppers into remote mining sites. He married Virginia and they had a son, Rupert, and eventually moved to Mission Beach in far North Queensland. Andy continued to fly helicopters, but eventually he retired, bought a boat and now spends most of his time cruising around Australia.

In April 1995 the medal injustice was finally corrected when Andy Perry received his Silver Star in Townsville. The commander of the US 7th Fleet, Vice-Admiral Archie Clemins, complete with an honour guard, pinned the medal to his chest aboard his flagship, the USS *Blue Ridge*, in Townsville Harbour.

The US citation, dated February 28, 1973, reads:

Reason: For gallantry in action: Sub-Lieutenant Perry distinguished himself by gallantry in action on 18 May 1970 while serving as pilot on a UH-1H Helicopter, 135th Aviation Company, Royal Australian Navy. On that date, Sub-Lieutenant Perry monitored a radio call stating that his unit was engaged in night combat assaults against a strong and hostile force and that several aircraft had been knocked out of action. Without thought to his own safety or the arduous hours of flying he had already accomplished that day, he contacted command and control aircraft and offered his assistance. Sub-Lieutenant Perry joined the flight as lead aircraft and carried one lift of Vietnamese troops into the landing zone. On the approach, the flight was raked by heavy fire, causing damage to several aircraft. Sub-Lieutenant Perry's aircraft was struck repeatedly, knocking out both chin bubbles, several important instruments, the side window and part of his pedal controls. The second aircraft in the flight was knocked out of action and could not continue to fly. Grasping the situation, Sub-Lieutenant Perry announced that he would continue as lead. Despite the damage to his aircraft and the fact that he was bleeding from the face and had lost feeling in his right foot from the impact of enemy bullets, he led the flight back to the pickup zone and then into the same landing zone two more times. Each time heavy enemy fire was received, but by his courage, flying ability and cool commands of leadership, the flight of aircraft never faltered and the insertions were completed. Sub-Lieutenant Perry's conspicuous gallantry in action was in keeping with the highest traditions of the Royal Australian Navy and reflects great credit upon himself and the military service.

Chapter 7

The Spearhead

Bayne 'Gus' Kelly is not at all bitter that it took more than 40 years for him to receive an American gallantry medal that he earned for courage under fire in Vietnam in June 1971, but he is highly suspicious about the ratio of awards given to national servicemen like him compared to regular soldiers.

More than 1050 Australian soldiers, sailors and airmen received honours and awards during the 11-year war. More than 640 went to regulars, or 'regs', compared to just 107 to national servicemen, or 'nashos'. That is a ratio of about 6:1, which bears no relationship to the ratio of regulars to nashos who actually served in the war (23,000 regulars and 18,000 nashos) — 55:45.

When it came to being awarded an imperial medal in Vietnam the hurdles were significant, and foreign awards were rendered almost impossible by red tape and bastardry. First there was the politics, then there was the imperial honours system (then in force in Australia) and its quota system that left the nashos at the bottom of the heap when it came to receiving awards.

Kelly was awarded the United States Commendation Medal for Valour for his heroism at the battle of Long Khanh, north-east of Saigon, during Operation Overlord in June 1971. Yet, despite saving several men from a burning helicopter full of ammunition, treating the wounded, calling in artillery fire and engaging a superior enemy force for more than nine hours, the 21-year-old conscript did not receive any Australian award. It was only because Operation Overlord was a joint US–Australian action that Kelly was recommended for the US award.

Bayne Kelly was born at St Luke's Hospital in Sydney's Kings Cross in January 1949. His dad, a doctor in Bellevue Hill, died at the age of 34, leaving a widow and two young children with a third on the way. The family moved from the well-to-do eastern suburbs to the hamlet of Bilgola Beach on Sydney's northern beaches, and young Bayne began his schooling at Avalon Public School. At the age of eight he was enrolled as a boarder at Oak Hill College in Castle Hill, where he stayed until he obtained his Leaving Certificate in 1965.

After starting work as a cadet with the petroleum firm HC Sleigh Limited, he was drafted in 1969 while he was studying business marketing.

He had been in the army cadets at school but any thoughts that his past 'military' experience might be an advantage were dashed by the grumpy drill sergeant who met the batch of wide-eyed conscripts at Marrickville on their way to Kapooka recruit training centre near Wagga Wagga in southern NSW.

The sergeant asked for a show of hands from all those who had been in school cadets. Up shot Kelly's and several others. 'Right, if I hear that fucking word once again I'll have you down for 1000 push-ups. It [cadets] doesn't have anything to do with the army,' the sergeant barked.

After they arrived at Kapooka at about 11 pm that night, they were thrown into a room and told to be up at 6 am. On the parade ground the next morning the sergeant yelled at Kelly, who wore glasses, 'You, Cyclops, go in there and tell all those blokes to shave their side levers right above their ears.'

'I walked into the block and said, "Righto guys, I've just been told to tell you to get your hair cut."

'"Get fucked, piss off!" So we went out on parade and about four of us had our side levers up so we were sent back in to tidy up. The rest of them had to stay there and do press-ups in the cold with just a pair of pyjama pants on — welcome to the army.'

The first lecture the new recruits received from Sergeant Grumpy was about the military totem pole. 'I just want to tell you blokes where you stand,' he said. 'First you've got the general, you are never going to see any of them; then after the general, you've got your brigadier, then you've got your colonel and lieutenant colonel and you'll see a few of them because they run battalions, then after lieutenant colonel, you've got the major, then you've got the captain, then after the captain you've got a first lieutenant, then you've got a second lieutenant, then you start with the non-commissioned officers, warrant officer class 1, warrant officer class 2, staff sergeant, then you've got a sergeant, remember they run the bloody show, then you've got a corporal, then you've got a lance corporal, then you've got a private, then you've got the rats and the mice and the worms and the lowest things on earth, and then they've got you, the recruit. Remember it, that's what you are for the next ten weeks.'

After surviving recruit training, the new privates were supposedly given the choice of a corps and, because the army needed infantrymen for the war, most 'chose' infantry. (In fact, the recruits had little choice in the matter.) From Kelly's platoon of 50 about 40 were assigned to infantry battalions and he and one other went to artillery.

The buses left Kapooka carrying the grunts to the infantry training school at Singleton in the Hunter Valley, and the two artillerymen to the training battery at Holsworthy near Sydney.

Bayne was not a big fan of the World War I vintage digs and facilities at Holsworthy, so he successfully applied for a transfer to the School of Artillery at North Head near Manly. He drove his old Volkswagen Beetle (four forward gears, no reverse) across Sydney to what was regarded as one of the best located army establishments in the country, for 14 weeks of glorious harbour-side training to be an artillery signalman. Gunner Kelly then joined the army's oldest unit, 'A' Field Battery of 12th Field Regiment of the Royal Australian Artillery. 'A' Battery started life in 1871 as part of the NSW colonial defence force and first saw service in the Sudan and then the Boer War.

After live fire exercises at Puckapunyal in Victoria and High Range west of Townsville in North Queensland with 3rd Battalion, whom they would support in Vietnam, Kelly's unit was sent to the jungle training centre at Canungra near Brisbane before the final exercise with the battalion at Shoalwater Bay near Rockhampton.

'We were exceptionally well trained, there is no doubt about that,' he says. 'You work with the unit for seven or eight months and it becomes like a team.'

12th Field Regiment consisted of 'A' Battery, equipped with six 105 mm howitzer guns, 104th Battery, and the headquarters battery. After a brief period of leave they were assembled in Townsville and at 11 o'clock one fine night, with the band playing

'When Johnny Comes Marching Home', 21-year-old Bayne Kelly marched off to war.

The Boeing 707 jet stopped over in Singapore where 120 soldiers disembarked and changed into civilian clothes (to prevent the enemy knowing they were going to war) for their arrival at the world's busiest airport at the time, Tan Son Nhut airbase in Saigon, South Vietnam.

January 1971 was a seminal period in the Vietnam conflict. US troop numbers were at their highest level (525,000), other foreign force numbers were at their peak, including Australia with 8000 on the ground, and support for the war was evaporating very publicly back home.

Bayne's first job was with the D and E (Defence and Employment) Platoon as a signaller to his artillery officer Terry Nolan. 'I carried the radio pack and my job when you got into contact with the enemy was to sit with the officer or the assistant, work out our grids and then send our messages back to the fire support base, which was probably ten to 12 miles [15–20 kilometres] away,' he says. 'If you wanted pressure — and I remember the great cricketer and former fighter pilot Keith Miller saying that pressure was having a Messerschmitt up your arse — at 21 years of age, you imagine trying to call in 105 mm rounds from maybe seven or eight miles behind you, and make sure they weren't going to hit your own people. I mean it was seriously hard work.'

After the main force arrived in February 1971, Kelly moved across to the battalion lines to join Bravo Company as an artillery forward observer. He says he was shocked by the pecking order in the battalion where the platoon sergeants ruled the roost and the tough senior diggers, many of them seasoned veterans, bullied the young officers mercilessly.

'They [officers] were treated like the lowest form of life, not by their own troops — we looked up to them — but those platoon sergeants were so powerful within the unit that they controlled those officers,' Kelly says. 'I mean to the way they spoke to them … I felt quite affected in the first couple of months as to how these young guys were treated, and I saw them at the end of their year's service in Vietnam, they were badly affected. I still see one of them and I think he remains damaged by the way he was treated in Vietnam.'

The platoon sergeant is the senior soldier and usually the hard man of a platoon. Many had been to Vietnam before and were hardened warriors compared with the raw young Duntroon graduates who were supposed to command them.

'They were really hard pieces of work, some of them incredibly good, but like anything in life, some of them incredibly bad. I saw at the end of operations, coming back in, a sergeant take his stripes off and get into a punch–up with one of the blokes who disagreed with him. Amazing stuff.'

The anti–war protests reached their zenith in Australia in 1971 and, like many troops serving in Vietnam, Bayne Kelly began to be affected by the discord and the lack of support back at home. Early in the year 100,000 people marched in Melbourne and just before Anzac Day 80,000 hit the streets of Sydney to protest against Australia's involvement.

US President Richard Nixon's sudden announcement that he would visit China, without any prior consultation with Canberra, was another of the straws that would break the camel's back for Australia in Vietnam. Prime Minister William McMahon announced that the nation would accelerate the draw-down of its forces during the year.

'I knew that I was going to be there for a year, I knew I had to be switched on all the time. I started to see some of the right-wing elements of "We should be in Vietnam because we are stopping the communists et cetera" move a bit,' Kelly says. 'As we got towards the middle of the year the message that was coming down from the high command was, "Whatever you do, no more casualties."' Gun-shy politicians had already affected operations.

In April 1971, 6 Platoon came across a juicy target in the form of a large enemy training camp. 'The patrol commander said, "This is what we've found, we've seen the camp, we can see people moving, we are all ready to go, we just want the command."

'My commanding officer was a serious warrior, he would have been in there in a flash, but he got orders from his boss, "Do not touch ... No more casualties."'

Just a few days later, the company received orders that it was moving out of Phuoc Tuy province and into neighbouring Long Khanh province. Leave was cancelled and a very unhappy group of diggers mounted helicopters for the short hop into an area where allied troops had not been for 18 months.

Kelly and his mates didn't realise it at the time, but the decision had been taken to withdraw the Australian task force from its base at Nui Dat, and they were being sent out to test the enemy's strength in advance of the final withdrawal.

Naturally the men thought that if the politicians and the generals didn't want any more casualties then they would hardly send them deliberately into harm's way. 'So B Company, there we were, first night, June 5, all day go around, didn't find a thing, next day, June 6, all day everyone is pissed off. We'd been out in the bush for nearly four weeks, they'd cancelled our leave so we could go up to this new province so you can imagine how happy everyone was,' Kelly said.

That evening, as darkness began to fall over the thick jungle and their thoughts turned to hacking out a sleeping position and battling the real enemy — leeches — the forward scouts spotted a couple of enemy in a dry river bed.

'As you come into your position, you had a pair of secateurs, you cut a bit of earth, that's where you were sleeping for the night, dug a little hole around it to stop the leeches coming in. I mean leeches were worse than the enemy, leeches on your eyelids, on your old fella — no one wore underpants in Vietnam, it was just too hot — you even put salt around it so they wouldn't come in,' he says.

A few shots were exchanged before the platoon commander ordered his men to ceasefire and to get ready to harbour up for the night and call in artillery.

'We started calling our battery in from about five o'clock to about 11 o'clock, so no one had any sleep. Platoon strength was probably about 30, should have been about 37 but about 30, and the idea was at first light we'd get up, move forward, find out where the enemy soldiers basically were, and just see what was there,' Kelly recalls.

'Everyone was thinking there might be something there, so we fired probably 300 to 400 rounds of artillery into this area. First light was at 6.30 so you get up and you have "stand-to", where you sit with all your webbing on, because if there is ever an attack, it is usually at first light or last light.

'We were ordered into an arrowhead formation and off we went. We probably got about 100 metres and it just erupted. I'd never heard a noise like it; they were shooting at us, we were shooting at them. Probably within the first ten minutes we had maybe three casualties; a young bloke from Adelaide got shot in the throat. He was just in front of me and I thought for all intents and purposes the poor guy is dead.

'If someone gets shot, initially they don't feel anything; it is just the shock, so he's screeching out, and I am pleased to say he survived as did 97 per cent of wounded soldiers, if they could get them out of the ground by medevac, back to hospital and operated on within an hour.'

The men had stumbled onto an enemy bunker housing a mixed North Vietnamese Army and Vietcong force. They were well dug in.

'We hit the ground and of course there wasn't much cover but at least we could get helicopter gunships in, so the Bushrangers [gunships] came in, and the battle started at about 6.30 am and it was still raging at four o'clock that afternoon,' Kelly says.

There were a number of casualties, including his boss and the platoon's forward observer, 22-year-old nasho Second Lieutenant Ian Mathers from Brisbane. By midday the Australians were beginning to run low on ammunition.

Mathers was a resident of St Paul's College and a graduate of the University of Sydney where he studied economics. With limited infantry experience, he made the error of exposing himself in a fire lane and was shot twice and killed.

'He was engaged to be married to a very nice girl at St Vincent's Hospital; a nice bloke, I feel to this day terribly sorry for him, because he didn't really have the skills because we were so short in forward observer officers. I think I had had four before Ian came out with us, so he probably had three weeks' training,' he said. 'So number one, even though he could call brilliant artillery, he hadn't lived like an infantry soldier for six or seven months; what he did, he looked around the corner but he was right in a fire way, and he was giving me orders. I was firing them back to the gun position. I looked around, I could see he was gasping but he'd been shot twice, he looked around into a fire lane … it was just an intense sort of day.

'The adrenaline comes up to the eyeballs. A lot of people have asked, and I don't discuss it that often, people asked, "Why would you do some of the things you did that particular day?" My only reaction is, if you didn't, what would happen to the poor people that were wounded?'

Bayne Kelly witnessed a lot of bravery that day in the jungle but none more so than that of a platoon sergeant and two-tour veteran, Edouard Desfontaines, who had in his kit an old red balloon left over from the Korean War.

In Vietnam, air support was usually delivered after coloured smoke was deployed so the gunship or fast jet crews knew exactly where friendly troops were located. 'We were in three-storey high vegetation with all this enemy in front of us in fixed positions in bunkers, how could you tell a Bushranger gunship where the enemy was? Smoke couldn't get up through the canopy, so he pulled this balloon kit out of the plastic bag and it had all these instructions. You poured water on it and it created hydrogen and it went into this red balloon. You then put it on a rope and whoosh, it went up through the canopy in the jungle, so all the choppers could see that the enemy were 20 metres in front of that red balloon and that's what saved us.'

Once the enemy fire was suppressed by the gunships, the transport choppers carrying vital supplies made their run into the battle zone to deliver ammunition and other essentials.

'Everyone was worried about ammunition because everyone had just been firing,' he says. 'By four o'clock that afternoon there had been so much open fire coming through that it just levelled the jungle.'

As Kelly watched the supply chopper coming in, it suddenly lurched sideways and rolled and to his astonishment the loadmaster tumbled out of the machine and fell about 30 metres, screaming all the way down, into the jungle.

For a 'loady' to be untethered by a safety harness was strictly against regulations, but that was the furthest thing from anyone's mind, as soon after the Iroquois helicopter itself crashed through the canopy. 'It was just like looking up underneath a giant Victa lawn mower, bloody big blades going, you can see part of them. It just sort of rolled over, then fell through the jungle onto its side.'

Kelly and the platoon medic, Corporal Ray 'Walshy' Walsh, ran to the downed and burning machine and extracted the dead pilot and a terrified co-pilot before they turned their attention to the crew in the back. With 200,000 rounds of ammunition and under intense fire, time was of the essence. Both door gunners were alive but one was trapped by his harness and pinned underneath the wreckage and he couldn't be released before the wreck was overcome by fire.

Kelly had the awful job of placing the three dead men into body bags as Walshy tended to the dozen or so wounded, including the loadmaster who had fallen to earth and a digger who had been shot in the stomach. The loady had broken numerous bones, but went on to survive the war thanks largely to the efforts of Ray Walsh, who was awarded the Military Medal for his courage that day. Most of the other injuries were shrapnel and wood shard injuries caused by the incessant hail of rocket-propelled grenades slamming into the jungle.

By now, US Cobra gunships had arrived overhead and were pounding the enemy bunkers with rocket and machine-gun fire.

'They [Cobras] were serious stuff, they had rockets on each side, Gatling guns on each side; they were the Rolls Royce of helicopter warfare, these Cobra gunships,' Kelly says.

Finally, after more than nine hours of intense fighting, the enemy's guns fell silent.

'I honestly thought at some stage there was no way I was going to get out of it, because I couldn't move anywhere. I've got my forward observer, Lance Bombardier Peter "Bluey" Maher, behind me, he was calling on one net [radio frequency] and calling in the gunships, mortars and artillery. It was like a cricket match.'

These days Bluey Maher lives a hermit-like existence near Geraldton in Western Australia, but every June 7, on the anniversary of the battle of Long Khanh, he phones Bayne Kelly for a chat about their war days.

There were several moments during the day-long gun battle when Kelly believed that his time was up, but thanks to large doses of adrenaline he also felt a strange sense of calm invincibility. 'I was remembering prayers I'd learned in catechism as a kid.'

He also made all sorts of promises to God regarding just how good he would be if he were spared on the battlefield. 'I thought, you know, "What is going to happen, I'm 21, where am I going to go from here?" But fortunately it didn't happen that way.

'But I was fearless. I got into a little bit of strife from the air force bombardier Maher later on. He said, "Gus, you are fucking crazy." I said to him, "But the adrenaline was up here, I was untouchable, I didn't think anyone could shoot me."'

Fortunately he was right.

'You can't hear anyone, it is so noisy, people screaming, you can see their mouth moving but you can't hear a thing, but we were so well trained that everyone had a role,' he says. 'You know, it was the most uncomfortable awful thing to do to be a grunt, but by gee you were a good survivor at the end of it.

'I got into a zone where I thought, "I've got to survive but don't ask me how I'm going to survive", but I reached above, you sort of got onto that next level. I had to be reasonably accurate with artillery, especially when using the American guns. They are coming over your head, lolling into 30 or 40 metres in front of you, they were like an express train. They were huge, the noise was unbelievable, that must frighten the shit out of the poor Vietnamese.'

Kelly reckons there were at least a couple of hundred enemy located in the bunkers. 'When we went in the next day to go through the bunker system, there was a hospital, there was a training room ... Mind you, the big Centurion tanks got up late that afternoon and put the old barrels down a few of them. There were some unusual sights when you went through there the next day.'

When the operation finished several days later and the men made it back to camp, there was a pall of sadness over the place. 'There were a lot of people wounded still in hospital and you were thinking, "Oh, how is that poor girl going to go that was engaged to Ian; what does your family think?"'

'Years later I looked up reports of the battle and it took up a few inches on page 2 of the *Herald*. If that had happened in Afghanistan, it would have been page 1, 2, 3, 4, 5, 6, 7 and 8, but because the government was looking so bad they were just trying to get Vietnam off the front page.'

It was clear to the Australians who fought in Operation Overlord that the enemy force was the spearhead of the final advance towards Saigon by the communist forces. 'In another 12 months the whole show was over, so they were coming down and they were obviously establishing themselves. No one had been through Long Khanh province for 18 months, so they'd just gone down there, set up and used it as a training ground.'

More than 40 years after the battle, Kelly was told that there had been intelligence about enemy forces active in the area. Just like the battle of Long Tan in August 1966, the information was not passed to the troops on the ground. 'They weren't going to tell the ordinary soldier why we were going up there. They knew by June that they were going to start withdrawing Australian troops by end of 1971. No one was going to tell us.'

Despite his valour in the battle of Long Khanh, not only was Gunner Kelly not recommended for an Australian award, but even the lower-level Mentioned in Despatches eluded him.

Bayne Kelly's war ended in November 1971 when he was trucked down to the port at Vung Tau and put on the 'silver plane' bound for Australia. 'That's the sad thing, that's why a lot of people had major issues — they got on the silver plane, they didn't say goodbye to their mates still in Vietnam, they came back, they got discharged out of the army, half of them went back to work straight away. A couple of doctors would say, "Give us a look at your ears, your eyes."'

Like many Vietnam veterans he found it difficult to relate to the civilian world and to even explain to his friends what he had been through.

'You are so used to one thing and all of a sudden it stops and you can't explain to your friends what you've been through because they think you are a bloody wanker,' he says. 'I remember standing down here at the Lord Dudley [hotel] nearly getting into a blue one night, with some bloke saying, "What the fuck were you guys doing over there?"'

Kelly says the Vietnam deployment was supposed to be voluntary for nashos, but in his experience there was no real choice.

People often asked him why he chose to go, given that he was a conscript and supposedly had a choice. He says it is difficult to understand the pressure brought to bear on young men in front of 100 or so other young men trained to go to war.

Some cranky sergeant asks for a show of hands from those who don't want to go. Those who put up their hands would be ushered to front of the room: 'All right girls, out the front.'

'You stand in front of all these people, you're not going to Vietnam but they are, that was the greeting if you said you didn't want to go to Vietnam,' Kelly says.

This pressure was applied in the context of the 63,000 young men who were conscripted into Australian forces between 1965 and 1972. Just 18,000 went to Vietnam and of those about 10,000 were frontline soldiers.

As well as the critics and the 'baby killer' jibes, Kelly and many other veterans had to endure ignorant comments such as, 'Gee you must have loved Vietnam, wasn't it beautiful?'

'They didn't understand that we arrived at Tan Son Nhut airbase in Saigon, flew up to Nui Dat, walked around in the jungle for 364 days, came back to Saigon, got back on a plane and flew back to Australia.'

Kelly says he was luckier than most because after he was discharged from the army he left Australia for an 18-month European sojourn where he didn't have to speak to anyone about Vietnam.

A decade after his return Bayne Kelly received a letter from the Australian Government notifying him that he had won the United States Commendation Medal for Valour for his efforts at Long Khanh on June 7, 1971. 'As you are aware Australian serviceman cannot receive overseas awards under the auspices of the British government,' the letter said.

A decade later the rules changed so that Australians were permitted to receive and wear foreign awards, although they must be worn on the right side of the chest, away from the Australian awards. Kelly had still not received his medal, so once again he put it to the back of his mind as life moved on.

In 2000 there was a reunion, and a former B Company soldier who worked in the Philippines mentioned that he had told his American mates about the Kelly story and they had been outraged.

'So all this correspondence started going everywhere and my old commanding officer Ivan Carr was ringing me up saying, "Gus, I want to organise a presentation for you, have you got the award?" I said, "No Ivan, I've heard nothing."

'Then I got all these letters from American veterans saying, "Mr Kelly received this prestigious award and we want someone to present it to him."'

In 2007 the medal was minted and sent to the Department of Defence in Canberra where it languished in the bureaucracy for 18 months before someone found it in a safe and posted it to him.

'I still couldn't wear the medal until it had been approved by the Governor–General,' he said.

So more letters to Canberra were followed up with a phone call seven months later because he wanted to wear the medal on Anzac Day 2009. It took another year before he received a letter signed by the Department of the Prime Minister and Cabinet saying that he was entitled to wear the award.

Finally, in May 2011, the US Ambassador to Australia, Jeff Bleich, presented Kelly with his medal before his wife Margaret, their three sons and a handful of old Vietnam mates, in a low-key ceremony at the US Consulate in Sydney.

Sitting in his comfortable villa in leafy Woollahra in 2012, Bayne Kelly reflects on that extraordinary time 41 years before.

He doesn't spend much time thinking about his medal, but every day he thinks about the men who were lost in the jungle far from home, especially Ian Mathers. 'I did what I had to do and I was lucky to survive it.'

Kelly is not angry about the decades it took to right his personal wrong, but like many veterans he does question the honours and awards system.

'I reckon I saw some feats that mightn't have been VCs, but they were definitely Distinguished Conduct Medals or Distinguished Service Cross,' he says.

On the other hand, he is also sceptical about some of the awards that were made. 'For example a Distinguished Service Order [DSO] to a lieutenant colonel [who was] a battalion commander, that fucking dropped his map out of a helicopter so they sent him two platoons for a week to try to find it and he gets a DSO? I can't fathom that, but that's the way it's always been.'

Chapter 8

Responsibility

For almost 40 years Keith Payne VC had the honour — and shouldered the burden — of being the last Australian soldier to be awarded the Victoria Cross for conspicuous gallantry in the face of the enemy.

These days, after the 2009 death of Ted Kenna VC, the final surviving Victoria Cross recipient from World War II, Payne is the sole living Australian holder of the imperial VC.

He has now been joined in the ranks of the bravest of the brave by SAS soldiers Mark Donaldson and Ben Roberts-Smith and 6 RAR infantryman Dan Keighran, who received the new Victoria Cross for Australia during the 12-year Afghanistan campaign.

A total of 96 Australians have been awarded the imperial VC, and the three from Afghanistan are the first to receive the Victoria Cross for Australia, which superseded the imperial version in 1991.

By far the most VCs were awarded to Australian soldiers in World War I — 63 men were bestowed with the top medal.

177

More than 70 men who were recommended for VCs were denied by the review process.

The stories of famous VC winners, such as Albert Jacka at Gallipoli, are welded into the national narrative. Tales of the dozens of selfless acts of courage that on paper at least appear to be worthy of the top honour, but were knocked back, are less well known. They are men such as Lieutenant John Patrick Tunn from the 9th Battalion AIF who recovered a dropped live grenade and lost his right hand as he saved his mates from the explosion. He did not receive any award.

At least Lieutenant Norman Frederick Bremner of the 47th Battalion was granted a Distinguished Service Order, after he was recommended and denied a VC for his gallantry at Messines in Belgium in June 1917. As the acting adjutant, Lieutenant Bremner volunteered to extricate his company after it had become isolated with the loss of all its officers.

His citation is a remarkable narrative of bravery under fire and has a similar tone to that of Mark Donaldson 95 years later.

He made his way over unknown country through an intense enemy artillery barrage to the company and found the surviving officer [Lieutenant Mendoza] lying severely wounded and unable to move. Lieutenant Bremner extricated the company, enabled it to capture 80 prisoners and ultimately the objective.

He returned for Lt Mendoza and carried him back under heavy machine gun fire and intense enemy artillery barrage. He was attacked whilst carrying this wounded officer by five Germans (four of whom he killed), he wounded the fifth and took him prisoner. His prompt and gallant action altered the situation, saved the company and imbued fresh spirit into the men.

However, those above Bremner in the command chain did not believe his actions deserved a Victoria Cross. In contrast to the Great War, just 20 VCs were awarded to Australians during World War II, along with six in the Boer War, two in the Russian Civil War and four during Vietnam.

Keith Payne's is a tale of persistence as well as sheer guts. In May 1969 in Kontum province, South Vietnam, Warrant Officer Class 2 Payne was serving with the Australian Army Training Team Vietnam, in command of the 212th Company of the 1st Mobile Strike Force Battalion. This consisted mainly of native Montagnard (mountain people) fighters and several foreign advisers.

Payne's citation takes up the story:

On 24th May 1969, in Kontum Province, Warrant Officer Payne was commanding 212th Company of 1st Mobile Strike Force Battalion when the battalion was attacked by a North Vietnamese force of superior strength. Under this heavy attack the indigenous soldiers began to fall back. Directly exposing himself to the enemy's fire, Warrant Officer Payne, through his own efforts, temporarily held off the assaults by alternately firing his weapon and running from position to position collecting grenades and throwing them at the assaulting enemy. While doing this he was wounded in the hand and arms. Despite his outstanding efforts, the indigenous soldiers gave way under the enemy's increased pressure and the Battalion Commander, together with several advisors and a few soldiers, withdrew. Paying no attention to his wounds and under extremely heavy enemy fire, Warrant Officer Payne covered his withdrawal by throwing grenades and firing his own weapon at the enemy who were attempting to follow up. Still under fire, he then ran across exposed ground to head off his own troops who were withdrawing in disorder. He successfully stopped them and organised the remnants of his and the second company into a temporary defensive perimeter by nightfall.

Having achieved this, Warrant Officer Payne of his own accord and at great personal risk, moved out of the perimeter into the darkness alone in an attempt to find the wounded and other indigenous soldiers. He finally collected forty lost soldiers, some of whom had been wounded and returned with this group to the temporary defensive position he had left, only to find that the remainder of the battalion had moved back. Undeterred by this setback and personally assisting a seriously wounded American advisor he led the group through the enemy to the safety of his battalion base. His sustained and heroic personal efforts, in this action were outstanding and undoubtedly saved the lives of a large number of his indigenous soldiers and several of his fellow advisors.

Warrant Officer Payne's repeated acts of exceptional personal bravery and unselfish conduct in this operation were an inspiration to all Vietnamese, United States and Australian soldiers who served with him. His conspicuous gallantry was in the highest traditions of the Australian Army.

Responsibility is a common theme with most, if not all, high-level gallantry award holders. Every soldier is trained to take responsibility for the safety of their mates and that is what it boils down to. Yet some reach deeper.

British Field Marshal William J. Slim famously drew a distinction between moral and physical courage. 'I have known many men who had marked physical courage but lacked moral courage,' Slim wrote. 'Some of them were in high places but they failed to be great in themselves because they lacked it. On the other hand, I have seen men who undoubtedly possessed moral courage very cautious about taking physical risks, but I have never met a man with moral courage who wouldn't, when it was really necessary, face bodily danger. Moral courage is a higher and rarer virtue than physical courage.'

The eminent British historian and author Antony Beevor regards many of the men who have been awarded VCs as examples of both physical and moral courage. He says there is a clear difference between the two, but when a person who is obviously physically courageous talks about responsibility that is an example of moral courage.

'Often the most physically brave men are absolute moral cowards,' Beevor says. 'Bismarck made the very perceptive remark, saying the moment a German puts on a uniform he loses all moral courage, which again emphasised the difference between physical courage and moral courage. Of course Hitler realised this in his sort of brilliant way of seeing the vulnerabilities of others and that's why the Nazi party was so keen on getting the children into uniform, because they knew that was one way that moral courage would evaporate.'

A lack of moral courage on a vast scale allowed the Nazi Party to persecute and murder millions of Jews, but Hitler's systematic dehumanising of them was another example of his evil genius.

'He was very, very clever in the way he didn't attack the Jews all out to begin with, he just did it step by step so that people started to accept it,' Beevor says. 'When they [Jews] were first ordered to wear yellow scarves there was tremendous sympathy for months from Germans for the Jews, but funnily enough, even those who felt sympathy at that particular stage soon lost it as a result of the distancing of the Jews, separating them from the rest of the German people, and then they thought, "They are not us, they are not Germans any more."'

Keith Payne has a clear view. 'I look at it as responsibility, and if you read the citations, or whatever the blokes say, they will always come up with, "Well, it was my job, I was just doing my job, it was my responsibility." And I believe that that is so,' he says.

He cites the example of Private Ted Kenna, who was awarded the Victoria Cross while fighting near Wewak in New Guinea in May 1945. His citation reads, in part:

> On his own initiative and without orders Private Kenna stood up immediately in full view of the enemy less than fifty yards away and engaged the bunker, firing his Bren gun from his hip. The enemy machine gun immediately returned Private Kenna's fire with such accuracy that bullets passed between his arms and body. Undeterred, he remained completely exposed and continued to fire at the enemy until his magazine was exhausted. Still making a target of himself, Private Kenna discarded his Bren gun and called for a rifle. Despite the intense machine gun fire, he seized the rifle and, with amazing coolness, killed the gunner with his first round. A second automatic opened fire on Private Kenna from a different position and another of the enemy immediately tried to move into position behind the first machine gun, but Private Kenna remained standing and killed him with his next round.

His action was described as 'magnificent bravery' that ensured a successful assault on an enemy position that minimised friendly casualties.

Payne regards this as a classic example of individual responsibility. 'His responsibility was to pour out ammunition and neutralise the enemy. So when the gun ran out of ammunition and he had no ammunition, he got a rifle and carried on, so his responsibility was to do that.'

Similarly, he sees it as having been Mark Donaldson's responsibility to save the life of an Afghan interpreter. 'Well he was out of the vehicle, for a start, he's seen the interpreter go down ... He would have been the first person to see the interpreter go down; being the first to see him go down, he's the first person to go pick him up. You've got to go pick them up, he was bloody well wounded — "I've got to go pick him up." [He's] part of the team, if it would have been one of his own blokes who's down, he's got to go pick him up. The fact he was an Afghan interpreter wouldn't have entered Mark's bloody brain anyhow. For a start, "They are my soldiers."'

And in the case of Ben Roberts-Smith, Payne says, 'Ben was doing his job. If you ask him — "I was doing my job."'

It is true that the most common phrases of gallantry or bravery award winners is, 'I was just doing my job,' or 'Anyone would have done the same.' But most people reading the citations would have grave doubts that they could ever possibly do what the bravest of the brave did to earn their VCs.

Keith Payne says that as the company commander he had responsibility for the safety of every man he led into battle. 'If I'm taking people into a firefight, all my planning and everything must be such that I can commit my troops with the least amount of casualties and to ensure that casualties do get out,' he says.

That situation is further complicated when dealing with foreign troops such as the Montagnards who were under Payne's command. The native fighters were already spooked by some serious contacts during the previous days. To add to his difficulties Payne couldn't converse with the mountain people.

'My interpreter was definitely not coming with me, no, he wasn't going to be part of that,' he says. 'I knew I had to have communications, and my radio man never came all the way with me, so I had to get that damn radio. Without a radio I was nothing, I was somebody running around the bloody jungle — I had to have a means of communication. So there were two factors at play: I needed a radio and I had to go up and get it, and I had to extract casualties.'

With so many wounded and confused men on the hill, the radio very quickly became a secondary issue of responsibility. 'The primary objective was to get as many as I could off the hill and get them back to the safe area,' he recalls. 'I just did what I had been trained to do on approaching ground like this. I was able to pick up two blokes very quickly and pull them down out of the way to where Charlie [the Vietcong] wouldn't find them.'

After three trips back up the hill, and with the enemy advancing in numbers and taking out wounded as they advanced, Payne decided to withdraw.

'I had to make a decision whether I was going to continue this, or abort and take back the people I had got,' he says. He recognised that if he stayed he stood a fair chance of being killed, 'because it was starting to get a bit dangerous', and of losing those he had already rescued.

His decision to withdraw was based on three factors. First, the enemy had already spotted him; second, the enemy was moving all over the hill; and finally, would there be anybody left alive to rescue if he made it back up?

'I was feeling a little tired and weak and everything because I'd lost a bit of blood and I thought, "Well, the best thing to do is abort that mission and grab hold of these blokes and get them back to a secure area."'

Payne doesn't regard what he did necessarily as an act of valour but rather an act of responsibility.

'You are weighing up a situation, doing what you think is responsible, what you are responsible for even though the situation is a very bad one, so you take your decision to carry out your responsibility, that's the big one.'

* * *

In 1954 Queen Elizabeth II and the Duke of Edinburgh launched the Remembrance Driveway along the Hume and Federal Highways between Sydney and Canberra when they planted two plane trees in Macquarie Place, Sydney.

Thousands of trees were planted subsequently along the old Hume Highway and its replacement the Hume Freeway, and in the mid-1990s the Remembrance Driveway Committee decided to establish a series of rest areas and memorial parks along the freeway to honour the memory of the 24 men awarded VCs for World War II and Vietnam.

So far, 16 rest areas have been built, allowing travellers to take a break on the 320-kilometre journey and to reflect on the courage and sacrifice of these brave men and all those who have fought and died in war.

Ted Kenna and Keith Payne, along with the three VC winners from Afghanistan, will have rest areas established in their honour in due course.

A sign at those already in use provides a summary of each man's official Victoria Cross citation and a brief biography of each of the ordinary men who, through one or more extraordinary act of personal courage, have been immortalised on the list of national heroes.

One of the most delightful of the roadside stops is situated on Roses Lagoon just off the Federal Highway between Goulburn and Lake George. Overlooking the rolling paddocks and a bird-rich lagoon, the park contains cypress, oak, willow, gum and poplar trees and is a living memorial to Australia's first VC recipient in World War II, Corporal John Edmonson from Wagga Wagga in southern NSW.

The 27-year-old's citation is a sobering summary of a brave man's last selfless act on this earth as he fought with the 2/17th infantry battalion at Tobruk in Libya on 13 April 1941.

The citation, published in *The London Gazette* in July 1941, says:

On the night of 13th–14th April 1941, a party of German infantry broke through the wire defences at Tobruk and established themselves with at least six machine guns, mortars and two small field pieces. It was decided to attack them with bayonets, and a party consisting of one officer, Corporal Edmondson and five privates, took part in the charge. During the counter-attack Corporal Edmondson was wounded in the neck and stomach, but continued to advance under heavy fire, killing one enemy with his bayonet. Later his officer had his bayonet in one of the enemy and was grasped about the legs by him, when another attacked him from behind. He called for help, and Corporal Edmondson, who was some yards away, immediately came to his assistance and in spite of his wounds, killed both of the enemy. This action undoubtedly saved his officer's life. Shortly after returning from this successful counter-attack, Corporal Edmondson died of wounds. His actions throughout the operations were outstanding for resolution, leadership and conspicuous bravery.

Corporal Edmonson is buried in the Tobruk War Cemetery.

Each citation accompanying VCs and other high-level gallantry awards makes for extraordinary reading and is a testament to the capacity of human beings to undertake remarkable feats of courage and sacrifice.

Chapter 9

The Perils of Hindsight

Gary Bornholt knows a thing or two about courage. As a former brigadier and infantry officer he commanded Australian forces in the Middle East during the post 9/11 intervention in Afghanistan.

As the head of military public affairs at Defence headquarters during the 2001 'children overboard' scandal, it was Brigadier Bornholt who sat before a subsequent Senate committee and told the truth about the doctored photographs that the Defence Minister at the time, Peter Reith, had released to support the Howard Government's false claims about children from a refugee boat being thrown into the sea.

He told the Senate he had advised Reith's office that the photos were from another incident. The boat sank just days before the 2001 federal election that was fought and won on immigration and national security issues, two months after the September 11 al-Qaida terrorist attacks in the United States.

Bornholt also confirmed that he had been present in the office of acting Defence Force chief Air Marshal Angus Houston when Houston had told Reith directly by phone that children had not been tossed into the water from a refugee boat.

* * *

The independent Defence Honours and Awards Tribunal was established by the Rudd Government in July 2008 and became a statutory body in January 2011. Its job is to examine medal issues, ranging from proper recognition of past service to the retrospective issuing or upgrading of awards.

A member of the tribunal, Bornholt is well placed as both an observer and an ex-miltary man to deal with the tricky question of historical honours and the emotionally fraught push for retrospective medals.

By far the most controversial case so far has been the tribunal's inquiry into acts of gallantry or valour performed by 13 sailors and soldiers. These men included Private John Simpson Kirkpatrick at Gallipoli, who is immortalised as Simpson from 'Simpson and his donkey', and Leading Seaman 'Teddy' Sheean, who during World War II went down with HMAS *Armidale* after strapping himself to a ship's gun.

Bornholt co-authored the tribunal's 2013 report, *Unresolved Recognition for Past Acts of Naval and Military Gallantry and Valour*. After an exhaustive examination of all the evidence, the tribunal decided against recommending any individual awards. Instead it opted for two unit awards for the World War II warships HMAS *Yarra* and HMAS *Perth*.

Like many professional officers Bornholt brings a hard-nosed approach to the issue and he believes strongly that valour is a far higher calling than simple bravery or courage that are part and parcel of a soldier's job description.

In the executive summary of its report the tribunal stated that numerous submissions, including those from past senior military officers, politicians and the RSL, argued that to award Victoria Crosses or other gallantry honours retrospectively would undermine the integrity of the Australian honours system.

'The tribunal agreed that this would be the case unless the evidence was compelling,' the report says. 'But a major problem exists in trying to find compelling evidence, sometimes up to a century after the event, to support a recommendation that an individual should be awarded an honour. In all the submissions and in its own research the tribunal found no case where allegedly new evidence proved acceptable or compelling. Further, there was the matter of equity. If one individual was singled out for a retrospective honour, every other alleged case would need to be examined, and every other previously awarded VC would need to be reconsidered with the possibility that one or some might need to be withdrawn. As one submitter stated, such a task would be "beyond the capacity of any tribunal or any other body".'

Given the iconic status of some of the 13 individuals involved in the review, including Kirkpatrick and Sheean, it was always going to be a controversial outcome.

The tribunal found that Simpson's Mentioned in Despatches (MID) was an appropriate award, given that his 'initiative and bravery' was representative of all other stretcher-bearers of the 3rd Field Ambulance serving at Gallipoli in 1915.

'Contrary to some views, Simpson was not nominated for a VC, nor was there any material in letters, diaries or anecdotes from the time that could reasonably be used to describe Simpson's actions to a standard of gallantry that would have resulted in a VC recommendation being successful,' the report says.

Regarding Sheean, the tribunal concluded that his actions displayed 'conspicuous gallantry' but did not reach the particularly high standards required for a VC recommendation. 'If Sheean had lived he might have been recommended for a higher imperial honour [such as a second- or third-level gallantry award] rather than the fourth level MID, but such intermediate honours were not available posthumously in 1942, and the equivalent level Australian gallantry honours should not be recommended now.'

The tribunal concluded that recommending honours for actions that took place many years ago 'should only be considered if there is a clear case of maladministration or, if proper process had been followed, compelling new evidence has emerged since the original decision was made'.

'Retrospective or revised gallantry honours should only be recommended when the potential recipients meet all the stringent requirements,' the report says.

With the backing of several Tasmanian politicians and serving and retired navy personnel keen to see the senior service obtain its first VC, Teddy Sheean's family and supporters reacted angrily to these conclusions and have vowed to fight on for what they, and many in the Royal Australian Navy, regard as justice for the 19-year-old from Tasmania.

The review did uncover maladministration in the case of the World War II navy sloop HMAS *Yarra*, sunk while battling a superior enemy force south of Java in March 1942 with the loss of all but 13 of her 151-man crew. It said that inaction by the Australian Commonwealth Naval Board in not recommending the ship's company for a gallantry award was a clear case of maladministration and recommended that the *Yarra*'s crew be awarded the Unit Citation for Gallantry.

A key finding was that extreme practical difficulties, such as gathering reliable evidence and second-guessing commanders of the time, made retrospective recognition not only difficult but likely to damage the integrity of the Australian honours and awards system.

Gary Bornholt makes no apologies for the hard line taken by the Honours and Awards Tribunal. The wording of the report reflects the view of many military officers, who regard award retrospectivity with a fondness normally reserved for gastric flu.

Bornholt argues that a lot of courageous conduct revolves around quick actions where someone reacts to a situation that may or may not be life-threatening and acts in a brave fashion. Valour or gallantry, on the other hand, usually involves a sustained effort under circumstances of extreme peril.

He uses the example of a soldier in a six-man section whose mates are all killed and his rifle is lost. The soldier returns to the lines, gets another rifle, turns around and immediately gets back into the fight.

'When you have a look at the job that was done by [Ben] Roberts-Smith for example, recently … It wasn't an action that took a matter of seconds, it was an action that took a long time and he just kept at it,' he says. 'I don't detract from those that have got lesser awards, but this gallantry piece is something that is on another level to what most people understand about brave conduct.'

Bornholt conducted detailed research for the review and he is convinced that the only people who understand what courage, gallantry or valour is about are those who were there to witness the action and who truly understand the culture and values of service.

'What's brave, what's valour and what's gallant to a civilian might just be everyday work to a soldier,' he says. 'You are not expected to just sit there like a wimp and expect it all to happen, you are expected to get off your arse and do something, that's what your job is.'

He says the risk is that well-intentioned people see situations that blow them away and they can't believe that someone could do that as part of their job. 'He is doing it bloody well and bravely, but it's his job.'

Bornholt cites the example of a three-man team made up of a machine gunner and his offsider and a rifleman. 'A sniper shoots the machine gunner so his number two moves to the gun and gets it going because that is his job,' he says. 'He also gets shot and the third bloke decides that he should get the gun going. Now that is not his job but he does it anyway. He knows what is going to happen to him and he could just sit there and do nothing, and he wouldn't be criticised because it wasn't his job to get the gun going, but what he does is he gets off his arse and he gets that gun going. Now that's an element of how you can distinguish between brave and gallant conduct, when you've got choices.

'That's why over all these years, the only people who can be judges of gallantry and brave conduct are those people who were actually there at the time, who look at it and say, "That is above and beyond what any of us could do."'

Sometimes even those who were there on the ground and in the fight can't agree on who should get what. Bornholt regards the Long Tan medal saga as a classic example of the minefield awaiting the unwary who have to deal with revisionism and retrospectivity.

He says the commander of Delta Company at Long Tan in August 1966, Major Harry Smith should have started agitating as soon as the battle was over. Bornholt maintains that Smith was wrong to wait until the war had ended to start his campaign, which included accusing the commander of the 6th Battalion, Lieutenant Colonel Colin Townsend, of rejecting some of his recommendations.

'What Smith was asking years later was to play a part in this nomination system that he never ever had when it existed, so he wasn't part of it. All he could do was give his list to the CO [Commanding Officer] and cross his fingers and influence the CO as best he could.

'If the CO doesn't push in the first place, it's not an injustice. If he then puts your name up and someone says no, that is not corruption. Saying no is the nature of the system. You've got a whole bunch of people, a whole row you've got to convince about the particular act, and that's why it's so hard. That is why there are so few of them [valour awards].'

Bornholt believes that commanders must follow their recommendations from the moment they put them forward, in order to influence the outcome. 'In my own case, on returning to Australia late in 2002, I discovered some of the recommendations for gallantry and distinguished service had been blocked in the chain of command,' he says.

So he went straight to Canberra, bypassing the command chain, and walked into the office of the Chief of the Defence Force, Peter Cosgrove. 'I told him my concerns. He picked up the phone right then and said to one of the chiefs, "A little bird just told me … Fix it!" Recognition for all came along later. I was satisfied. Trying to do this years later would have been problematic.'

Bornholt points to the more than 70 Australian soldiers from World War I who were recommended for the VC but missed out. Many received no awards at all despite being recommended for the highest of them all. That is the nature of the system, he contends, and because no witnesses are left alive and unless there is compelling new evidence to support a claim, Bornholt believes there is little anyone can do.

The tribunal's findings were also informed by the experience of the imperial honours system in which decorations for gallantry and meritorious service would not be considered retrospectively without 'exceptional' circumstances. No case for the retrospective awarding of an imperial VC has ever been successful and since 1947 there has been no recommendation for any case more than five years old.

As the tribunal notes in its lengthy and comprehensive report, 'No system is perfect. For every VC recipient, there are many others who could have received the honour.'

Bornholt thinks one of the biggest problems over the years has been the lack of an immediate review process whereby those with a grievance can raise it and have it dealt with while the memories of those involved are still fresh and clear and witnesses are still alive. That way people don't have to wait for 40 years and be miserable because they feel they were dudded.

'You draw a line in the sand, set up an expert review panel and invite people to come forward with their grievances. The review might take two or three years but it is done,' he says.

Bornholt says many of the issues with post-war trauma can be traced back to the fact that soldiers have not been afforded the opportunity to get this stuff off their chest. Perceived injustices about honours and awards can eat away at a person like a cancer. 'It would allow all these people who haven't been heard to have their say, and they are just as entitled to do that, there is a gate closed and we move on. A process has to be put into place to deal with the whole thing, because if it's not, and if it's not seen to be fair, it's seen to be an in-house thing, or politically motivated, you may as well not go through the process.'

He says the review should be supported by Defence but not run by it, due to the obvious conflict of interest and the fact that the military never takes kindly to serving members airing dirty laundry in public.

Few people in Australia have been more intimately involved in the system of honours and awards than Gary Bornholt. After all his experience as an infantry officer and commander at war and following years of research on the topic, he does not believe there are specific, identifiable traits that can point to the potential for an individual to commit an act of conspicuous valour.

'There are no traits. You don't do a course on this stuff, it just happens on the day and some people make it happen better than others. You could probably come up with some common traits but it wouldn't get you anywhere,' he says. 'There are circumstances and situations that cause the act of valour to occur and you just can't predict them. I think that's a good thing because if you could, we would all be out there trying to do it.'

AFGHANISTAN AND THE AGE OF TERROR

Chapter 1

For Valour

September 2, 2008, was an historic day for the Australian Army and the SAS Regiment in particular. For his actions that day, SAS Trooper Mark 'Donno' Donaldson was awarded the first Victoria Cross for Australia.

Donaldson was part of a multi-vehicle convoy mounted on American Humvees in the Khas Oruzgan area of Oruzgan province, near an American patrol base called Anaconda. The Australians had killed a number of insurgent fighters during the days leading up to the rolling ambush.

His citation not only provides a chilling insight into the calm professionalism of the modern-day special forces soldier but tells the tale of a man of deep compassion.

On 2 September 2008, during the conduct of a fighting patrol, Trooper Donaldson was travelling in a combined Afghan, US and Australian vehicle convoy that was engaged by a numerically superior, entrenched and coordinated enemy ambush. The ambush was initiated by a high volume of sustained machine gun fire coupled with the effective use of rocket-propelled grenades. Such was the effect of the initiation that the combined patrol suffered numerous casualties, completely lost the initiative and became immediately suppressed. It was over two hours before the convoy was able to establish a clean break and move to an area free of enemy fire.

In the early stages of the ambush, Trooper Donaldson reacted spontaneously to regain the initiative. He moved rapidly between alternate positions of cover engaging the enemy with 66mm and 84mm anti-armour weapons as well as his M4 rifle. During an early stage of the enemy ambush, he deliberately exposed himself to enemy fire in order to draw attention to himself and thus away from wounded soldiers. This selfless act alone bought enough time for those wounded to be moved to relative safety.

As the enemy had employed the tactic of a rolling ambush, the patrol was forced to conduct numerous vehicle manoeuvres, under intense enemy fire, over a distance of approximately four kilometres to extract the convoy from the engagement area. Compounding the extraction was the fact that casualties had consumed all available space within the vehicles. Those who had not been wounded, including Trooper Donaldson, were left with no option but to run beside the vehicles throughout. During the conduct of this vehicle manoeuvre to extract the convoy from the engagement area, a severely wounded coalition force interpreter was inadvertently left behind. Of his own volition and displaying complete disregard for his own safety, Trooper Donaldson moved alone, on foot, across approximately 80 metres of exposed ground to recover the wounded interpreter.

His movement, once identified by the enemy, drew intense and accurate machine gun fire from entrenched positions.

Upon reaching the wounded coalition force interpreter, Trooper Donaldson picked him up and carried him back to the relative safety of the vehicles then provided immediate first aid before returning to the fight.

On subsequent occasions during the battle, Trooper Donaldson administered medical care to other wounded soldiers, whilst continually engaging the enemy.

Trooper Donaldson's acts of exceptional gallantry in the face of accurate and sustained enemy fire ultimately saved the life of a coalition force interpreter and ensured the safety of the other members of the combined Afghan, US and Australian force. Trooper Donaldson's actions on this day displayed exceptional courage in circumstances of great peril. His actions are of the highest accord and are in keeping with the finest traditions of the Special Operations Command, the Australian Army and the Australian Defence Force.

It is a beautiful summer's day in Canberra in January 2009 and Mark Donaldson, his wife Emma and daughter Kaylee are joined at Government House, Yarralumla, by a battalion of top brass, politicians and special-forces troops, for the VC investiture by Governor-General Quentin Bryce.

Donaldson looks strangely out of place surrounded by Prime Minister Kevin Rudd, Chief of the Defence Force Air Chief Marshal Angus Houston and a who's who of the nation's military and political elite. He sits bolt upright as the audience hears the tale of his courage under fire, Emma sits proudly by her husband's side and Kaylee wonders what all the fuss is about.

There is a lot of reflected glory in the nation's first VC for 40 years and, after Donaldson poses for numerous photos with the long list of stakeholders seeking a piece of the action, it is time for the dreaded post-ceremony press conference.

The assembled reporters are keen to hear what it was like to be under fire and to establish why a man would risk his life in such dire circumstances to save a colleague, and an Afghan one at that.

The modest boy from Dorrigo in northern NSW, who looks as if he'd rather be anywhere else, plays down his feat in typical fashion. 'I'm a soldier, I am trained to fight and that's what we do. It is instinct and it is natural,' he says. 'You don't think about it at the time, you just do what you've got to do.'

* * *

The son of former Western Australia Supreme Court judge and ex-Army Reserve Major-General Len Roberts-Smith, Ben, or 'RS' as his mates call him, is an extroverted, heavily tattooed man-mountain, while Mark Donaldson is a quietly spoken man of compact stature.

They represent the yin and yang of SAS troopers. Just as the nature of yin and yang is not static but lies in the interaction between the two, so does the SAS Regiment exploit different personality types as a means to the same end — winning in battle.

But when it comes to what is deep inside, one of their former commanding officers, Lieutenant Colonel Paul Burns, doesn't see them as so very different. 'Oh, but I think down to their hearts and souls, they are exactly the same. It's what's in their hearts and what their values are. They don't wear them on their sleeve. Ben is big, robust, but deep down he would die for his mates and he would die for his country. Mark Donaldson is a slighter build, but deep down he would do exactly the same. You don't wear this on your sleeve. That is what the [SAS] selection course does, it sort of identifies — because you are broken down physically so the selection panel can see inside your soul to see what you are really about.'

No one was more relieved when Roberts-Smith was awarded his VC in January 2011 than Mark Donaldson. Not only had one of his regimental brothers been recognised for outstanding valour, but also there was someone else to share the dazzling public spotlight that comes with a VC.

Roberts-Smith had already been awarded the Medal for Gallantry in 2006 for an earlier action in Afghanistan and so became the most highly decorated soldier in the Australian Army. A warrior with a fearsome reputation, he peeled enemy fighters off his back and dispatched them during one action. Roberts-Smith or 'Big Ben' as he was tagged by one media outlet, was an instant hit with the Australian public.

During one interview with Channel Seven he was asked if he was prepared to die for his country. 'Very much so ... I don't mean that in a theatrical sense, or I'm not being silly about it. I know what we are doing is actually stemming the flow of terrorism into this country,' he said. 'I think if I go away and I was to get killed on the next trip, and that was the way my life was meant to play out, then so be it. At least I've done it serving my country. And making this country that we love, all of us, a better place for our children.'

Statements such as this, coming sincerely from the heart of a warrior hero, are music to the ears of politicians, who faced a growing struggle to convince the Australian public of the merits of the war in Afghanistan. When the nation's most decorated soldier, who came close to death numerous times during the VC mission, says the war is making Australia safe, the nation listens.

'RS' first realised that his patrol might be in trouble when the US Black Hawk in which his team was flying on June 11, 2010, began to take heavy fire from the ground.

He was hanging out of the helicopter providing covering fire to his mates already on the ground, who had disembarked from another helicopter, when an insurgent fired a rocket-propelled grenade (RPG) and it passed just below his feet. 'That's probably the most vulnerable I felt all day because you are not in control,' he said.

After two Australians were wounded, the Black Hawk landed so that his team could assist in securing the area for a medical evacuation. They married up with the main force and the squadron commander decided they would assault the enemy position in the 'green zone'.

Afghanistan is dominated by desert ('dasht') with verdant green zones running along the river valleys. These small, fertile areas feed the people, and the orchards and tall crops of corn, and other vegetables, as well as prolific marijuana plantations, provide excellent cover for insurgent fighters who blend in with the local farmers and their families.

This presents a major problem for the Australian soldiers, who must pursue the insurgents without harming the local people. 'There is no way that we could risk any type of civilian tragedies,' Roberts-Smith explained to the media after the award ceremony. 'We always make sure we are as surgical as possible to achieve that.'

They began to push forward. 'We started to progress through the green, the trees, the orchards and our lead element, or our lead patrol, got hit by machine-gun fire straight away and essentially pinned down,' he recalled.

Unable to identify the enemy's location behind the walls of a compound due to the density of the vegetation, the patrol was trapped in position for about 20 minutes.

'My patrol commander decided that he had had enough and said that we were going to go and have a crack at whatever this position was; at that point we weren't really sure, we thought perhaps one gun, maybe two.'

They moved in single file up a slight hill through a dense fig orchard and after about 80 metres they were hit by an intense weight of fire.

'At that point we realised we had actually hit up against three … machine guns and a number of other insurgents with small arms or rifles,' he said. 'What happened initially was that we got split as a patrol because of the lay of the ground; some of the guys were moving around to a flank and they ended up engaging other insurgents out of the trees and three of us ended up in front of the guns, so we began to fire and move forward supporting each other.'

They got to within about 40 metres of the enemy position and the incoming fire was so great that they were forced to crawl to within about 20 metres.

'A couple of grenades were thrown, one of the other lads just headed up in front of all these guns and put in a magazine of fire, which was incredible to watch, and he had a magazine stoppage,' Roberts-Smith said. 'He had drawn fire to himself so they were focusing on him, and I believe at that point perhaps the grenades had knocked out one of the [machine] guns, so we still had two and the fire hadn't stopped.'

While the soldier was dealing with his magazine stoppage and a third man was pinned down by enemy fire it was apparent to RS that he had the best cover.

'I just looked across, saw my mates getting ripped up and decided to move forward. I wasn't going to sit there and do nothing, thought I'd have a crack, not let my mates down. I got to the wall, engaged the first machine gun, about nine metres on there was another one, engaged that, from there the second mate next to me, we began mopping up positions and decided to push the advantage while we had it.'

That was the turning point in the battle, but it took another six hours to finally silence the enemy. When the dust settled, more than 20 enemy lay dead and five machine guns and numerous other weapons had been captured.

'Every single bloke in that troop, as I said earlier, was at some stage fighting for their life, every single person there showed gallantry, the decisions I saw made were heroic. Just watching some of my mates who had been wounded by frag [shrapnel] just keep firing, just ignoring the fact they were drawing fire to themselves, it was certainly an amazing squadron effort and a good result. We were always hearing these stories about ambushes and things, losing good Australians, but we won, we won and we hurt the insurgency and it was an enduring defeat so I'm very proud to be part of that.'

Did he feel fear while he was out there, in the heat of battle? 'Oh sure, everyone feels fear and anyone that says that they don't is probably either crazy or not telling the truth.'

As for being bombarded by ammunition, he said, 'I think as anyone would tell you, at the time it doesn't mean a lot to you. You are conscious of it, so trying to position yourself to avoid being hit, you also are concentrating on the fight. You are listening for the sounds of weapons, where they are moving, what your boys are doing, if someone has a stoppage, just trying to help everyone else there. I think afterwards, when you look at the bloke next to you and think, "He's copping a pasting," you feel sorry for him. Then you get back and say, "Gee mate, you were copping a pasting." You don't really focus on yourself.'

* * *

In 2012 Corporal Dan Keighran became the first Australian infantry soldier in more than 43 years, and the first member of a regular army battalion since World War II, to be awarded a Victoria Cross.

All four Vietnam VCs went to members of the Australian Army Training Team Vietnam and the two earlier Afghanistan VCs to members of the elite SAS Regiment.

So it was a matter of great pride for the wider army and a huge honour for a modest man from Nambour in Queensland when the VC was pinned to his chest by Governor-General Quentin Bryce in Canberra on November 1, 2012, before a crowd that included Prime Minister Julia Gillard, the military's top brass and a bunch of Keighran's mates.

Corporal Keighran arrived in Afghanistan with 6 RAR in February 2010 and was working with the Mentoring Task Force in August that year, operating with the Afghan National Army's 1st Kandak (battalion) of the 6th Brigade 205 Corps, known as the 'Hero Corps'.

It was during an operation at the village of Derapet in the Tangi Valley that Corporal Keighran and several of his mates earned their medals; it was also where, tragically, another of his mates, Lance Corporal Jared MacKinney, was killed in action. The combined coalition force knew that the enemy was in the area — in fact, they deliberately drew the enemy out — but they were not prepared for the numbers of enemy fighters and the intensity of their attack.

Dan Keighran's citation is a testament to selfless soldiering and a level of commitment to his mates that separates him from other men.

Early on during the attack and despite accurate enemy fire, Keighran and another digger moved to an exposed ridgeline where they could identify enemy positions and direct the machine guns fire onto them. Corporal Keighran deliberately drew enemy fire moving over the ridgeline so he could positively identify targets for the machine gunners. Under persistent enemy fire he continued to lead his team and move around the ridge both to direct the fire and to move his men to more effective firing positions.

He moved back up the ridgeline to direct fire support being provided by the 30mm guns of Australian Light Armoured Vehicles in a nearby overwatch position. That fire silenced many of the enemy guns and turned the tide in the favour of the combined Australian–Afghan patrol. On several further occasions Keighran deliberately exposed himself to draw enemy fire and shoot at enemy positions.

The citation reads:

> Realising that the new position provided a better location for the patrol's joint fire controller, Corporal Keighran moved over 100 metres across exposed parts of the ridgeline, attracting a high volume of accurate enemy fire, to locate and move the fire controller to the new position. He then rose from cover again to expose his position on four successive occasions, each movement drawing more intense fire than the last in order to assist in the identification of a further three enemy firing points that were subsequently engaged by fire support elements.
>
> During one of these occasions, when his patrol sustained an Australian casualty, Corporal Keighran with complete disregard for his own safety, left his position of cover on the ridgeline to deliberately draw fire away from the team treating the casualty. Corporal Keighran remained exposed and under heavy fire while traversing the ridgeline, in order to direct suppressing fire

and then assist in the clearance of the landing zone to enable evacuation of the casualty.

Corporal Keighran's acts of the most conspicuous gallantry to repeatedly expose himself to accurate and intense enemy fire, thereby placing himself in grave danger, ultimately enabled the identification and suppression of enemy firing positions by both Australian and Afghan fire support elements. These deliberate acts of exceptional courage in circumstances of great peril were instrumental in permitting the withdrawal of the combined Australian and Afghan patrol with no further casualties.

What the citation did not mention was that the patrol had, according to one soldier who was there, been let down by a lack of fire support, such as artillery and air strikes, at crucial stages during the battle. An email to News Limited newspapers from a digger who fought at Derapet revealed deep anger at the perceived level of fire support made available to the troops that day.

The soldier also questioned the value of intelligence reports that gravely underestimated the strength of the enemy force lying in wait for the diggers. He blamed the coalition's fear of collateral damage and civilian casualties for placing the lives of soldiers at risk. The only consistent fire support, he says, came from Australian Light Armoured Vehicles parked on a nearby hillside in an over-watch position.

Mortars, artillery (one round all day) and air support (Apache attack helicopters) were limited due to the close proximity of civilians and the risk of casualties, but that didn't stop the soldier from claiming that the lone Australian casualty of the battle, Lance Corporal MacKinney, would have survived had mortars been used.

'That contact would have been over before Jared died if they gave us f...ing mortars,' the email states.

The army, of course, denied the soldier's allegations and blamed his reaction on the emotion of battle and the loss of a mate. What is not in dispute is the courage of Dan Keighran and the other soldiers awarded medals for their gallantry at Derapet.

Keighran is the least talkative of the three modern-day VC winners. A quiet country boy, he prefers to duck the limelight. He left the army in 2012 and chose to work underground in the mines at Kalgoorlie in Western Australia.

Such is his modesty that for two years he avoided telling his wife Kathryn the grim details of the action at Derapet, but he was forced to confess after he was informed that he had been awarded the VC.

Due to a bungle within army headquarters his award was delayed by more than two years. High-level valour awards are supposed to be presented as soon as possible after the action, so a two-year delay is highly unusual. He was originally nominated for the Star of Gallantry, one level below the Victoria Cross for Australia.

What is not unusual for a VC winner is the level of moral and physical courage that Dan Keighran displayed during the battle. His actions not only suppressed the enemy but undoubtedly saved lives, as did the actions of four others that day: Lieutenant James Fanning, who was awarded the Distinguished Service Medal; Sergeant Sean Lanigan and Private Paul Langer, who each received the Medal for Gallantry; and Private Sean Parker the Commendation for Gallantry.

Chapter 2

Gallantry at Derapet

Sergeant Sean Lanigan, who was awarded the Medal for Gallantry (MG) for his actions at Derapet, is in utter awe of what Corporal Dan Keighran did that day.

The 36-year-old Lanigan was on the opposite flank to Keighran and his section during the firefight. As well as trying to stay alive and keep his troops safe, he was charged with mentoring the Afghan soldiers attached to the patrol.

Lanigan was a late starter in the Australian Army. After quitting university and working for some years as a farm labourer, hay carter and in hospitality, he wanted some direction in his life, and the army was the answer for the then 26-year-old from Port Fairy in southern Victoria.

As a mature and motivated individual his progression was quite rapid and after a tour to East Timor with the 2nd Battalion he undertook a sniper's course and joined the specialised world of the sniper platoon. 'It was another little world within a world, something new, a whole new skill set to learn,' he says. 'Some of the guys had been in special forces for some time so we were in a really highly motivated environment. I look back now and see that people on that course shaped me and the way I operate as a soldier. I wanted to be like them. They were fit, professional and all those blokes have gone places.'

After just four years in the army Lanigan was promoted to corporal in 2004 and posted to the school of languages in Melbourne for a year in 2006 before he transferred to 6th Battalion RAR in Brisbane.

'I always wanted to work in Brisbane and on my fifth day at work in 6 RAR I was in East Timor and that began this tempo of sniper courses, promotion courses and going to Timor, Iraq and Afghanistan all within four years in 6 RAR,' he says.

Lanigan regards his time with the 6th Battalion as the best years of his life. Certainly, in terms of the post-Vietnam Australian Army, he had a dream run. Thousands of professional Australian soldiers had been in the army for decades and had gone nowhere, and suddenly the new generation was undertaking almost back-to-back deployments.

'You couldn't have had a better time, I don't think, as a soldier in the regular army, it was like living in paradise. It was unbelievable.'

He was promoted to sergeant in 2009, and was the sniper platoon sergeant as the preparation for Afghanistan got underway. After brigade level exercises where he was attached to the headquarters, Lanigan was posted to Mentoring Task Force Number 1 and began his preparation for Afghanistan as a member of a mentoring/reconnaissance team.

He deployed in February 2010 and in July his team, Mentoring Team Alpha, was sent from Patrol Base Wali in the

Mirabad Valley — to the east of the main base at Tarin Kowt (TK) — to the Deh Rawood region in the west to replace French troops who had pulled out.

'It was a massive deal because the furthest base from TK at that time would have been roughly 30 kilometres away and that feels like bloody 600 kilometres in Australia,' he says. 'We were going into an area about 60 kilometres away, so I was very grateful to be part of that historical thing.' When the team departed TK and entered the desert, Lanigan says he felt as if he was in a wagon train heading across the Wild West.

To date, the three months from June to August 2010 were the most deadly for Australian forces in the entire Afghanistan campaign. In just three months ten young Australians were killed in action, including five in July and four in August. Among the dead were four of Sean Lanigan's mates from 6 RAR — Privates Nathan Bewes, Tomas Dale and Grant Kirby and Lance Corporal Jared MacKinney. The death of Private Robert Poate in October 2012 would take the battalion's killed-in-action list to five, making 6 RAR the Australian battalion to suffer the highest losses of the campaign (up to early 2013).

The death of Nathan Bewes on July 9 hit the troops hard, but the worst knock came on August 20 when Tomas Dale and Grant Kirby from Mentoring Team Charlie were killed by an improvised explosive device (IED).

'We had this little patrol base and all we had was each other,' Lanigan says. 'It was another kick in the guts but we were very, very aware of where we were and how we were feeling. We all thought, "Let's just keep our resolve hard for our mates." We were sad for our mates.'

That resolve was a definite factor during the next few days as the team began to encounter enemy fighters around the village of Derapet. Their first contact was on August 22 and by the time they left Wali on the 24th they knew something would be on.

When the engineers, who patrolled ahead of the diggers to clear the way of IEDs, reported that the civilian population was fleeing they knew it was 'game on' and they would probably get an opportunity to avenge their mates.

As the platoon sergeant, Lanigan's day began very early and he clearly remembers the feeling of dread in the pit of his stomach. 'I felt physically ill with worry because they were all good young lads,' he says. 'I just felt it was going to be on when they went out and cleared that spot. I remember being really sick in the guts with worry.'

It wasn't long before his concerns would be fully justified.

The patrol of about 20 Australians and 20 Afghans left the security of Patrol Base Wali at about 8 am for the short patrol into Derapet.

'It was like walking into no–man's–land, there was no one around and it was a pretty eerie sort of feeling,' Lanigan says. 'I remember seeing a couple of little kids standing there and, looking back, they were probably spotters because they were the only two kids there.'

It was only about 70 metres from the last building to the green zone and as Lanigan, who was in the lead, got to within about five metres of the lush zone and its two–metre–high corn and marijuana crops, all hell broke loose.

'We were taking small arms from pretty close range and being up the front your first job is to regain the initiative.'

The enemy was only about 50 to 70 metres away and, as is often the case in Afghanistan, their fire was not as effective as it could have been. By the same token the Afghan soldiers in the patrol were also trigger–happy and they responded with a massive rate of fire from small arms and rocket-propelled grenades (RPGs) that presented another danger for the diggers.

Lanigan led his section into an aqueduct as he tried to establish exactly what his force was up against. It soon became apparent that an enemy machine gun was set up further along the aqueduct. Meanwhile, his Afghan troops were pouring fire into the enemy and he and his mates had to ensure that they didn't get caught in the back-blast of any friendly RPGs.

The team was now split in two, with Lanigan's section occupying the low ground and Dan Keighran's section the high ground. Four section moved to support Keighran and his men on the high ground when Jared MacKinney was hit. First reports said he had been shot in the arm, and Lanigan thought he would be OK. Only later did they discover that the enemy round had pierced his aorta, inflicting a fatal wound.

After about 25 minutes, during which time Lanigan and his mate Paul Langer had fired about five magazines each, they decided to assault along the aqueduct. Lanigan would eventually go through nine magazines of ammunition (180 rounds) during the battle.

'I just remember thinking, "Holy shit, we've got something big going on here," when I was up to about my third mag change,' he says. 'All I was thinking was, "We are mentoring the Afghan Army and we have got to try and teach them to fight."'

Lanigan is adamant that while he was awarded the MG, many other soldiers did exactly what he did that day.

'You are not there to get medals,' he says. 'You are just there to do your job. I got the MG but other boys made that split-second decision to move down that aqueduct. They [the Afghan Army] just lost their initiative and we were getting hit from different angles. I just remember going forward, firing at the enemy, I sort of got knocked off my feet and the fight was coming from the other place. Our ears were ringing but we were having the time of our lives really, to be honest. We were hooting, it was like we were in a real big fight and that was the adrenaline, it just all happened so quick. There was no thought of personal safety. You just have total confidence in the guys you have been working with.'

The loss of two mates on August 20, four days before the big battle, was a motivating factor for the diggers, who just wanted to get out there and kill the enemy. 'All the boys in our patrol had that mindset of trying to push forward.'

The official citation for his Medal for Gallantry says, 'Sergeant Lanigan's gallant actions in contact with a numerically superior and entrenched enemy, in rallying the soldiers and coordinating their return fire, gained time for both Australian and Afghan soldiers to move into supporting positions. He then bravely led a frontal assault under heavy enemy fire to clear the enemy from their entrenched position, and subsequently disregarded his own safety while coordinating the partnered patrol to defeat the enemy's counterattacks.'

The official citation of Private Paul Langer, who also won a Medal for Gallantry in the same action, is equally impressive.

'Private Langer's disregard for his own personal safety while suppressing the enemy in the initial stages of an enemy contact allowed both Australian and Afghan soldiers to move into supporting positions and return fire,' it says. 'His subsequent actions to clear the enemy from an entrenched position in an aqueduct while he was under accurate, sustained enemy fire, and to then hold this position against determined enemy action were outstanding. His selfless actions ensured the holding of the low ground from constant flanking enemy assaults for nearly three hours.'

But while his own bravery and the courage of the men around him that day was formidable, Sean Lanigan says it was nothing compared to what Dan Keighran did.

'Dan Keighran ran up that hill twice to support his mates, to get the medic up there and to help with marking targets,' he says. 'I remember walking out of there and thinking to myself, "Dan Keighran deserves something for what he did today."'

The firefights were gut-churning experiences for Lanigan and his men, but he regards the threat from IEDs as the worst experience in Afghanistan.

'Walking through a crack in the ground and thinking you are going to get blown up churns your stomach way more than being in a firefight,' he says. 'I reckon every young Australian who went over was a brave lad. They went over looking like 17-year-olds and they came back home looking like men. So much happened, wandering those fields, bombs everywhere.'

Chapter 3

Towards Ana Kalay

Troy Simmonds always wanted to be a soldier. After moving to Australia from England as a young boy with his parents, Margaret and Clive, the family settled in the Adelaide Hills, where both Mum and Dad worked as art teachers before Clive was bitten by the winemaking bug and joined a winery in McLaren Vale. Young Troy enjoyed an idyllic rural childhood helping at the winery, exploring the hills with his mates from the Strathalbyn High School.

He wanted to join the army straight from school, but he was doing well in his education and his folks and his mates talked him out of it. He enrolled in an Arts/Law degree at Flinders University in Adelaide and, later, the University of Adelaide.

'I still had the idea in my mind that I wanted to serve my country and be in the army,' he says. 'My dad was in the National Service in England as a volunteer and he hated the army. He had a lot of adventures in the army, but he hated it! He was in the medical corps and because of his artistic background he specialised in making gruesome make-up of disembowelled casualties for the medical training, which he loved.'

His uncle — his father's brother — spent 23 years in the British Army, and his grandfather served with the Royal Air Force during World War II. The message handed down to young Troy was that the army was not great, but when he was about eight years old his dad told him that if he could have his time over again he would try to join the British Special Air Service.

'I said, "What's that?" He said, "Oh parachuting and all this action-packed secret stuff. I would have loved to have done that if I'd have been a volunteer." So I kept asking him and whenever I'd ask him about army stuff I would ask about the SAS,' he says. 'He finally bought me a book on the SAS, the British SAS, and I studied that as a young fellow. Later on I found out Australia had an SAS and I remember when I was at uni, I went down to the recruiting officer and asked them about the SAS.

'The recruiters were cooks and Ordnance Corps so they had no idea about the SAS, but they said, "Oh yeah, join, you can go straight to the SAS."'

They also said that as a university student he should probably go to the officer corps, but that officers didn't usually stay in the SAS for long, while other ranks, or non-officers, could stay in for much longer.

'I did my research from what they said and thought, "Yep, just join as a soldier." I had been studying, I didn't want to study again at Duntroon, I wanted to go and be a soldier and be a full-time SAS guy and have all the adventures,' he says.

To the dismay of his parents and friends he quit university and enlisted in the Australian Army. 'I quickly realised you couldn't go straight from the army to SAS so I ended up doing five years in infantry. I thought infantry was a good start to get my background, so went to the 1st Battalion.'

He was preparing to attempt the arduous SAS selection course when the 1993 Somalia famine happened and the battalion was deployed to the Horn of Africa to help stabilise the security situation there. After returning from Somalia he reapplied for selection to the SAS, but on day three of the incredibly demanding course he dislocated his shoulder and was out. After shoulder reconstruction he applied again in 1996, and this time he was successful.

SAS entrants must complete the 'reo', the reinforcement cycle of training. At this stage there are basically two choices — to become a water operator (diver and water warfare specialist) or a free-fall parachutist. Troy Simmonds was never the world's best swimmer so he chose the free-fall troop and added signalling as his second speciality. Each SAS trooper must be either a medic or a 'sig', or 'chook' (signaller).

'As you progress in SAS it's better to have been a signaller because once you get to patrol command level, you work hand in hand with your signaller,' he says. 'If you can understand the reason why we can't suddenly pick up and go because he's got his wire out and if you are continually asking the signaller, "Have we got comms yet?"; if you can understand the processes you are going through, you have a much better relationship, whereas some of the medic patrol commanders who are former medics had to really learn extra stuff to comprehend that. So it's not a bad thing.'

After qualifying as a sniper he joined Number 2 SAS Squadron in 1998 on counter-terrorism operations to begin preparing for the Sydney 2000 Olympic Games. In those days the SAS was responsible for the military's national counter-terrorism (CT) response, known as TAG (Tactical Assault Group) West, based at SAS headquarters, Swanbourne, near Perth. Each squadron would spend a year rostered on to CT duty. These days there is also a TAG East based at 2 Commando Regiment at Holsworthy barracks, near Sydney.

While preparations for the Olympic Games were underway, the 1999 East Timor crisis kicked off. Simmonds would ultimately undertake three tours of the troubled former Indonesian province.

The year 1999 marked the beginning of the busiest period in the regiment's history since the Vietnam War, with Afghanistan in 2001–02, Iraq in 2003 and Afghanistan again from 2005 to the present day. Troy married his wife Lia in 2002, the same year as the first of his six deployments to Afghanistan.

Based at the huge US airbase at Bagram, north of Kabul, 2 Squadron's main role in the early days of the post-9/11 campaign was to conduct clandestine patrols in search of al-Qaida leaders in the mountainous regions south-east of Kabul where it was thought the world's most wanted man, Osama bin Laden, was hiding out.

Due to a limited supply of the regiment's primary mode of transport — specially modified, six-wheeled, long-range patrol vehicles — the troop conducted most of its work on foot. Their bread and butter was observation and that meant tramping for days through the cold, desolate and steep mountains, undetected, to reach a point where they could spend even more days on end sitting in the one spot observing a road or a building, looking for targets of interest.

'Our arse was hanging out, we just walked day and night,' he recalls. 'We walked all night then you slept for a couple of hours during the day because we were trying to be concealed. We'd sneak in between rocks and pull some brush over the top of us and sleep like that for a couple of hours, basically just hiding. The sun was just smashing us and goats would come around and try and eat the shit that covered us and at night we'd move again when it was dark enough and we dared move again, and there were always people around, and we have to be totally clandestine so it's pretty hard.

'One time we were up there, they wanted us to watch this particular road. There was supposed to be a particular person of interest on this road; they had us waiting there for ages and we literally ran out of water,' he recalls. 'A vehicle patrol came and they couldn't drive up the hill, obviously, so they parked at the bottom as close as they could and sent guys carrying water to re-supply us. They got up there and were saying, "We can't believe this is what you guys are doing all the time."'

All Troy and his mates were thinking was how wonderful it would be just be to be able to get a ride in a vehicle.

The years between 1999 and 2013 were a new golden age for the SAS Regiment. If not on operations, then the sabre (operational) squadrons would either be preparing to deploy or go off on another adventure in the jungles of Papua New Guinea or the wilds of northern Australia.

'Plus every year you get a new officer in there, or, every couple of years, your troop commander, and that's his chance to make his mark so he can come back as squadron commander,' Troy says. 'Even though all the other guys and all the NCOs [non-commissioned officers] have been around for years, it's sort of, "Righto my priority is fitness, everyone is going to do all this fitness stuff," or, "We are going to be the best people at walking long distances."

'Most of them are pretty good, but they do have to make their mark and I suppose when we are busy on operations they get the opportunity to make their mark. That's really great for them and their career; if they've got the talent they deserve it. In peacetime I suppose they have to still make that mark and they haven't got the operation to hang it on.'

* * *

The 'fog of war' is a serious occupational hazard for combat soldiers. It is not easy recalling exact details from a battle where terminal danger combined with survival and success have generated confusion and vast amounts of adrenaline. When most of the participants have been wounded and evacuated from the battlefield, and indeed the country, the situation becomes even more blurred when it comes to the sensitive issue of honours and awards.

The battle of Ana Kalay in the Khas Oruzgan region of Afghanistan on September 2, 2008, and the gallant deeds of I Troop Number 3 SAS Squadron, has become part of Australia's rich military folklore due to Trooper Mark Donaldson's 80-metre run across open ground under withering enemy fire to rescue the gravely wounded Afghan interpreter.

Nine of the 13 Australian soldiers (11 SAS and two from the Incident Response Regiment) operating alongside American special forces troops that day in the Khas Oruzgan region were wounded, including SAS patrol commander Sergeant Troy 'Simmo' Simmonds, who was shot twice and blown up by a rocket-propelled grenade.

Two of the SAS operators were very badly wounded, one shot in the chest and another through both legs. One American soldier was killed when he was shot in the head; as two SAS men dragged his body towards a vehicle, the already dead soldier was shot twice in the back as well.

Several times during the battle the enemy fire became so intense that the soldiers literally had nowhere to take cover, so movement, accurate fire and the occasional air strike was their only defence.

Days before, the Australians had conducted a classic sniper–weapon-initiated ambush in a neighbouring valley. Their American colleagues had been hunting insurgent leaders in the Khas Oruzgan area for months, but two valleys to the east and north-east of US patrol base Anaconda remained virtual no-go zones for coalition troops. The entire district was a hotbed of insurgent activity and the base itself had been attacked on several occasions.

Anaconda was built on a knoll about 800 metres from the first mud qalas (dwellings) of the district capital, Khas Oruzgan. In August–September 2008 when the Australians from Number 3 SAS Squadron arrived to support the Americans the area was regarded as 'tiger country' (enemy territory).

I Troop consisted of four six-man patrols designated India 1, 2 3 and 4. Each had a patrol commander, a second-in-command, scout, signaller, medic and joint terminal air controller (JTAC). Supporting them were communications specialists, engineers from the Incident Response Regiment, explosive ordnance detection dogs and an interpreter, or 'terp'.

The diggers and the Americans devised a cunning plan for August 29 that would see the SAS operators walk into the valley to the east of the base overnight and establish sniper positions on the high ground. The Americans would drive their armoured Humvees in early next morning to draw out the enemy. Whenever the Americans conducted overt vehicle patrols, Taliban fighters would mount a speedy ambush to try and catch the infidels.

'The Taliban would go down the rat lines [routes used by insurgents] and set themselves up to ambush the Americans but we were already in position, where we could ambush the Taliban getting into their ambush position,' Troy Simmonds recalls. 'We got into position undetected and the next day the Americans drove out in their convoy. The Taliban told all their mates, "The Americans are coming out, let's get them."'

American and Australian troops were able to easily monitor all enemy communications. 'The Taliban all started massing, coming down their rat lines, and at three o'clock in the afternoon we were in a position to ambush them. We had three guys come along initially and we knocked them off and then there was a lot of radio traffic.'

This is widely known as 'ICOM chatter', named after the primitive hand-held radios used by the Taliban that are easily intercepted.

'It's not exactly a high-tech interception of communication,' Simmonds explains. 'You've just got to buy a Motorola and you can understand what they are saying.'

More enemy fighters flooded in on the back of a sports utility vehicle to try and find what had happened to their three mates. 'As soon as we saw the vehicle and that they were all in the back with RPGs and various weapons that tied in with the communications we were intercepting about their intent, my patrol ended up knocking over 11 Taliban in one initiation,' he says. 'The Americans didn't get attacked — they [the enemy] thought it was the Americans, they didn't think it was us that were hidden in a hide on the side of the hill so we were able to sort them out. It had a good impact with the Americans because [the dead] included two Taliban regional leaders and one particular guy they were after.'

Photographs taken by the troops show Taliban dead strewn around a Toyota utility riddled with holes. In one shocking image virtually the entire brain of one of the dead insurgents can be seen in the console between the two seats.

Confident about their chances of nabbing a bomb-maker after their success on the 29th, and the capture of Taliban shadow governor Mullah Bari Ghul, the combined US, Australian and Afghan troops decided to mount a patrol on September 2 into the north-east valley near the village of Ana Kalay in a bid to lure the enemy from their mountain hideouts, on a mission codenamed Operation Katnook.

And lure them out they did.

Chapter 4

A Bad Valley

The physical contrast between an isolated valley in southern Afghanistan and Belfast in Northern Ireland couldn't be greater, but the signs of imminent and grave danger were all too familiar to Australian SAS soldier Rob Maylor.

The 46-year-old Kiwi-born special forces operator had served with the Royal Marines in the early 1990s, and in 1993 he was deployed for the first time to Northern Ireland. During foot patrols through the streets every move the squaddies made had been monitored and reported by spotters, whom the British called 'diggers'.

As the combined Australian, American and Afghan National Army (ANA) force moved into the valley of Khas Oruzgan on September 2, 2008, it was subject to some heavy-duty 'digging'. The force included four six-man patrols and the troop headquarters. Patrols India 1 and India 2 walked in overnight with the headquarters and India 3 (commanded by Troy Simmonds) and India 4 (which included Mark Donaldson) drove in with the Americans at first light that morning.

'If you go to Northern Ireland you are being watched; they strategically place people on corners, on shops, on high ground to observe what you are doing and report on your movements, and the Brits used to call it "digging",' Maylor says. 'So basically we were getting "digged" from several Taliban in that area and they were paralleling us, watching every move we made, basically, counting numbers, looking at vehicles, trying to find weaknesses and probably formulating a plan on how they were going to attack us if we came back through that same area.'

Just before lunch, Maylor, armed with his sniper rifle, joined a foot patrol up to the high ground. They didn't observe much movement from their observation posts high above the valley floor and the lush green zone, but they picked up a growing level of ICOM chatter on their radios.

The Australians realised something big was being planned for their return journey so they had asked the Americans in the Hummers to try and find another route back to Anaconda base. None could be found, so once they married up back at the vehicles they discussed staying the night and escaping early in the morning. But as the ANA soldiers had no night-vision gear, the decision was taken to retrace their steps and head back to base.

'As soon as they [the enemy] saw the vehicles breaching the narrow entrance back into the valley, the ICOM chatter went nuts,' Maylor recalls.

It was ideal ambush country. There was only one narrow track, and a series of washouts (where rain had swept down sand and gravel) and very steep ground prevented them from heading to the right and away from the green zone and the qalas built close to the road.

'We had to bridge the road a couple of times, just to get the cars around those big washouts, and we ended up stalling a couple of times and that stopped progression at times because we had to get into some of these washouts, to guide the cars through and move boulders out of the way, just to keep us away from that green zone and that heavy weight of fire, just make a path for the vehicles to go into the washout and back up through the other side,' he says.

The convoy was made up of ANA-manned vehicles in front and at the rear, Maylor's vehicle with patrol commander Troy Simmonds and some American troops second in line, followed by Mark Donaldson's mixed Australian–US vehicle, then an American vehicle ahead of the last Afghan Hummer.

As they passed a series of compounds they heard the Taliban commander telling his fighters to wait until they had passed a particular building. 'They had already planned where the ambush was going to start, and the first car rolled through then our car copped the full brunt of the initial contact,' Maylor says. 'The other cars were quite a way behind us, and up on a little bit of an elevated position, they had a little bit of sporadic fire, but we copped the brunt of the mortars and machine-gun fire. Luckily at that stage it wasn't that accurate but you could see it getting closer and closer, and it was at that point we had to get onto the road to get around one of those washouts.'

Thus began a fight for survival as the patrol fought its way out of the valley and back to base. Maylor's vehicle immediately began to take 'effective fire', where rounds consistently strike within one metre of the target.

'Rounds were hitting the car, they were splashing around the car, mortars were landing closer and closer so were bracketing onto us. We did bust out because that car was just a fucking magnet. So we got off; we didn't actually get too far away from the car, but we had to try and find some cover either beside the vehicle or on the ground, using depressions in the ground or rock formations, which there weren't too many of. Once the vehicle started rolling ... we'd jump on again, so we got around the first washout and that's when we heard one of the Taliban leaders say, "Kill them, kill them all."

'That's when you got that horrible sick feeling in your gut, "Oh shit, that is not looking good." We had a really long way to go at that stage and the other cars behind us started to attract some effective fire as well. They all got past the washout then the effective fire slowed down.'

The words of the Taliban commander would haunt Rob Maylor for the next two hours.

Once the targets had moved past the first killing zone the enemy fighters ran to the next choke point and set up for another attack. Maylor says at one point the Green Berets just stopped the vehicle and poured heavy fire into the enemy positions.

Coming from the mobility troop, the Australians were well drilled in either breaking contact or going on the attack, but always supporting one another using the basic drills of fire and movement and conserving ammunition.

'But you are firing and moving in vehicles, so one vehicle is moving, the other one is stopped and shooting, it's covering your withdrawal or your advance,' he says. 'This didn't really happen that day and I don't think a mobility operation is a strong point of the Green Berets; their strong point is guerrilla warfare, so, you know, both sides, I think, learned quite a serious lesson that day.'

As he sits in the den of his comfortable house in the tree-covered hills of the Gold Coast hinterland, it is difficult to reconcile this quietly spoken family man, relaxing on the sofa as his wife and daughters unpack groceries in the kitchen, with the warrior fighting for his life in a dusty, violent Afghan valley.

Maylor believes complacency played a definite role that day. 'We got caught unawares and they [enemy] did a very good job.'

It took the patrol almost four hours to fight its way along several kilometres of valley against a force that grew to an estimated 150. Maylor was armed with a sniper rifle rather than a carbine, so his main job throughout was surviving and helping to keep the convoy moving. Every time he and another SAS sniper moved away from the vehicles carrying their specialised, long weapons, they would attract an enormous rate of fire, preventing them from finding adequate cover to bring their weapons to bear.

'Trying to find a target lying down and getting shot at, just wasn't fun because you are forever sort of moving out of the way, or moving your body position out of the line of fire. You could just see the line coming in, getting closer and closer coming swinging beside you, landing in front of you, so you had to crawl or move out of the way,' he says. 'I tried that several times, but it didn't work so I went back to the car because I was getting absolutely hammered by small arms fire.'

As he arrived back at the vehicle he noticed that the American JTAC, Evan, who was specially trained to call in fast air or helicopter fire support, was completely focused on a laptop and two radios in his hands and oblivious to the mortal danger he was under as rounds hit all around.

'He was looking at the map of the area ... on his computer so he could find likely locations or actually pinpoint enemy targets ... so he could relay that grid back to the aircraft that they could drop bombs on it,' Maylor says.

Because he had been ineffective with his sniper rifle, Maylor decided to look after Evan, who was possibly the most vital member of the entire team at that point and was in grave danger. Evan was also controlling two American fast jets that were crucial to the survival of the patrol.

'If we had lost him there was no one to control the aircraft because by that stage we'd had a couple of our guys severely wounded,' he says. 'I thought, "I need to keep this bugger alive because he is going to keep us alive by controlling those aircraft." So I ran out there, grabbed him on the shoulder, pulled him down and said, "Mate we've got to get out of here, you are attracting a lot of fire."'

They moved to the vehicle where Donaldson was located and Evan began to take target indications and pass them on to the pilots of the jets. 'As we were moving past the vehicles everyone was shouting target indications at the poor bugger … but we did get a couple of clear targets that he'd identified and one of them was where the mortar base plates were,' Maylor says.

Evan relayed that information to the first aircraft, which engaged the target with a 250-kilogram air-burst laser-guided bomb. Then he switched his attention to the second pilot.

'All of a sudden the first pilot he was talking to said, "Impact five seconds," and you hear, "Oh shit take cover, incoming!" As soon as he said that, this fucking thing exploded. It was a huge explosion, because it was "danger close",' Maylor says. 'You could hear the shrapnel whizzing over our heads, it was that close, but it stopped the mortars.' Had the soldiers not reacted when they did and hit the dirt some would almost certainly have been killed by the white-hot metal.

Evan and the fast jets would play a vital role once more as enemy fighters began to mass in a creek bed. This time the 250-kilogram weapon was set to ground-burst and the mob was eliminated before they could attack the patrol, which was now under sustained fire from at least three sides.

'If [they] hadn't been seen we would have had more casualties, we would have been in a lot more trouble than we already were in and I think by that stage we'd had multiple casualties.'

The pair finally made it back to the vehicle where they married up with Simmonds and another SAS operator, as well as Sarbi, the explosive ordnance detection dog, and her handler. The five American Humvees still had about four kilometres to go to reach the safety of Patrol Base Anaconda.

Patrol commander Simmonds convened a quick meeting with his remaining soldiers at the rear of his vehicle, which was second in the order of march. His second-in-command had taken over the gun position in the turret and was busy supressing enemy fire and monitoring the battle. Just as they began to weigh up their options an enemy RPG landed right in the middle of their huddle.

'Luckily the force of it went underneath the vehicle but the blast got all of us,' Simmonds says. 'I remember Mark Donaldson saying he saw it from the vehicle behind and he thought the vehicle had hit an IED [improvised explosive device]. He saw the back of the vehicle lift up and a massive dust cloud and us just tumble and he thought we'd hit an IED and we were all in pieces.

'I can remember the ground was like a thick cloud of dust all around me, feeling numb and trying to feel for limbs. I went to grab my left arm and I was thinking, I was scared for a fraction of a second that it wouldn't be there. It was there and after a while the feeling came back. We kind of shook ourselves off, my weapons had sort of spun around ten times and landed in the dirt and we were OK but we got fragged. I got quite a few pieces of shrapnel in the left side of me and Rob Maylor got heavily fragged, he got a lot of pieces of shrapnel in him. But nothing stops for that, the battle is still going on, we kind of shook ourselves off and got back into it again.'

As well as the RPG that went under the car, another three landed around them, according to Maylor. 'One overshot the car, one dropped short, one went underneath and exploded and the fourth overshot us and landed about a metre beside me. Luckily I was the opposite side of the blast direction so all the main blast went away from me.'

Maylor and his SAS mate were lifted off their feet, while Sarbi went on the run after her wounded handler had to let the frightened dog off the leash so he could be more mobile.

'It was quite surreal, there was instant heat from the explosion and everything sort of went quiet and into slow motion,' he says. 'I saw the two sniper rifles hitting the deck, we hit the deck. "Fuck, what was that!" Then the sudden realisation that we'd been hit. It was like someone had sort of smacked me with the flat end of a cricket bat, so we got up, dusted ourselves off a bit, and then I remember saying, there was another volley of automatic machine gun fire came in and I said ... "There are too many people around this car, we need to go to that one there."

'We'd identified the front car and it wasn't attracting any fire whatsoever, so we said, "Let's go."'

Before their brief chat had been so rudely interrupted they had decided that Maylor and another soldier, Trooper H, would move across 150 metres of open ground to get the lead vehicle moving again after its Afghan crew had taken a wrong turn and were being smashed by enemy fire. This was delaying the entire five-vehicle convoy, and delay meant only one thing in the valley of Ana Kalay that day — certain death.

The two men were both wounded, Maylor with serious frag injuries and the other with a bullet wound across his backside, but they covered the 150 metres to the Afghan vehicle in Olympic qualifying time. As they reached it, the Hummer was hit by a splash of rounds so Rob Maylor ran past the vehicle and took cover in a washout. His mate told the Afghans to drive up and provide cover so he could rejoin the vehicle.

'I was looking through the scope and trying to find targets,' Maylor recalls. 'And I could just see splashes of dust and rounds kicking up in front of me and I could feel the dirt coming inside the washout from rounds hitting the edge of the washout and just looking at the ground and I thought, "This is it, we are done for. Are we ever going to get out of this?" Then it was quite comforting to hear a familiar voice, "Get up here," and there was the car, ten metres away. It was good.'

'I'm pretty sure that the fire that was hitting the car followed me, which enabled Trooper H to stay by the car and eventually manoeuvre or convince the driver to move the vehicle closer to me so it was blocking the fire from the high ground and let me get out of the washout and get to the car as some sort of safety.'

In their panic the Afghan soldiers had locked the doors, so the two diggers were banging on them as the Afghans were staring at them all wide-eyed.

'"Can you fucking open the door you pricks?" The driver opened his door which then prompted the guy in the back to open the back door for me,' says Maylor.

The second SAS man reefed the ANA driver out of his seat. 'We just said, "We've got to get this fucking thing moving," and we did.'

Up to that point Troy Simmonds had been unable to talk to the American special forces captain in charge of the operation so he made his way towards him to discuss the situation.

As we sit in the dining room of Troy's comfortable bungalow in suburban Perth, on timber chairs that he built in his shed, eating a tasty lunch that the accomplished amateur chef has prepared, it is bizarre to be talking about a life-and-death struggle in a far-off war-torn land.

'All of a sudden I saw two characters up on the high ground and I had a crack at them with my rifle,' Simmonds says. 'Next minute my rifle just smashed me in the side of my head, and I had a look at it and a bullet had hit the working parts [just above the trigger] and destroyed it.

'Shortly after that I just crumpled on the ground. I had been shot through the side of my buttock and the bullet went through my hips. I just fell on the ground, blood was everywhere but I was bloody already from the previous injuries. I knew I'd been hit somewhere. I hoped it wasn't a vital organ and just, yeah, just got back up again and sort of pushed my way around. All the time bullets were either side of my head.' The bullet had passed through his body and remains embedded in his hip to this day.

'I got to [the American captain], opened up the door and he had two [radio] handsets on his head, talking to two different agencies, telling his boss about what is going on, trying to talk to someone else as well, absolutely flustered but doing a great job and I said, "My guys are trying to get that lead vehicle going that is bogged down, we need to get out of here, if we can't get out of here we have to come up with some contingency." And I was thinking in my head if we couldn't get out of there, going into one of the compounds and doing a bloody wagon wheel [putting the vehicles in a circle] or something to defend ourselves, [if] basically for some reason we couldn't get out of there.'

At this stage there was an enemy force estimated to be 150 strong attacking the vehicles and the 37 men attached to them.

By now it was getting very late and Rob Maylor had identified a compound where they might be able to organise some cover and wait for darkness before calling in the aeromedical evacuation (AME) choppers.

'As we got closer and closer to this compound, the valley was coming to a bottleneck and we were just attracting more fire, and at that stage it was coming from everywhere, so we decided it was too much of a risk to go to that compound, we need to keep moving.'

It was as they were heading out of the valley that Simmonds managed to wedge himself between the bullbar and the bonnet of his patrol's Hummer — the only place he could fit — wearing a 'helmet' improvised from the vehicle's towing chain.

As they approached the last feature in the valley, Maylor's vehicle stopped to provide covering fire for the other vehicles, but the Afghan on the Mag 58 machine gun had a stoppage. Maylor recalls that just then an American vehicle rolled to a broadside halt next to them and took up the fight. He says, 'We were then able to start breaking contact out of there, car by car, it was almost like a rolling break contact but once we were out of the valley we were still getting hammered. I wouldn't say it was effective fire but we were still attracting a lot of fire from the green as it tapered off towards Anaconda.'

Maylor's vehicle was one of the last to arrive back at the base and the sight that greeted them shocked him. The ground was covered in wounded soldiers from the other vehicles, including one Australian with critical chest and abdominal wounds, another with serious leg wounds, and several others, including Afghans, with a variety of gunshot and shrapnel injuries.

Maylor himself had serious shrapnel wounds in his back and strong pain in his stomach, so he was added to the makeshift triage ward awaiting the first American AME Black Hawk helicopter for the 20-minute flight back to the surgical unit at Tarin Kowt.

'I was grazed a couple of times by rounds but also had a lot of frag in me, my abdomen was a bit sore and that sort of prompted the medics to mark me down as a priority one case because they didn't know how far the actual frag had gone through my back into my stomach,' he says. 'So they said, "Let's get this guy out of here real quick." Simmonds was in the same boat, they didn't know where the round was and obviously [Trooper G] had breathing complications and major trauma to his chest and liver, and [Trooper J] had horrific wounds to his legs.'

He thought Mark Donaldson had been wounded as well because he was covered in blood, but as it turned out it wasn't his own blood. Donaldson had picked up an American helmet when the fire intensified and the blood of the dead American dog-handler ran down his head and shoulders, making him look badly wounded.

Numerous soldiers had minor wounds from bullets or shrapnel that had missed vital areas by millimetres.

Rob Maylor has no idea why they had been so lucky. But he says that every man did his job with great courage that day.

'The American medic was fantastic and if it wasn't for him, [Trooper G] probably wouldn't be alive,' he says. 'He had total disregard for the fire that was coming in as he worked to save his life.'

Fortunately the insurgents were mostly using armour-piercing rounds, so most of the diggers who were shot received 'in and out' rather than expanding wounds. 'That's probably what saved [Trooper G] because the round entered his chest, but for some reason its trajectory has diverted so it's dipped down underneath his heart, through his liver, as it's sort of come down in the middle of his guts there it started to come back up on exit, but if it had continued on its entry trajectory it would have gone straight through his heart,' Maylor says. 'I can't figure out why we were so lucky, mate. If that RPG was two metres off it probably would have killed me because it would have landed a metre the other side and I would have copped the full blast.'

All the training in the world does not take account of luck, and on that day in an isolated valley in Afghanistan, Lady Luck sure was smiling on the Australians and their mates. Of the 37 coalition troops on the ground just one was killed in action despite the vast weight of fire poured into the men and their vehicles. Nine Australians were wounded, four seriously, and several Americans and Afghans were wounded to varying degrees.

After the battle, there were reports from intelligence sources that around 70 enemy fighters had been killed, including Chechen snipers who had been operating in the valley.

As well as luck, Rob Maylor puts their success down to teamwork. 'You are fighting for your own personal safety but you are fighting for the other guys too,' he says. 'After a situation like that the team becomes even closer. If you were lacking motivation to watch your mates' back previously, it doesn't happen any more.'

Chapter 5

Too Stubborn to Die

Troy Simmonds's wounds were serious enough for him to be flown home to Perth for treatment and recovery. As a consequence, he was unable to participate as patrol commander in the operational debriefings and the discussions regarding honours and awards.

It was three months after his return before Simmonds had any formal contact with the regiment and by then the awards had been done and dusted.

Honours from the battle were Donaldson's VC; two Medals for Gallantry; a Distinguished Service Medal (DSM); and a Commendation for Gallantry, but no award went to Troy Simmonds or to some others, including Rob Maylor, who helped save the day (and their lives) and whom Simmonds recommended for high honours following the battle.

Simmonds also recommended his second-in-command for a Medal for Gallantry, but the trooper received the DSM instead, which is awarded for leadership in action, for taking over command of the patrol from Simmonds — despite the fact that Simmonds had remained in command until almost the end of the battle.

'I didn't get wounded until right at the end and it wasn't like I handed over command sort of thing. I was the commander right until the end even though I was wounded,' he says. 'It wasn't like I was like, "Oh take over, fellas." I literally was only out of action for just the final couple hundred of metres before we went through that pass.'

He also recommended Rob Maylor and Trooper H, who covered 150 metres of open ground under intense fire to get the convoy moving again, for the MG, but Maylor missed out. He had left the regiment and written an unauthorised book entitled *SAS Sniper*. His mate had stayed in, and after months of lobbying by Simmonds, Trooper H did receive the Medal for Gallantry; one of the engineers from the Incident Response Regiment was also awarded a Commendation for Gallantry.

'Those two guys went 150 metres through heavy fire, machine-gun fire ... Both of them were already seriously wounded and got the whole convoy going,' says Simmonds. 'I really feel happy and proud, particularly for Mark Donaldson, for what he got. I think it wouldn't have been inappropriate for a couple of other guys to at least receive a commendation. I did push hard and I was very pleased that one of my guys, my signaller, did receive a retrospective Medal for Gallantry, because often, particularly in very significant events, it's easy for very brave actions to be overshadowed by something such as a VC.'

His persistence came at a cost. The regimental sergeant major even recommended psychological counselling to help him get over his 'issue'. There is a strongly held perception by some in the SAS that a session with a 'shrink' is tantamount to admitting weakness and should be avoided. This is despite the fact that nowadays every operator is required to see a psychologist to prevent bigger issues occurring down the track.

Troy says he is particularly proud to have been associated with Donno's Victoria Cross. 'I realise it's not all about medals, but this is a pretty significant event and I was the patrol commander there and I was cut out of all the discussions because I was injured and most of my patrol were injured. It kind of leaves a bit of a sour taste in my mouth.'

Says Lieutenant Colonel Paul Burns, at that time Commanding Officer of the SAS Regiment, 'No one is saying he [Simmonds] wasn't brave for what he did and the bravery and valour that he showed, and courage, is absolutely incredible. Sometimes we don't always get it right, sometimes there isn't always an award that fits precisely to recognise that performance on the battlefield, and … there are guys not being recognised. Sometimes recognition by your peers is just as important.'

Simmonds says he is happy that all the Australians survived what could easily have been a much darker day for the SAS Regiment and for the nation. None of them died despite having men being shot through the chest, across the top of the head and in his own case across his neck, through his back and into his M4 carbine, not to mention numerous shrapnel wounds from RPGs.

'There were heaps of other guys that just got clipped, but if it had been a few millimetres the other way they would have lost their heads, so it was more luck than anything. It could have been the worst military disaster in years,' Simmonds says.

Of the enemy, he says, 'Even though we took a few casualties, they got smashed on that thing, and now MTF [Mentoring Task Force] have been pushing up that valley, so I guess in the long term it had an effect.'

Recognition comes in many forms. The sole American soldier who lost his life in the combined operation that day was working-dog handler Sergeant First Class Gregory A. Rodriguez from Michigan, aged 35. His specialised search dog Jacko survived the ambush.

In a subsequent email to Simmonds, which he shared with other members of his patrol, another of the American soldiers who fought with them that day wrote the following:

… Troy, there is nothing to thank me about. We were there together working for the same reason and although we had casualties and one KIA [killed in action], we accomplished a great mission together. I am really proud and honored to say that I have worked with such caliber soldiers like you and your whole team.

Troy, I think about SFC Rodriguez (Rod) all the time. Sometimes I wake up and spend hours thinking about what I could have done to avoid that incident. I can only say that episode made me a better soldier and I use that experience now to train and prepare others for our next trip out there. It is also good that you are doing the same running the selection course and training. Use all that experience, be hard and fair, but do not cut any slack.

I am really glad to hear about Donaldson's award. Your whole team deserves that same award and more, because what you did that day was not only an act of valor, but it made a difference in the world at the end.

Troy, we not only worked as a team together that day, but I believe we created a relationship that will last forever. Again, I am really proud, honored and grateful that I served with you and the team. Tell our mates that we are always here.

In his Anzac Day address to the SAS Regiment in 2009, Paul Burns reflected on the meaning of the Anzac legend and asked whether the regiment was upholding it: 'Surely, on this momentous day we should be honest with ourselves — turn our binoculars inward, and reflect on this question.'

In his mind, he said, scrutiny of the history of the Anzacs in action revealed three core traits: 'Those traits are courage, boldness, and perseverance.' Citing historical examples of each trait, he compared those actions and individuals with the actions and individuals of the SAS Regiment in Afghanistan.

For 'courage', he compared Mark Donaldson's valour with that of World War I hero Albert Jacka VC. 'Albert Jacka showed us how courage transforms into the decisive action that can alter fate's intended outcomes. We know of his legendary savage bayonet charge at Gallipoli for which he won the Victoria Cross. What is generally not as well known is his action at Poziéres, where he led his small depleted force, severely wounded, directly into a large German counter-attack, with the bayonet and grenade, in a way that was so frightening, to the enemy, that it turned a local defeat into a victory.

'Mark Donaldson reminded us all that courage is alive in the SAS Regiment, when last year, in Southern Afghanistan, he conducted an individual action that saw him win the Victoria Cross. He reacted instinctively to aid his wounded comrade — knowing how slight his odds were on that open ground, strafed by multiple entrenched machine guns and RPG. Despite this, he went. And in so doing, he saved the life of his comrade. With men like Mark, and others among you, courage is very much alive in this regiment.'

To illustrate 'boldness', Burns compared the famous Operation Jaywick raid on Singapore Harbour in 1942 with an SAS raid in

2009, in which a small foot patrol from 2 Squadron had infiltrated a Taliban stronghold and killed a key bomb-maker.

'Operation Jaywick remains one of the defining points in the evolution of Australian special forces,' he says. 'The men of 'Z' Special Unit proved to all that a small group of men, carefully selected and highly trained, can shake the earth. During this perilous mission, a small and diverse crew from 'Z' Special force boldly infiltrated Japanese territory by conducting a 5000-mile epic in a small fishing vessel — the MV *Krait*. They executed an action that not only destroyed 40,000 tonnes of maritime assets, but Japanese morale and confidence. This skilful, daring act, dangerous beyond measure, against a dominant enemy, is one of our great benchmarks for boldness.

'Our unit cap badge, Who Dares Wins, embraces the spirit of boldness. Only a few weeks ago a small foot patrol from 2 SAS Squadron clandestinely penetrated an enemy stronghold to identify and subsequently neutralise a key IED facilitator at very close quarter. This was a mission that could not or would not have been undertaken by any other force due to the extreme, but calculated risk involved in such an audacious and daring action.

'If it wasn't for this SAS boldness, this cowardly bomb maker would not have met his end and the threat to our coalition partners would not have been reduced. Boldness is an often unacknowledged element of all our missions but is what makes the men in SASR truly special.'

Then he turned to the third quality, perseverance. Here, he compared the performance of Troy Simmonds and his troops in Afghanistan with that of the 2/2nd Independent Commando Company, which waged a year-long guerrilla campaign against the Japanese in East Timor during World War II.

'The 2/2nd Independent Company was stoic in its refusal to surrender during Japanese occupation of East Timor,' he said. 'In 1942 when the Japanese commander asked for their surrender, the 2/2, in a famous retort, declared, "Surrender? Surrender be stuffed!" (Or words to that effect.) Instead, they took [to] the hills, re-postured, built a radio out of broken parts, and cracked on. For the better part of a year, they persevered, resolute in the knowledge that as far as they were concerned, Australia hadn't surrendered and neither would they.'

Turning to Simmonds's example, he said, 'The only thing that kept Troy alive in that ambush last year was perseverance. Troy persevered to command, despite a situation bordering on hopeless. His patrol was corralled in a Taliban ambush — a killing ground that stretched for miles. He was engaged from all sides, and from above and below. He was wounded three times, and had his main weapon destroyed by enemy fire. Despite this, Troy maintained the small amount of fire and manoeuvre available to his team, he maintained command and control, and he pressed on. The presence of this quality alone saw him bring his patrol through what were truly odds uncounted. This is an act of perseverance in spades.

'We should be mindful that the lens of war is always selective. We know that there are countless other equal or possibly greater acts which will forever remain unspoken. Knowing this and being at peace with it is equally important to the Anzac legend as those deeds that are seen; that are recognised.'

Troy Simmonds returned to fight again in Afghanistan after being wounded. He left the army in September 2012. 'I'm enjoying the civilian life now,' he wrote from his new job in Western Australia in early 2013. 'I have no regrets about the amazing 22-year adventure I had in the army, but I feel equally content to have now put it behind me.'

On the issue of the awards, he feels he has moved on. 'It would have been good and appropriate if a few more of us had been recognised at the time, but now it's history and it's no longer high on my priority list. I wouldn't want to create any embarrassment to Defence or the regiment by pushing any harder for recognition than I have done already.'

Chapter 6

The Golden Hour

Damien Thomlinson is a young man whose life was changed in one violent instant on a dusty track a long way from home.

The tall, blond-haired, blue-eyed surfer from the NSW Central Coast was on patrol with his mates from the 2nd Commando Regiment in Oruzgan province, Afghanistan, in April 2009 when an insurgent bomb shattered his body.

Few manifestations of courage are as inspiring or emotional as a gravely wounded soldier who overcomes horrendous injuries inflicted by an unseen enemy.

Thomlinson joined the special forces in 2005 under a direct entry scheme. This allowed men with the physical and mental attributes required to join the Commandos without having to serve the normal 'apprenticeship' in a regular army battalion. Applicants still have to pass basic and advanced infantry training to qualify to join a Commando regiment, but they don't have to serve the usual several years 'internship' as a foot slogger in a battalion.

He is not sure what attracted him to the army's elite band of warriors, but as a 24-year-old male who had always been good at sport he regarded it as a challenge. His family and many of his friends were mystified, but their doubts evaporated once he set his mind to the task.

Military service was always in the background of the young man's life. Both his grandfathers served during World War II, and a great-grandfather fought in World War I.

'It was something that I think was always an option when I was looking for a secure type of job,' he says. 'I noticed a recruitment scheme while I was looking for things on the internet and from there I decided I would be more than happy to give it a crack. It was something I thought I would be suited to, but not many people that I ran it by thought that I was suited to in any way whatsoever, but I thought I was and I was willing to give it a go. I didn't think the physical aspect was going to be too dramatic to get through, it was always going to be more the mental side, so when it's one of those type of challenges it takes it into a different sort of ball park.'

While his parents' reaction was more of a nervous laugh than a shriek of horror, many of his mates understood and respected where he was going with his life. 'They saw a different side of it, they saw me training, they saw me not drinking as much when we were out, all the little things to try and make the pieces fall in, whereas my parents still saw this kid running around breaking stuff.'

He made it through the tough selection process and, after his initial training, was posted to the 2nd Commando Regiment at Holsworthy to undertake reinforcement, or 'reo', training before he joined an operational company.

After operational deployments to Fiji on HMAS *Kanimbla* and to East Timor, Thomlinson arrived in Tarin Kowt in Afghanistan in March 2009.

'I was pretty excited to be there. I mean, you train for so long and you train so hard for it,' he says. 'It was the focus of the entire year before our deployment. It was entirely focused on what we were going to do when we got over there. There was an overwhelming sense to be finally there, I guess.'

About three weeks later, his troop left the Special Operations Task Group base at Camp Russell for a disruption operation targeting enemy commanders deep inside 'tiger country'.

Thomlinson was driving an open, non-armoured patrol vehicle when the driver's side front wheel detonated a large improvised explosive device. With no memory of the explosion, he has only pieced together what happened via the recollections of his mates on patrol with him that day.

'My memory stops at some stage in the days prior,' he says. 'I did look up at one stage [in hospital] and see someone who wasn't actually out in the field with us and I asked him what he was doing there, but then I passed out.'

He is not sure if the memory loss is related to the heavy nerve treatment he received to deal with massive trauma or whether it is linked to the concussion he sustained from the huge explosion. Either way his memory is wiped, and it is probably just as well. But long discussions with his mates, especially the ones who saved his life on the dusty battlefield, not only allowed Thomlinson to piece together some of the detail of what happened, but was important therapy for those soldiers as well.

'I wanted to be as much a part of the recuperation that they were going to require. So having them talk about it, sitting there listening to them talk about it I think was a big thing for me. The only information I really got about what happened, about any of the events, has come from the guys around me.'

The explosion tore his right leg off about two-thirds of the way up the femur and his left foot was literally hanging by a thread. Both his arms were fractured and he had a broken nose and torn mouth, but it was the damage to the right leg and the blood gushing from his severed femoral artery that was causing most concern as his mates moved quickly, despite their own injuries, to administer combat first aid. Their own injuries included a perforated eardrum and a serious leg gash, but they instinctively fell back on their combat first-aid training and applied tourniquets high up on his thigh to stem the flow of blood.

Black humour is a vital defence mechanism during trauma on the battlefield, so there were some comments made about protecting his 'family jewels' as they applied the custom-made battlefield tourniquets to stop the bleeding.

His left foot was still attached, but X-rays at the field hospital showed that most of the bones in the lower leg had been pulped, forcing doctors to amputate the leg below the knee.

The only reason Thomlinson is still alive today is because of the standard of first aid administered to him, firstly by his wounded comrades and then by the highly trained combat first aiders who kept him breathing until the medevac chopper arrived to fly him to a British field hospital.

He can't speak highly enough of the soldiers who applied that crucial first aid. 'You have to be really good at what you do, to be able to deal with something like that,' he says. 'Let's face it, you can't train anyone to see one of their mates that they've spent the last year in the build-up cycle with, have half of him sitting on the ground next to you and then be able to switch straight into the mindset of "Let's make this work and make this happen." I mean it is a really critical time, early.'

Adding to the pressure was the fact that it was a night mission, so they were working on him in the dark. Time is of the essence for badly wounded battle casualties and Thomlinson's initial treatment and rapid evacuation within the 'golden hour' — the first hour after injury — undoubtedly saved his life. Such was the extent of his wounds that during his first emergency operation at the trauma unit at Camp Bastion, the main British base in nearby Helmand province, he required six times the volume of blood normally carried by a human being just to stay alive.

By the time of his second surgery at Bastion his condition was so critical that if the operation had been unable to repair him adequately for the long plane journey to Landstuhl Regional Medical Center in Germany then, he says, his life support system would have been switched off.

His first memory after the incident was waking up in Ramstein and seeing an enormous frame around his right arm. The arm injury alone was very serious — the elbow, the radius and ulna were all broken and the humerus was in about six pieces. The arm had a plate running its entire length to hold all the repairs together.

His time in Germany was a haze of heavy painkillers and surgery, so the full extent of his injuries did not become clear to him until after he arrived home in Sydney and was admitted to the intensive care unit of a private hospital.

His parents and his partner, Brazilian biochemist Tisha Agostini, worked around the clock in shifts to sit by the bed and operate his morphine machine so he could rest. 'Otherwise I'd wake up basically I think every ten minutes, so they had it down to a little timed situation where they would sit up next to me and push the button for me. I mean they've been just awesomely supportive.'

Soon after he arrived home, Thomlinson set himself his first goal: to be standing on the airport tarmac to greet his mates when they returned home from duty in Afghanistan.

'The first thing that I wanted them to see when they got off the plane was me standing there. There is no better message,' he says. 'Anyone can tell you that he's doing really well, anyone can tell you that, but until you have seen it with your own eyes it is not one of those things you take as seriously. So I thought it was most important that I am there standing for the whole team when they get off that plane, that's the first thing they see.'

That was a huge motivating factor as he recovered to the point where he could be fitted with prosthetic legs. 'The initial part of the rehabilitation was all about getting on the legs and making them work, having everything function well enough so that I could be there,' he says. 'I mean, eight weeks after the hit I was standing and walking on both legs. That's fair motivation for the guys that I had been that close to for that long.'

The homecoming was a huge day for Thomlinson. The Special Operations Commander, Major General Tim McOwan, stood beside him at Sydney airport as the commandos filed off the charter jet. McOwan says that as the aircraft came to a stop, Thomlinson was so nervous he could barely stay upright.

'He wasn't sure how they would receive him. He was concerned about the fact that he thought he had left his mates behind in the battle,' McOwan says.

The young soldier needn't have worried: his presence at the airport was a great surprise and an inspiration to the returning warriors. He stood there to greet every single person who left the plane, and each one shook his hand with a beaming smile. His team members hugged him and almost dragged him off his new legs.

'I think everyone who was there was really happy to see me there,' he recalls. 'It was a really, really good experience for me, I think, and a good experience for them. Speaking to them afterwards they said that it really did help everyone that was involved, so that makes it, makes all the effort worth it when you get a pay-off like that.'

By December 2009, he was back working two days a week in the development cell with the Commando Regiment at Holsworthy Barracks. 'Coming in and getting out of the cycle of having to stay at home, which, as appetising as it sounds to some people, really isn't that flavoursome after an amount of time, it was a big thing, a good mental step for my recovery to be back at work and seeing everyone that's around me,' he says.

His return to work became the focus of his rehabilitation. In the safe and private world of Commando headquarters he was able to get back as close to normal as was possible under the circumstances.

In late 2010 Thomlinson got a call from Ray Palmer in Queensland, whose son Scott had been killed in a helicopter crash in Afghanistan in June 2010. Palmer had been on patrol in April 2009 and was one of the first on the scene after the blast that hit Thomlinson.

In July 2011 Thomlinson told Sydney's *Daily Telegraph* that Scott had phoned his dad and told him he didn't think 'Thommo' was going to make it. Palmer senior told his son's mate that he and Scott had always planned to walk the Kokoda Track in Papua New Guinea and he wondered if Thomlinson might join him for the trek.

It comes as no surprise that Thomlinson completed the arduous walk across some of the toughest and most infamous mountain country on earth. By that stage of his recovery he was so adept at getting about on his man-made legs that he walked with an unusual gait but only a slight limp.

During the trek a stranger asked him if he had twisted his ankle playing footy.

'No, drove over a bomb,' came the reply.

The stranger laughed. 'Seriously, twist your ankle playing footy?'

'No, seriously,' he replied. 'Drove over a bomb.'

By early 2012, it had become apparent to Damien Thomlinson that his army career was over. He had already developed a new life and had become an inspiration to tens of thousands of Australians through his many activities, including driving a rally car for charity, walking the Kokoda Track and fundraising for the Commando Trust Fund.

In April the keen snowboarder received a call from the Australian Winter Paralympics coach with an offer to try out for the Winter Games in Russia in 2014. After discussing it with Tisha, he decided to give it a go.

His training schedule includes daily swims at Bondi Icebergs near their Sydney home. Early in 2013 he packed his special 'snow legs' and snowboard and went to Utah in the US to begin his bid for Olympic glory.

No one who knows this courageous former soldier would be silly enough to bet against him.

Chapter 7

Weighing up Valour

The boss knew that he was dealing with something outside of the ordinary when he saw the magazine from Ben Roberts-Smith's M4 carbine. The SAS troops had just arrived back from a place called Tizak and it was clear that they had had a busy day at the office.

Their commanding officer, Lieutenant Colonel Paul Burns, had monitored the fight from his headquarters at Camp Russell in Tarin Kowt and knew the SAS patrol had fought an intense battle against an insurgent stronghold and won.

'I asked Ben how the fight was and he just pulled out the magazine and it had just one round left, and it was the last round,' he says. And that was after having borrowed even more ammunition from his mates during the battle.

Over the next few days, as the emotion of the firefight wore off and the troops began to relax, it became clear that what 'RS' had achieved that day was something quite extraordinary.

'All the excitement has gone away, all the noise, the buzz, the dust, it's all gone away and then you start to open your eyes to what else happened around you that day,' Burns says. 'Because in some of those situations, there is a degree of sensory overload. All you know is what is going on in front of you, but over the next couple of days, pieces start coming together and other people have other snippets of, "Oh shit, yeah, we were over here ... I didn't know that."'

As an experienced commander with probably more time in action than any other 'half colonel' (lieutenant colonel) in the Australian Army, he was acutely aware of the commander's responsibility to get the issue of post-action citations and recommendations for awards 100 per cent right.

'You can't stuff it up, and I will say we don't always get it right either,' he says.

He understood better than most the need to sift through the chatter and seek out the nuggets of information that would provide a totally accurate picture of what happened during the battle of Tizak. He had commanded the SAS squadron that roamed the western desert of Iraq during the 2003 war. The squadron was awarded the first Unit Citation for Gallantry (UCG), the highest unit award in the Australian military.

Having himself received the Distinguished Service Cross (DSC) for his exemplary command in Iraq, Burns well knows the importance of harnessing the power of teamwork. 'If the organisation isn't really fine tuned and working closely together it's going to fall apart,' he says. 'Units get destroyed because the enemy will exploit a crack and just bust it wide open. In Iraq, because we chose to operate as a squadron group and very rarely broke down into troops or patrols, we were always able to support each other. We were very calculating in tactics to make sure we always had the advantage. Why would you go into a significant fight with a knife when it was a gunfight? You always walk in well prepared, more prepared than the other guy. You are not there to lose.'

Several other individuals from the squadron received high-level awards for their work in Iraq, including a Medal for Gallantry and a Distinguished Service Medal, but he regards the Unit Citation as the most significant of them all.

The then commanding officer's one regret is that the 'enablers', the support team who worked so hard to keep the fighting team operating, could not be officially part of it, because to receive an award for 'gallantry' you have to be shot at by the enemy.

'So the logistics guys didn't get recognised as part of the UCG, although they were a critical enabler and we couldn't have done what we did without them. But it is still for gallantry, that's the difficult thing, and it causes a degree of friction because they didn't get recognised,' he says.

He dedicated his own DSC to the entire team. 'I was very blessed by having the squadron that we had and in particular having my squadron sergeant major, who got a Distinguished Service Medal,' he says. 'The moral component is critical — and the leadership of it all, at every level. Two troop commanders got awards as well because they were the one who actually harnessed the full power of their organisations. The goal is to create an outcome that is greater than the simple sum of the parts.'

One reason why the military does not always get the official awards right is the citation itself. Burns says the wording is the most important part of the process. 'If you don't put the right words in in terms of "valour", "selflessness in the face of battle" and "little disregard for his own safety", you know if you don't put those things in to describe the actual events accurately, then it's not going to get through the process,' he says. 'At the end of the day it is the citation that will tell the story of the action for all in perpetuity and is the primary tool by which the award will be assessed. If the citation doesn't speak to you and totally convince you, then it's probably not right.'

Paul Burns is in the unique position of having been Mark Donaldson's direct unit commander as CO of the SAS Regiment when Donaldson was awarded the Victoria Cross for Australia, and then the overall commander of the Special Operations Task Group when he nominated Ben Roberts-Smith for his VC.

In addition to managing the process and all the challenges involved, there is the more important requirement: to manage the man and his career. In the past, VC winners have been pulled out of the fight to fulfil myriad public duties and effectively barred from returning to the frontline.

Mark Donaldson and his CO were determined to break that mould, so they sought and received agreement from army chief Lieutenant General Ken Gillespie that Donaldson would be allowed to return to Afghanistan.

'We knew there would be a lot of pressure upon him, public implications, a lot of pressure not to go back to Afghanistan, but he worked really hard to make sure that he did go back to Afghanistan, because he joined the army to fight. That was really important to Mark,' Burns says.

After 12 months of constant public engagements where he virtually became the face of the army and a powerful recruiting tool, 'Donno' returned to Afghanistan and has been back several times since, and was wounded in action for a second time.

Burns says the precedent set by the Donaldson experience was extremely positive because it showed the guys that even receiving the nation's top award did not take them out of the fight.

On the day of the Tizak battle, after Roberts-Smith showed the boss his last round, he and his mates immediately began reloading their magazines and preparing to return to the fight.

'"The job is still on, the commandos are still in the fight in Chenartu. Reload your magazines; I need you on stand by again to support the commandos just in case they get into trouble." And so it was just business as usual,' Burns says.

During the next few days word began to spread around the mess at Camp Russell about exactly what RS and the other operators had achieved at Tizak. 'I said to the OC [officer in command], "Just let the process run its course, so get from the guys [their views about] who they think deserves recognition as a result of that incident." And then the names came back and they gave a verbal on who they think did what. "OK, now go away and write it up, write up the ones that you think are deserved,"' he says.

Burns and the regimental sergeant major adopted a clinical process for dealing with the recommendations. 'They were dropped off on our desk, we read through them, and then we made our own judgements and we got the OC back in and some of the key guys back in and said, "Tell me exactly what happened here,"' he says. 'We got several briefs of how the position on the ground unfolded and that there were potentially two Victoria Crosses.'

After a month of further discussion and review, the list of potential award winners was sent to the commander of Task Force 633, Major General John Cantwell, at his headquarters in Dubai, where a further review was undertaken. From there, any such list is sent on to the Chief of Joint Operations in Canberra and finally to the Chief of the Australian Defence Force and the Minister for Defence. Three eyewitnesses must support the citation and once it has gone up through the chain it is again reviewed by a board back in Canberra.

'People die for those sorts of medals; their honour needs to be maintained. That medal cannot be compromised, it's so important,' Burns says. 'So for your mates around you who say, "You deserve a Victoria Cross", it's got to be the highest honour. Apart from being awarded by the Governor-General and all that sort of stuff, the biggest honour will come from your mates, to say, "What you did on the battlefield today, unbelievable, unbelievable selfless valour." Then that drives the moral fibre of your military, your fighting forces in the future because you'll be held up as an example of what to do on the battlefield.

'It's important … for a young bloke going to Kapooka today to be told about the honour, the trust, the courage, the valour of Ben Roberts-Smith and Mark Donaldson — that's what you want to live up to when you are fighting for your life and fighting for your mates around you. It's about being selfless in the service of your nation.'

Burns says the system is far from perfect, but that there really is no easy way to conduct the process. 'For a commander who is in the fight for the first time and it is the first time he's dealing with this, everything's a big deal, everything is bigger [because] he doesn't have a benchmark,' he says. 'I've been lucky to command on two significant occasions so my benchmark is going to be different to the guy who is the first time he's ever been in a fight. So I'm probably going to be a bit harder on the awards. That's why I go back to the citations. You've got to read the citations before you make your judgement. You can get it wrong [and] it's going to bite you in the arse down the track.'

He describes the process as 'tortuous'. 'You've got to sit down and give it 100 per cent of your mental focus to get these awards right, because this is an enduring thing,' he says. 'It's not just another report that you write, it's something that means a lot to the recipient, it's going to mean a hell of a lot to the other guys and then when you are standing around on Anzac Day regaling what happened on the day, it's got to hold up to that rigour and critical analysis.

'In actual fact that's probably where the most of the analysis comes out, standing around on Anzac Day!'

* * *

When the system gets it wrong the commanders might spend years or decades trying to make it right. Another big factor, particularly when there is a potential VC involved, is the historical precedent. Already in the ranks of veterans there is some disquiet about the fact that three Victoria Crosses have been awarded for Afghanistan when just four were awarded during the entire Vietnam War, all to members of the Australian Army Training Team Vietnam.

The ratio of VCs to total troop numbers has dropped significantly since World War II when it was about one per 60,000, and Vietnam where it was one to 12,000, to about one to 7000 in Afghanistan.

It could easily have been four for Afghanistan as the soldier who fought alongside Ben Roberts-Smith at the battle of Tizak was nominated for the top award and then downgraded to the next level — the Star of Gallantry. Or the number might have remained a two had Corporal Dan Keighran's initial nomination for the Star of Gallantry not been upgraded to the VC.

'There is always pressure on the Victoria Cross,' Burns says.

Historically most VCs have been awarded posthumously, and the British military have awarded just two in Afghanistan, including one posthumously to Lance Corporal James Ashworth, 23, despite having more than six times Australia's troop numbers and fighting in some of the bloodiest battles in some of the most dangerous parts of the war-ravaged nation.

New Zealand has awarded one, and Canada not a single VC despite also having many more troops deployed than Australia and losing 158 killed since 2002.

'You want to make sure it is right so you don't discredit the medal ... Who we give the VC to has to be beyond reproach,' Burns says.

The other big issue for a commanding officer is resisting the temptation to judge an issue when not having been present at the fight. 'I refuse to judge anyone because I wasn't there, and it is not my place to do that because when we talk about valour on the battlefield, it's a hugely personal thing. The noise, the confusion, the fog of the unknown, you don't know what is going on around you, the explosions, your own internals, and that's why you need to capture the actions immediately, then allow several days to let it distil,' he says. 'It's not my place to judge or second-guess what would have happened, or this is what I would have done.'

Another thing that his service with the SAS taught Burns is never to judge a book by its cover. 'In my free-fall patrol there was a small, slight-built guy that we used to call "the operator". You'd look at him and would think, "There is no way he's an SAS warrior," but on the battlefield he is the most tenacious, courageous individual that I've ever seen. But to look at him just walking around the unit, he is just a smallish sort of bloke. [You might] wonder how he got through the selection course — it's all mental and in your heart.'

Burns describes valour as a willingness to be selfless, to put others before yourself and to be willing to die for a higher ideal. 'When you openly espouse that and consistently demonstrate it in training, then it's likely you are going to do it in battle,' he says.

'It's about service first, their contribution, how they measure their self-worth. They do not measure their self-worth through a pay rise or promotion, they measure it by the contribution they make to their mates and the service to their country in battle.'

He says this is what separates them from the self-seeking careerist who puts self before service. 'It is not the rank you achieve, but rather what your contribution was at that rank that counts and what you will be remembered for,' he says. 'Commanding soldiers in action is a privilege, not a right or something to simply wait your turn for so you can tick a box. When soldiers are willing to die in the service of their nation they deserve commanders who understand that commitment intimately. Displaying moral courage in every decision, even if unpopular or at your own personal detriment, is essential and is also a form of valour.'

Moral and physical courage was displayed in spades during the battle of Tizak. The troop commander running the show on the ground could have chosen to withdraw and call in close air support to bomb the enemy, but he chose not to because there were civilians mixed in with the enemy.

'The fact that he made a decision to fight on and not call in close support because of the civilians there meant that he made a conscious decision that the lives of those civilians were more important than his troops,' says Burns. 'I reckon that is incredible.

'He could have easily said, "No, these Afghans aren't worth it, we'll call in close air support because Australian soldiers' lives are more important than the lives of civilians here," but he didn't. That's valour. He wasn't the guy storming the pits but he was responsible for telling the boys to assault multiple machine guns. It's important to acknowledge that he would have been held responsible for their deaths if the assault had failed. That is a significant weight to bear for a young officer. He was recognised with a Distinguished Service Medal for leadership in action. Although not a medal for valour per se, the decision he was faced with was very, very similar — a conscious decision that something else was greater.'

Paul Burns says valour is about putting everything else ahead of yourself. 'It might be to achieve a mission, you will stop at nothing to achieve that mission; it might be to put yourself in the line of fire, or to be prepared to die for the mate next door to you, because you consider that his life is more important than yours and it's a belief in a greater cause, that is the service of your nation is more important than your life. "I would rather die for you, so that you have the chance to live with your family in peace and prosperity – I would die for you." That's valour, you know, it's unbelievable really. What the boys are fighting for in Afghanistan is so that you can sit here and have coffee, so you can drive to work without getting blown up; they are prepared to die for you, it's truly amazing.'

He says the moral component is the most important part of valour and is what guides the conduct of wars for a first-world army. He also believes it is possible to train an operator or soldier in what he sees as the three essential traits of courage, boldness and perseverance, to come up with unique ways of doing things 'outside the box', to do whatever it takes to win within the guidelines of the profession of arms and the laws of armed conflict.

'There is still a degree of chivalry involved — we are not criminals. There is still a warrior's code.'

In the same Anzac Day address in which he cited Troy Simmonds's actions at the battle of Ana Kalay as a shining example of perseverance, Burns paid tribute to SAS signaller Sean McCarthy, killed by an improvised explosive device in Afghanistan on July 8, 2008, aged 25.

It was, he said, well known that he had served the people of Australia with distinction, with passion and enthusiasm, and with outstanding professionalism. What was not so well known were his actions during the patrol in which 33-year-old SAS Sergeant Matt Locke had died, nine months prior to McCarthy's own death.

'Only a few of us know that it wasn't Sean's turn to head out on that particular patrol, but after discussions with his opposite number, he requested that he take part in the mission, feeling that he had had a lighter workload than the other bloke.'

While conducting the task, the troop — E Troop — became heavily engaged by the enemy, taking fire from three sides, and with a man down almost immediately. They were at risk of being cut off from support. Throughout the contact, another patrol on a mountainside was in a position to provide fire support, to potentially enable the troop to shift to a more favourable position.

'Distinguishing friend from foe in the green — especially at a distance — is difficult, if not impossible,' Burns said. 'Without a marker, the supporting patrol were unable to accurately engage the enemy without putting their mates' lives at risk.' So the supporting patrol requested that E Troop mark their position so that they could accurately determine their location.

'Without being asked, Sean immediately broke from his position of relative safety to place a marker panel in the open where it might potentially be used as a reference for fire support. On returning to his covered position he discovered that the patrol could still not see the marker panel. So again without request he moved out into the open, under heavy fire, recovered the marker panel and climbed a tree to place the panel in a position where it would hopefully be seen.'

The panel was shot out of his hands. He recovered it, climbed the tree again and finally moved to cover, where it was confirmed that the patrol on the mountainside was able to locate the troop's position and start giving fire support.

'These actions assisted in the prevention of loss of further life and the medevac of Sergeant Locke from the battlefield. In this single action we see all three traits of courage, boldness and perseverance. Sean McCarthy truly upheld the legend of Anzac.'

SAVING LIVES

Chapter 1

Into the Fatal Sea

As the navy Seahawk helicopter flew towards the site of the explosion in the northern Persian (Arabian) Gulf, Ben Sime, the aircraft's sensor operator, or 'senso', was looking at some disturbing images from the navy helicopter's powerful forward-looking infrared camera. They did not make for a pretty sight.

Just a few minutes earlier, a local vessel called a dhow had blown up as it was being approached by an inflatable boat with a crew of seven, operating from the 53-metre United States Coastguard patrol boat, USS *Firebolt*.

Leading Seaman Sime saw survivors and body parts floating among the wreckage near a large offshore Iraqi oil terminal known as Abot. This and other floating terminals were vital in keeping the flow of oil from Iraq's vast reserves to the outside world, and the US-led coalition was determined to protect them and keep the 'black gold' flowing.

As the Seahawk, callsign Hamish, from the frigate HMAS *Stuart* approached the site late in the afternoon of April 24, 2004, Sime left his monitor and moved to the open doorway for a closer look at the carnage below. As the machine hovered about 20 metres off the water, he focused on one American sailor who was conscious but fading fast due to massive head injuries.

After several unsuccessful attempts at winching the badly injured sailor out, Sime decided that the only way he would be able to save the man was to be alongside him in the tepid, oily sea.

As he weighed up his options, word came through on the radio that the scene of utter devastation metres below was the result of a coordinated terrorist attack involving several dhows packed with high explosives. While he processed that information, Ben Sime decided it was time to act. After gaining permission from the pilot to 'leave' the security of the hovering chopper, he removed his safety harness and the wires that attached him to the communication systems and shuffled towards the open doorway as the aircraft descended to about six metres above the surface.

By this time the man they had been trying to save was unconscious and face down.

'I'll be frank, there were decapitated bodies in the water, there was oil and all that sort of stuff, debris from the actual instigating vessel, which turned out to be a suicide bomber,' he says. 'By this stage it was getting dark, really dark. So anyway, I jumped from the aircraft and the aircraft went back up and conducted a circuit, a look around the area to see what else was going on. Once I got into the water I inflated my life jacket — not rescue gear, just air crew ensemble that you wear in the back of the aircraft.' He had his helmet, flying suit and life preserver on when he hit the water.

'I swam to the guy in the water — at that time he was unconscious — rolled him onto his back and commenced CPR as best I could for the position in the water,' he says. 'I tried to make him responsive, I kept his head out of the water, I tried pumping his chest, just trying to get him to respond, shouting in his ear all that sort of stuff you do. Anyway, I wasn't successful in that, he was not responsive in the water, so I stayed there with him until a rescue vessel arrived.'

Floating among the detritus of war in the Persian Gulf was a long way from Ben Sime's quiet upbringing in Queensland. After finishing Year 11 on Bribie Island he decided to join the navy, and at the tender age of 16 he left home for the recruit training college at HMAS *Cerberus* on Victoria's Mornington Peninsula.

After a stint on board the frigate HMAS *Hobart* he decided to transfer to the navy's firefighting service and was posted to HMAS *Albatross* base at Nowra in NSW.

After he'd spent two years in the job, the firefighting branch was disbanded in 1999 and Sime decided to leave the navy to become a policeman back in his home state. As he was contemplating his future course of action a navy colleague suggested he take a look at transferring to aircrew. He took the advice and moved across to the world of navy helicopters in the year 2000.

Following 12 months of intensive training he was posted to 816 Squadron at HMAS *Albatross* to work in the navy's Seahawk helicopter fleet. The Seahawk carries three crew members: pilot, aviation warfare operator and sensor operator/crewman. The chopper, a true multi-role machine, is used as a transport for people and cargo as well as its main roles of anti-surface ship warfare and anti-submarine warfare.

'You wake up in the morning on the ship, and you might be tasked to do "potatoes and chaplains" [transport supplies or a padre], as we say, or media or PR, or to surface-search over the horizon for a target or a search with a submarine,' he says. 'The most challenging part of it is the reactive part. If you know you are going to be doing something a week away, you have got that time to prepare for it, whereas the reactive side of things means you need to pull out that certain cartridge and put in another profile cartridge, so you can operate in an effective manner in the environment.'

After more training and several postings to Fleet Base West at HMAS *Stirling* near Perth, Ben Sime decided that the east coast was for him, so he transferred permanently back to *Albatross* in Nowra, where he, his wife Stacey (a police officer) and their two children still live.

The Seahawk fleet had been through a large upgrade after 2005, and Sime was closely involved in fitting the choppers new electronic warfare kit, .50 calibre machine guns and optical sensors to assist with their counter-piracy role in the Persian Gulf and the Horn of Africa, known officially as the Middle East Area of Operations (MEAO).

The main task of a ship's helicopter during a deployment to the MEAO is to provide a surface picture of ship movements and daily life in one of the world's busiest waterways, close to the border between Iran and Iraq, one of the most volatile borders on the planet.

During Sime's 2004 deployment, in addition to the oil tankers moving in and out of the terminals there was other merchant traffic steaming around the area, as well as literally thousands of small dhows, traditional craft that have been plying the glass-smooth waters for centuries.

'There were thousands and thousands of these little dhows around that also represented some sort of a threat,' he says. 'We needed to report every single one of those back to the ship so they could gain a surface picture and have a look at patterns of life and all that sort of stuff.'

The normal routine for the aircrew was two sorties each day of between two and three and a half hours in duration. It was during a routine patrol that the crew received the call to go to the assistance of USS *Firebolt*'s rigid hull inflatable boat (RHIB), which had been hit by a waterborne improvised explosive device not far from the northernmost oil terminal, Abot.

Just after Sime had jumped, two more explosions occurred as part of a coordinated terrorist attack targeting the oil terminals. 'At the end of the day it didn't really matter because we had a scenario in front of us and that was what we had to deal with, getting these people back onto their vessel and getting assistance to them,' he says.

Sime had already established that there were seven people in the water and most of them were already dead. As the only aircraft airborne at the time, the Seahawk was also providing crucial information to other ships and the command chain. While it circled above, Sime struggled to keep the big American sailor's head out of the water as he tried to save the gravely injured man.

Despite the horrific scenes all around him he says his main focus was on the man he was attempting to keep alive. His own safety was very much in the back of his mind. 'My main focus was to get this guy out of the water; I just wanted to make sure I could at least assist him until an RHIB arrived, or some sort of vessel or they could throw a life belt or something to this guy. I really didn't think about it at the time, to be honest with you.'

Darkness began to fall and he could hear the helicopter and see the vessels in the distance as he and his 'patient' floated among the remains of two boats and a number of human beings.

'I honestly can't remember how long we were in the water for, but it felt like a long time. The RHIB from HMAS *Stuart* was slowly coming towards us,' he says. 'I indicated to the RHIB that we have this guy, they took him from me and I got into the RHIB and we transited back to *Firebolt*.'

They transferred the coastguard sailor onto the stern of the patrol boat and began to apply CPR to him. Sadly he did not respond. Sime recalls the horror on the vessel as the crew tried to deal with the loss of several of their mates whose remains were being dragged back onto the vessel.

'They were recovering bodies from the water, and they were pretty badly damaged, these bodies, as a result, so there was a lot of screaming and all that sort of stuff on the actual vessel itself,' he says.

Sime and the casualties were transferred from the RHIB to HMAS *Stuart*, where the ship's doctor, Lieutenant Commander Jody Bailey, and her medical staff could treat the four wounded and pronounce the three casualties, including the man Ben Sime had stayed with throughout the ordeal, dead.

Due to confusion and a lack of communication, his helicopter had no idea that he was back on board the ship, so it flew back to the *Firebolt* to search for him. His whereabouts confirmed, the chopper flew to the *Stuart* to transfer the injured to hospital at Camp Doha in Qatar.

Adding to the confused picture was another terrorist attack, on the second oil terminal, Kaot, using a dhow. The explosion from that bomb was so big that the shockwave was clearly felt on board the Australian warship.

It was well after midnight when the chopper was finally back on board and secured. For Sime and the rest of the crew it was a long night as they remained at action stations, code red, for possible further terrorist attacks.

Two days later, as the *Stuart* was refuelling *Firebolt*, a local boat sped towards the two vessels. A pair of .50 calibre machine gun operators on the American boat and boarding party members toting machine guns on the *Stuart* prepared to engage as the boat sped ever closer.

Finally, just as their guns were about to unleash, the boat veered away and sped off. No one knows if it was another attack that was aborted due to the aggressive response of the ships, but the crews of both navy vessels remained on edge for some time.

As the mission wore on Ben Sime didn't give much thought to the incident or his role in it. It began to play on his mind a little as the deployment drew to a close, but it would be almost four years before a letter arrived from Government House to tell him he had been awarded the Medal for Gallantry, the fourth highest award for courage in action.

He was 26 years old when the incident occurred. Now, a decade later, he sometimes still wonders what might have been — if the man he had tried to save had made it.

'It does have an effect on me, and I might be sitting down talking to mates and all of a sudden I just wander off and start thinking about something else,' he says. 'I've got a lot of friends in emergency services too, firefighters and police; they see things as well, they deal with it differently. When they start talking about their stories, whilst I never bring mine up, I do wonder about it. I drift off and think about it, but I don't bring it up.'

Ben Sime doesn't regard what he did as being particularly brave. 'It was just a matter of doing my job and trying to assist this one guy. Unfortunately it didn't work out the way I wanted it to work out. I mean I would love to sit here and have a beer with him now, but unfortunately that didn't eventuate.

'We are out there to do a job, to save life, pretty much; I know it sounds like an advertisement, but we are there to do something and I'm pretty confident most people would have done the same. The end result would have been the same anyway, but at least I take comfort from the fact that we tried.'

While Sime does not believe that he did anything extraordinary in the dangerous waters of the Persian Gulf, he says that even to be recognised in the same way as some of the soldiers who have been awarded the Medal for Gallantry was a huge honour.

'To be put in the same breath as some of the guys that are risking their lives every day doing their job and to have that medal is probably the most amazing part of it. I am certainly not saying that I am on the same level as these guys, but just to be acknowledged in the same breath as them is very rewarding.'

It was almost five years after the action that Ben Sime had his medal pinned on by Governor-General Quentin Bryce at Government House in Canberra.

His citation reads in part:

On the night of 24 April 2004, terrorists in fishing dhows launched a series of determined attacks against Iraqi oil terminals. One dhow, packed with explosives, was detonated when a RHIB from USS *Firebolt* drew alongside to challenge it. Three American sailors were killed and four seriously wounded. *Stuart* immediately rendered assistance, ordering her Seahawk to close *Firebolt*'s position. On approaching the scene, Sime observed that the RHIB had capsized and that all of its occupants were in the water. Following several unsuccessful attempts to get survivors into a rescue strop lowered from the helicopter a decision was made for Sime to enter the water and provide direct assistance. Moments after he did so, two further attacks were launched against the nearby oil terminals. Sime continued to provide support to survivors throughout the unfolding action until he was himself recovered by *Stuart*'s RHIB. Leading Seaman Sime showed outstanding courage and remained dedicated to supporting a sailor in his care without regard for his own safety. His efforts were of the highest order and in the finest traditions of the RAN. In recognition of his deeds he was awarded the Medal for Gallantry.

Chapter 2

A Clandestine Swim

Justin Brown couldn't believe it when the vehicle pulled up on the beach and shone its headlights directly at where he was treading water.

It was October 1999 and the Royal Australian Navy clearance diver was just ten metres or so off a beach in the Oecussi Enclave of East Timor, providing overwatch for a team of divers operating in the dark depths below.

Some days earlier, a fearless 15-year-old local lad by the name of Lafu had carried a message concealed in his thongs through territory controlled by pro-Jakarta militia and their Indonesian backers, to Australian forces at Balibo on the West Timor border. The message told the International Force about on-going atrocities inside the isolated enclave.

Lafu, whose full name is Fredolino José Landos da Cruz Buno Silva, was later taken back home by boat and given a satellite radio so he could provide intelligence to the Australian-led International Force.

Oecussi is an accident of the island's colonial history and was hived off as part of Portuguese Timor when the island was divided between Portugal and the Netherlands centuries ago. Located to the south-west of Dili, East Timor's capital, the enclave is separated from the rest of East Timor and is surrounded by Indonesian-controlled West Timor and the sea.

Moving into Oecussi had always been on the International Force's agenda, but the dire situation around Dili and other areas of the former Indonesian province meant that it lacked the resources for an early push into the enclave. It wasn't until Lafu made his journey that senior personnel understood just how serious the situation was for the locals. As the situation stabilised around Dili, the Australian commander, Major General Peter Cosgrove, started to plan for an operation to liberate the people of Oecussi from their brutal occupiers.

Navy divers were called in to find a suitable location for Australian landing craft to carry troops and equipment ashore. This was the first phase of the plan to rid the enclave of militia thugs.

Justin Brown was born in Wollongong, NSW, and joined the Royal Australian Navy at 16 as an aircraft electronics technician. He completed his trade training at HMAS *Nirimba* in western Sydney and was appointed to 723 Squadron at HMAS *Albatross* at Nowra in NSW.

Brown grew up on the beach and in the water but he received his first taste of the underwater world during a posting to the Western Australia-based survey vessel HMAS *Moresby*.

'While I was on board they were looking for people to become ships' divers to help out part-time,' he recalls. 'If anything happened to the ship while in remote localities, the divers could get in the water and help resolve it. When I did the course I decided that I liked this diving thing so I came back and put my paperwork in to change over to become a diver.'

The year 1996 was a big one for Justin Brown. He completed his diving course and married his sweetheart, Nicole. The pair had maintained a long-distance relationship during his time in WA.

The so-called 'barrier test' for the navy diving branch is designed to weed out applicants who will not physically be able to meet the demands of the diver selection course. The test involves long-distance swims across Sydney Harbour in the middle of the night, canoeing in Pittwater, hiking around Sydney's myriad national parks weighed down by heavy packs and carting huge loads to the top of Barrenjoey Headland at Palm Beach. It also includes mental tests, teams tasks and sleep deprivation, all designed to test men who could go on to serve in one of the most demanding branches of the RAN. The divers also worked with SAS water operators and they knew their elite army brethren would give no quarter.

Navy clearance divers undertake a variety of tasks, including mine counter-measures, maritime tactical operations, underwater battle damage repair, explosive ordnance disposal, counter-terrorism with special forces, and training and support.

During the Afghanistan War, navy divers were regularly posted with Australian forces in the land-locked country to work in teams that would be called in to disarm or explode bombs detected by army engineers.

Despite being the oldest person on the course at 26, Justin was a fitness fanatic and so he passed the barrier test with flying colours. He was posted to Dive Team 1 based at HMAS *Waterhen* in Sydney.

282

Such was his determination to be a navy diver that he dropped back two ranks from petty officer to able seaman to make the change. 'Had I gone from working on aircraft electronics to working on a ship or a submarine working on electronics, well it's the same trade, it's the same job, but this was something totally different,' he says. 'Working with explosives and diving gear meant I had to get used to all that new equipment, so you can't go in there at petty officer level when you've got guys that have been in the diving branch for six or eight years who know what they are doing inside out, back to front. A petty officer in the diving branch is responsible for supervising diving operations and demolition operations. You are not actually just doing it, you are supervising it and making sure everybody else is doing it safely and correctly.'

During the seven-month diver training course the new recruits cover the spectrum of underwater activities, from deep diving on air to below 50 metres, to long days practising shallow diving on oxygen, as well as underwater navigation, a crucial skill for conducting beach surveys.

'You have to be able to navigate underwater with a fair degree of accuracy at night,' Brown says. 'The biggest thing to try and estimate underwater, when you can't see anything, is how far you have travelled. Bearing is OK, but how far have I travelled? If you are trying to get into something without being seen, you don't want to go popping your head up at the wrong time because, you know, a head popping up on the surface kind of gives the game away.'

Portable GPS receivers were not widely available in 1999, so the only way for dive teams to confirm their location was to surface and check landmarks.

After two hectic years with Dive Team 4 at HMAS *Stirling* south of Perth, studying beach operations and mine counter-measures, Brown had been looking forward to some stable family time in 1999 when he was posted to the ship maintenance branch. During this time he also travelled to Townsville to undertake an advanced underwater medical course. The dive teams have specialist medics, but more often than not they do not deploy so each member of the team must have some knowledge of advanced diving first aid.

'It gave us the ability to provide a higher level of care for guys for whatever incident may or may not happen while we are away. You don't have a medic, you're it, so you are able to patch them up and hold them together until they are evacuated or until highly trained medical staff can get hold of them,' he says.

Throughout 1999 a shortlist of divers was being drawn up just in case teams needed to deploy to Timor at short notice. Brown's call came on a Monday in August when he was placed on the shortlist and told to be ready to move at the drop of a hat. Fortunately the divers always had their gear packed and ready to go because the very next morning he was told that he would be shipping out at lunchtime that day.

'I'd ridden my bike to work so I borrowed a mate's car, brought my bike home and packed the rest of my gear, packed another bag and went back to work and away I went.'

Normally the divers travelled on a C–130 Hercules with virtually unlimited space, but on this trip they were flying on an RAAF Boeing 707 with much stricter cargo limitations. 'We couldn't take as much gear as we wanted so we packed three rubber boats, outboards, diving cylinders, for — it was an eight-man team — six sets of diving gear and probably a dozen cylinders,' he says. The men knew they would be joining a navy ship at the other end so they didn't need to worry about gas pumping equipment or compressors. 'Everybody was responsible for their own personal kits, so fins, masks, snorkels, wetsuits, weight belts, that is all part of your own kit,' Brown says.

They flew to Darwin via Adelaide and Richmond outside Sydney, and upon arrival their gear was placed on a truck and moved to Larrakeyah army barracks south of the city. Over the next few days Brown and another able seaman attended high-level briefings about the planned move across to Dili on board the navy's leased fast catamaran HMAS *Jervis Bay*.

The team made three nine- to ten-hour trips from Darwin to Timor on the *Jervis Bay*. One of their jobs was to secure any wharf area where the ship would be landing troops and supplies.

'It wasn't really expected we were going to come up against anything very technologically advanced, but it doesn't take much to put a handful of star pickets down the side of a wharf to really destroy the side of an aluminium fast cat,' he says.

They never knew their final destination until just before they arrived so their target wharf area could have been Dili Harbour itself or the refuelling wharf to the west of town, or elsewhere.

The team transferred onto the replenishment ship HMAS *Success*, which would become their base for most of the East Timor operation. 'We were living in one of their recreation spaces because they didn't have enough bunks for us, so we were living on stretchers,' Brown says.

Each day they travelled in and out of the harbour doing whatever was required. That mostly involved clearing wharf areas or landing spots for barges bringing troops and vehicles ashore, in the biggest military lift by Australian forces since the Vietnam War.

So the divers travelled around the province securing landing sites, and Brown was in Suai on the south coast on the day that an SAS patrol was ambushed close to the town. Landed in a Sea King helicopter from HMAS *Success*, the divers were taken to a secure zone until the battle was over and they could get on with diving to map a safe landing area for reinforcements to land on the troubled south coast.

It was after this that Cosgrove dispatched *Success* and the divers with orders to survey a landing site for an amphibious force at Oecussi that would relieve the locals of the burden of the militias.

On the night of 21 October, the ship hove-to over the horizon from the enclave and the divers left the ship in two rigid hull inflatable boats (RHIBs), each carrying six men, including three divers and two surface swimmers.

They stopped about two kilometres from the beach under a full moon in windless conditions. The sea surface was like a millpond, the worst possible conditions for surface swimmers and divers, who would be highly visible. Wind chop and an agitated sea surface provide much better cover for clandestine water operations.

Unlike today, when divers carry state-of-the-art waterproof GPS equipment, back in 1999 a diver used a hand–held device, purchased from a retail store and carried in double-sealed plastic bags.

Justin Brown and his commanding officer, Lieutenant Commander Peter Tedman, were the two surface swimmers. Armed with Steyr rifles, their job was to protect and support the unarmed divers operating below the surface.

The pair wore night vision goggles and carried depth sounders to monitor the depth of the water as they swam towards the beach. Timor being a volcanic island, the water depth goes from hundreds of metres to 50 metres and less over a very short distance. It is vital for amphibious operations that divers choose a landing site that will not trap the landing vessels as the tide recedes.

Night vision equipment works best in very dark conditions, so as they approached the shore with the full moon glowing the adrenaline was pumping.

'As you are getting close to somebody else's piece of dirt you become a lot more aware of what is going on,' Brown says. 'We could hear weapons fire, buildings were being torched; all the things that we'd seen in Dili and had been cleared up were being repeated in Oecussi. It still had that real pungent odour of things burning and it wasn't something we wanted to necessarily go and see again.'

The team knew there was a road just behind the beach; the spot was chosen so that the landing troops would have quick access into town.

Speed was vital. The militia thugs were tough when it came to bashing unarmed civilians and women and children, but as soon as they were confronted by trained and well-armed soldiers they usually fled back to West Timor rather than stand and fight.

It was just past midnight when Brown and the team reached a point about ten metres from the shore and started to deploy markers for the landing site.

Suddenly, a vehicle drove onto the beach and shone its lights directly at them. They knew it was highly unlikely that a frightened local was behind the wheel. There was a better than fair chance that the driver would be an armed militiaman.

'The whole idea of reconnaissance is getting in there and out without anybody knowing that you've been there,' he says. 'All of a sudden we swim in to do this thing and next thing you know we are lit up like Christmas trees.'

The men and their gear were well camouflaged, and the first reaction was to send the three divers back beneath the waves to continue their work. The two swimmers wore life jackets with a lot of gear in them so they were unable to submerge.

'You are just hoping then that nothing you are wearing is going to reflect,' Brown says. 'Cooler heads had to prevail — we couldn't go anywhere, we couldn't swim far enough away to outrun anything if it came down to it, so we just had to stay put. The more movement you make, the more chance you have of being seen. It was a matter of just sit there, be still, wait it out and let the heart rate do what it's going to do.'

As the two swimmers drifted slowly away from the shore they knew that they couldn't just keep swimming back to the RHIBs because they were the only armed protection for the divers below, whose bubbles were clearly visible in the moon and the car light.

After what seemed an eternity the vehicle left the beach and the men were able to swim to the rendezvous point further offshore and collect the divers before returning to the RHIBs and coming back in for a second swim. That swim went off without incident, the landing site was marked, and later that morning the landing craft went ashore to rid the enclave of the scourge of the militia.

Brown received the Commendation for Gallantry for his work that night and Lieutenant Commander Tedman was awarded the Distinguished Service Medal.

After the awards ceremony at Government House in Canberra, with all its lights, cameras and smiles, Tedman said he had seen the same 'rabbit in the headlights' look on Justin's face once before. This time it was TV cameras and spotlights but the previous time had been in a dark and hostile sea just metres from a dangerous shore — and those lights were definitely not friendly.

Justin Brown retired from the navy in 2005 and now lives at Rockingham in WA with Nicole and their children Joshua and Sarah.

Chapter 3

Burning Bridges

Matt Keogh understood just how dangerous his situation on the deck of the burning vessel was, but he also knew that he had to be sure everyone was safely off the boat that would later make headlines as SIEV 36.

The leading seaman and his crewmates on board the navy's Armidale Class patrol boat HMAS *Childers* were in a deep sleep after a long boarding operation on a foreign fishing vessel near Ashmore Reef in the Timor Sea when the boat's alarm sounded action stations.

Childers was due to take over the towing of the latest Indonesian fishing vessel from HMAS *Albany* at 6 am, to deliver a load of desperate asylum seekers to Australian shores. But the alarm meant that something had gone seriously wrong.

As Keogh shook off the fatigue and made his way on deck, the *Childers'* executive officer briefed him on what was going on with the fishing boat, officially known as Suspected Irregular Entry Vessel (SIEV) Number 36 for 2009.

Once on deck he saw a small boat about 30 metres away jam-packed with people. The boarding officer from the *Albany* was standing on top of the fishing boat's wheelhouse trying to calm a very agitated crowd. Keogh assembled his own boarding team and launched one of his patrol boat's two powerful rigid hull inflatable boats (RHIBs).

As the RHIB sped towards SIEV 36, the *Albany*'s boarding officer briefed him by radio. He wanted Keogh's team to try to quell the Afghan passengers, who had been told by a ringleader that the navy was going to turn them around and send them back to Indonesia. There had already been one incident involving threats by an asylum seeker to set the boat alight with a cigarette lighter. With petrol fumes seeping from every crack in the vessel, the situation was worsening by the second.

Fully kitted out with side arms, helmets, body armour and life jackets, Keogh's team boarded the boat on the starboard side.

Just 90 seconds after they scrambled onto the rickety, overcrowded vessel and begun trying to calm the situation, a huge explosion occurred. He remembers seeing the whole deck pop up and immense flames come straight out of it, then hearing a big bang.

'It was kind of a big whoosh,' he says. 'We got the shock of the actual explosion as well; I remember ducking away from it. I felt like I'd been horse-kicked. Lucky I was wearing [body armour], because I probably would have cracked a rib from the blast.'

Keogh describes the scene as utter bedlam. The water was littered with debris, burning fuel, and drowning and panicking people. 'It was phenomenal: the amount of debris and screams was intense, absolutely intense.'

One man emerged from the wheelhouse engulfed in flames from head to toe before he jumped into the water.

'I remember looking out in the water and there was shit everywhere, absolutely everywhere, and there was fire on the water and people screaming, people splashing. And I remember an old guy that I couldn't save, he drowned in front of me,' he says. 'There was a whole heap of people around him and they basically took him under. I was trying to move him away and ripped the chair out of the wheelhouse that was on fire and gave it to him, but that kind of just melted off my hand. I was kicking the boat, trying to break off some wood to give him something to hold on to.'

Matt Keogh came late to the military life. Born in Townsville, he spent the first nine years of his working life with a local trucking company before he decided to move to Brisbane and then to join the Royal Australian Navy in 2003. His grandfather had served with the Royal Navy and he says something about the senior service just clicked inside him.

Following his basic training at HMAS *Cerberus* in Victoria he was posted as a boatswain in the navy's replenishment ship HMAS *Success*. After deployments to the Southern Ocean, Singapore, Thailand and Hawaii he transferred back to North Queensland to join the heavy landing craft HMAS *Tarakan*, based in Cairns.

That posting rescued his career because at the four-year point he had almost been ready to move on again. 'The beauty of a small boat is that you can branch out, you can do other categories; that's the thing I love and I try to get the boys to try to think that way as well. You've got to make your job; you can't just get stuck in a rut. If you get bored with it, do something else,' he says.

After an enjoyable three years on the *Tarakan* doing everything from navigation to cooking, he decided to complete his small ship's navigation course and was posted to the patrol boat fleet. Once qualified and promoted to a leading hand and cleared by his commanding officer, that meant he could drive a powerful Australian-built patrol boat. 'Flying through the reef at 25 knots with 26 people asleep on the boat is a huge responsibility,' Keogh says.

These days, as the boatswain, or 'buffer', on board patrol boats, most of his sea time is spent on Operation Resolute, the government's asylum-seeker operation, in the waters between Darwin and Christmas Island.

As the fire took hold that night in the Timor Sea, Keogh was sure that most of his boarding party, and all 44 of the fishing boat's passengers and crew, were now in the water. Only he and two of his shipmates remained on board.

His immediate concern was for his two shipmates. One was on fire, so he helped him into the water, and the second was in a lot of pain from a broken ankle. Fortunately Keogh himself was not badly injured. He managed to jump into one of the RHIBs, then he accounted for all the boarding team and set about conducting the rescue.

'Once it [SIEV 36] exploded, there was nothing. The whole fucking boat was gone, it was just flames mainly, ten to 15 feet high,' Keogh says.

The navy sailors were criticised during the subsequent coronial inquiry for helping their shipmates first, but that is what they are trained to do. It is also instinctive to assist your friends first and that is precisely what the sailors would do if confronted with the same scenario again.

'You've got to remember they are your family at sea and anyone that goes through that stuff, you just automatically do it.

Khaz Oruzgan: During the rolling battle along the valley floor in 2008, nine SAS operators were wounded and a US operator killed. Mark Donaldson was awarded a Victoria Cross for his heroic actions in the battle.

SAS soldiers dressed in American camouflage uniforms patrol in armed Humvees, prior to the battle of Ana Kalay in Afghanistan in September 2008 that left 11 diggers wounded.

SAS Sergeant Troy Simmonds was wounded during the battle of Ana Kalay and was lucky to survive after being shot twice and hit by a rocket-propelled grenade.

This M4 Carbine, belonging to Troy Simmonds, was rendered inoperative when it was struck by an enemy round during the battle of Ana Kalay.

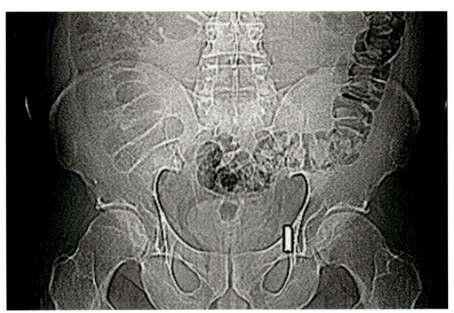

A round from an insurgent AK-47 assault rifle remains embedded in the hip of Troy Simmonds.

American Army dog handler SFC Greg Rodriguez, the only soldier killed in action during the battle of Ana Kalay.

SAS soldier and sniper Rob Maylor (left) helped save the day at Ana Kalay when a combined special forces patrol was ambushed and almost wiped out by more than 100 enemy fighters. He did not receive an award for his actions. (below) Maylor 'bombed up' and ready for action in a chopper in Afghanistan in 2008.
Rob Maylor

Veterans of the battle of Derapet in Afghanistan in August 2010: (from left to right) Corporal Lukas Woolley, Sergeant Sean Lanigan MG, Corporal Dan Keighran VC and Sapper Joel Toms MG at Victoria Barracks, Sydney. Sam Ruttyn, News Limited

Sergeant Sean Lanigan was awarded the Medal for Gallantry for his bravery in the battle of Derapet. Lanigan led his men from the front during the battle, and he and his team did not flinch in the face of a large and determined enemy. Sean Lanigan

Victoria Cross winner SAS Corporal Mark Donaldson with his wife, Emma, and daughter, Kayleen, at Government House for his investiture in January 2009. Donaldson was the first Australian to be awarded the nation's highest military honour since Keith Payne in 1969. Kym Smith, News Limited

Losing both his legs to an improvised explosive device in Afghanistan has not stopped former commando Damien Thomlinson from leading an active life. His prosthetic legs have allowed him to walk the Kokoda Track and snowboard in the United States.

Phil Hillyard, News Limited

'Big Ben'. SAS Corporal Ben Roberts-Smith showed a complete disregard for his own safety when he attacked entrenched enemy positions during the battle of Tizak in June 2010. He was awarded the Victoria Cross and is the most decorated soldier in the Australian Army.

Colin Murty, News Limited

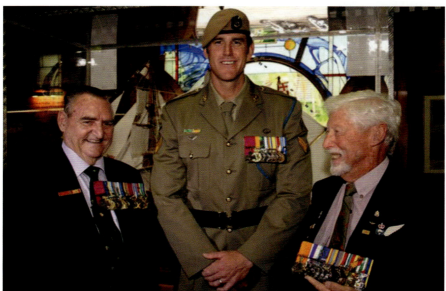

Former Lieutenant Colonel Harry Smith (right) compares his rack of medals, including the Star of Gallantry, with Victoria Cross holders Keith Payne (left) and Corporal Ben Roberts-Smith. Harry Smith

Australia's four Victoria Cross holders at the Pool of Reflection in the Australian War Memorial: (left to right) Mark Donaldson, Keith Payne, Dan Keighran and Ben Roberts-Smith. Gary Ramage

You've got to look after your mates. I was happy to take a hit for that if anything came out of it.'

Fortunately nothing did and after some initial criticism from lawyers and the media the sailors received universal praise for the way they handled the initial response.

The criticism had included some reports that sailors had kicked away Afghan asylum seekers as they attempted to save their shipmates. Keogh says that definitely happened, but if it hadn't, then some sailors would almost certainly have been drowned by groups of panicked boat people who could not swim and were not wearing life jackets.

Many of the victims had drifted towards the *Childers* and the patrol boat's crew were also using ropes and rafts to get people out of the water. 'I remember the XO [executive officer] telling me he tried to pull one guy out of the water and his whole skin came off his arms,' he says.

Keogh's RHIB delivered the injured sailors, including the boarding officer, who had been blown many metres from the roof of the wheelhouse by the explosion, back to *Childers* for medical attention before it joined the rescue effort with the boat's second RHIB and two from HMAS *Albany*, which had arrived back on the scene.

By the time the rescue was over, the sailors had 39 survivors and three bodies on board the *Childers*. Two of the dead could not be found.

The tiny quarterdeck of the 56-metre-long patrol boat was transformed into an overcrowded triage area, and its garbage compartment, the coolest place on board, became a makeshift morgue.

Keogh says the scene on the boat was surreal, with people crying and screaming and others in shock. The ship's medical officer, RAAF Flight Lieutenant Jo Darby, treated the most seriously injured with the assistance of medic Corporal Sharon Jager and other crew members, including Keogh, who stayed with the injured for ten hours until they were transferred onto the floating oil platform *Front Puffin*.

He describes the work done by Jo Darby in treating 39 injured people, including many with critical burns and fractures, with limited medical supplies, as 'absolutely outstanding'.

She received a commander's commendation for her efforts that reads, in part: 'Your actions were exemplary. Individual and collective acts of courage, compassion and bravery were embedded within a gargantuan team effort in the face of overwhelming circumstances. It is a testament to your efforts that every person recovered alive from the water that morning survived.'

For non-medical people such as Matt Keogh, the stench of burning flesh and the constant screams of the injured and traumatised over a ten-hour period made for a very intense experience after what they had already been through.

Another aspect of the event that amazed him was the activation of the national response. In short order a RAAF Orion aircraft was dropping vital medical and other supplies to the *Childers* and a Customs vessel was on the scene to render assistance.

'It was stuff you see in the movies. It was phenomenal, absolutely phenomenal, yeah. Then even Customs turned up at one stage — all these government departments just activating; it's good to see. You bitch and moan about everything, but when something happens and they all start helping it's a really good feeling.'

After the injured were transferred, the *Childers* set course for Darwin and the 28-hour cruise back to base at HMAS *Coonawarra*. That journey is a bit of a blur for Keogh, with a combination of physical and emotional exhaustion, adrenaline and dehydration knocking him and the other sailors flat.

Listening to his interview tapes and reading his statements later on, he realised that he had been virtually running on empty. 'I remember reading some of my statements from the federal police and all that, and listening to the radio; you can just hear it in your voice, you are just so shattered, you just don't even know what you are talking about,' he says.

Keogh says he has no lasting ill effects from the traumatic experience with SIEV 36. He has conducted numerous boardings since and while he doesn't like to think about what happened that day, he is heartened by the response of the entire team.

'I remember one guy, an air crew man, Norton his name was, he was there for six hours holding IV drips. It's a mediocre job, but he stood there for six hours holding drips. That to me was absolutely phenomenal.'

With typical modesty he even puts his own decision to stay on board the burning boat down to his training. 'There was probably a tenth of a second where I was shell-shocked and then bang, it just clicks.'

Apart from training, there is no doubt that something far deeper kicks in when human beings such as Matt Keogh decide that their own safety is secondary to the greater good.

'I believe everyone's got it, I believe everyone would have done the same and I have no doubt that one of my boys would have done the same if I was hurt or if I got blown off and they knew no one else was there,' he says. 'I think I made the decision because I knew I was the last one there. Someone had to stay there to make sure everyone was off, they had to make sure that all their mates were safe.'

The entire crew of the *Childers* received the ADF Gold Group commendation for their efforts that day. Matt Keogh was singled out for his courage by being awarded the Bravery Medal, given for acts of bravery in hazardous circumstances.

'I am a very big believer that day shouldn't be highlighted by one person and I do get frustrated when they don't acknowledge other people. The rescue itself, and looking after the guys, that was horrendous. And there were young guys, actually there was one guy, a young seaman, he was from *Cerberus* [training college] and he'd got a ride on our boat just to come out and have a look and that was one of his first experiences. You've got to feel sorry for someone like that.'

On the positive side, the young sailor witnessed the outstanding work of Keogh and his shipmates and that was reflected in one of the many letters Matt received following his award from the navy chief, Vice-Admiral Russ Crane.

'Your efforts to calm the tense situation and avert an emergency of the kind that eventuated are an outstanding example to our junior members of the qualities we need in the most trying of circumstances,' Crane wrote. 'Your courage and tireless energy in response to the explosion and over the many hours that passed until all casualties could be evacuated showed great fortitude and determination, but it is your selfless efforts to save the injured passengers in the water, while remaining on the burning boat until the end, which inspires us all.'

As he stood on the tiny quarterdeck of HMAS *Wollongong* in Cairns Harbour in 2012, preparing for another long patrol on Operation Resolute, Matt Keogh reflected on the events of April 2009 and the impact they have had on him.

The father of three believes that his actions that day were about personal responsibility and the safety of his mates.

'I'd rather something happen to me than them, and I think I'm always that way,' he says. 'Sometimes you've got to take that decision and once you make that decision you have to stand by it.'

Chapter 4

Too Bold to Die

Andrew Harris knew that if he blacked out, he and his mate would both probably die. Suffering from horrendous injuries, he dragged himself towards the burning wreckage of the Aero Commander aircraft where his friend was hanging unconscious over the nose of the plane.

'I just said to myself, "You have got to stay conscious." I was coughing to keep my heart going, a form of CPR — if you ever have a heart attack, you cough really hard, it keeps your heart pumping. So I was actually going through that,' he recalls.

'I kept saying to myself, "You are no good to him if you die." I didn't give a shit if I died, but my concern was that I was no good to him if I died. I didn't want to get halfway there and have us both die; that would have been a waste. As long as he was alive I didn't think about my death.'

Just as he reached his mate and grabbed his belt to pull him clear, the left wing fuel tank of the aircraft exploded in a ball of flame.

The plane crash that resulted in Andrew Harris being awarded the Star of Courage — the second highest honour for civilian bravery after the George Cross — was not the first near-death experience for the former Special Air Service soldier, TV personality, pub bouncer and colourful Melbourne identity and businessman with close connections to some of the city's most notorious underworld figures.

Andrew Harris was born into one of Melbourne's leading business dynasties and a well-connected military family. His father, George Harris, was the president of the Carlton Football Club and a minor figure in the demise of the Whitlam Government following the Khemlani loans scandal. He provided a key document to Carlton's number-one ticket holder, Opposition leader Malcolm Fraser, who tabled it in Parliament with devastating effect, including the resignation of the Treasurer, Jim Cairns, from the fracturing Whitlam administration.

George Harris was a POW at Changi in Singapore, incarcerated by the Japanese with his own father, Major Joel Harris, and his older brother, also called Joel Harris. Japanese authorities referred to them as 'E Joel Harris and sons'.

Andrew's mother's grandfather was General Sir Alexander Reid of the Indian Army. His great uncle was Sir Isaac Isaacs, the nation's first Australian-born Governor-General. Andrew says he was born a rebel, and for a man from such a background his life has taken a rather unorthodox path.

The Harris family's privileged existence among the mansions of exclusive East Ivanhoe came to a shuddering halt after his grandfather's death, when Joel senior's gambling debts were called in and his substantial property portfolio had to be liquidated.

George had just finished his dentistry degree and the family of four children found themselves in rented accommodation in less salubrious surroundings at West Heidelberg. His second son, Andrew, was determined to follow in the footsteps of his uncles and boyhood heroes. One was a top-grade player with Melbourne Football Club, the other a professional middleweight boxing champion.

For young Andrew the move to West Heidelberg and his father's decision to leave him at the exclusive Wesley College would be critical to his career choices. 'I hated Wesley. Living in one of the toughest suburbs in Melbourne in a purple [Wesley] uniform turns you tough,' he says.

When he was 13 he told his Uncle Joel that he was sick of being pushed around and asked him to teach him how to box. He became a good amateur boxer at about the same time as he realised that he and school were a bad mix, so he set himself on a path to leave the education system behind and get to work.

He soon applied his newfound skills as a pugilist to a teacher at Wesley and was promptly shown the door. From there it was on to McLeod High School, with the same outcome. The final straw was Preston Tech. Nobody ever got expelled from Preston, one of Melbourne's toughest schools, but young Harris managed it and at 16 he was free of the burden of school and began an apprenticeship in the rag trade.

It turned out that the tough guy from West Heidelberg had a flair for designing dresses and bikinis, and he went to work for a company called Waterside Swimwear. By 19, he was the manager of the business and studying industrial engineering, but again his restless nature intervened and he left the firm to drive interstate trucks for a company called BJ Hart. He also managed to obtain his pilot's licence, and a girlfriend who lived at Benalla in northern Victoria.

Harris had become an accomplished amateur fighter as well, and was earning some extra cash by bouncing at some of Melbourne's toughest pubs. 'I was really mixed up with the wrong crowd. There was myself and a fellow called Sugar Davis, another top amateur fighter; he lived in Reservoir and we were like brothers,' he says.

The two lads also became mixed up in the seedy side of the pub business and were introduced to the Melbourne underworld. Criminals ran the city and tough guys such as Andrew Harris and Sugar Davis kept the peace with their fists and concealed weapons.

'I remember going to the Waterside Hotel one night and a fight happened and I said to Sugar, "Get in the car and come home with me and give this the arse." He didn't, and next day's newspaper said he was shot in the back of the head with his arms tied behind his back,' he says. 'I thought, "Shit, I'm a tough kid hanging with the wrong people." Two or three had been jailed and that was my third mate killed in either a fight or by being shot. I was living in a very dangerous world, but I felt no fear; I've always had this absence of real heavy adrenaline or fear. My brain was saying, "God, I hope something changes in my life!" Well God bless national service, that kind of slapped me right around.'

It was 1971 and a pivotal year for Andrew Harris when his number came up in the national draft. He joined the Australian Army and was sent to Puckapunyal training camp near Seymour in Victoria to learn how to be a soldier.

'I seemed to find my whole meaning once I got into the army. I was in a structured environment, I liked the structured environment, we were doing things that were dangerous but controlled and enjoyable,' he says.

At Pucka he met an officer called Dave Christie, who went on to become an SAS officer. Christie spotted the potential in the new recruit and suggested he become an officer in the regular army. Harris took the advice and transferred to the Officer Cadet School at Portsea, from which he graduated in 1973.

With the Vietnam War over for Australia, the only operational deployment for a young Australian officer was in Papua New Guinea, where diggers patrolled the disputed border with the troubled new Indonesian province of Irian Jaya (West Papua).

Lieutenant Harris was posted to the 2nd Battalion and set about patrolling the region between Wewak and Vanimo as Papua New Guinea moved towards independence. The work of the Australian troops there is shrouded in secrecy, but Harris marks this period as one of the most rewarding of his life.

His commanding officer was Lieutenant Colonel Mike Jeffery, who would go on to command the SAS Regiment and eventually become Governor-General of Australia. Harris says that Jeffery wrote him up for an active service gong for his work in PNG, but when he arrived back in Australia he was sat down and told to forget about what he had done along the border because it was not public knowledge. He wanted to soldier on, so he kept his mouth shut.

Harris had become close to Jeffery and his family, and just before he left New Guinea Jeffery had asked him if he would come to Perth and try for selection into the SAS. In mid-1976, back home, he embarked on six months of hard pre-selection training.

SAS selection is probably the toughest physical and mental test for any soldier. Andrew Harris knew what was involved and what he would need to do get through it. At the same time, he was training for an Australian amateur boxing title, and the two objectives were highly complementary when it came to the brutal fitness regime.

After passing selection and doing some more training, he was posted as a free-fall parachute troop commander. He had been parachuting for years in the civilian world, where he was also a private pilot, so he was a natural fit for air operations within the SAS Regiment.

After another brief stint in PNG he was assigned to the newly formed counter-terrorist (CT) wing of the regiment and was sent to the British 22nd SAS Regiment at Hereford to study how the world's best special forces unit conducted its CT operations.

His career hit the wall in 1979 when he was posted to what was purgatory for an SAS officer — a desk job at Defence headquarters in Canberra.

'Here I am with bloody parachute wings of qualifications and operational experience coming out my bum, and instead of sending me to do operational training I was put in a shoe box at Russell Offices where my job was to write what would happen to logistics command in the event of desert warfare. That would have to be the most soul-destroying job, so the minute I got there I put my resignation in.'

Just before he went to Canberra he married his first wife, a former army sergeant, so here he was, newly married and about to throw himself on the mercy of the civilian job market.

He met with his superiors and put them on notice that unless he was given another job he would resign from the army. 'They didn't have me contracted in any way, so I had no return-of-service obligation,' he says.

The personnel officer asked him to settle down and think about it: 'We've spent literally millions training you, you are one of the highest qualified parachute instructors and CT instructors.'

Says Harris, 'I said, "What the fuck am I doing sitting here, then?"'

The officer made the cardinal error of saying, 'You won't resign,' so not only did Harris make good on his threat, but he also managed his departure with a great deal of flair.

As a natural-born rebel who didn't react well to injustice, Harris decided to leave the army with a bang. He convinced one of his mates at the local civilian parachute club to fly him over Russell Offices so he could jump onto the hallowed turf of Blamey Square and present his resignation letter in person to the Chief of the Defence Force, Admiral Sir Anthony Synnott.

He told the *Army News* and the *Canberra Times* of his plan to touch down at precisely 8.31 am just as the chiefs were having their morning parade on the square.

May Day 1979 dawned bleak and grey in Canberra with a cloud base of around 300 metres above Defence headquarters. Harris told the pilot to run in above Commonwealth Avenue and pull into the clouds to buy him enough height for a safe jump.

'I didn't want to splat myself; that's not going to prove anything,' he says. 'I had to get out slightly upwind of Russell Offices over the hill, so I probably got out at about 900 feet [above ground], fell in cloud for a couple of seconds and the minute I saw the ground opened my parachute.

'The journalist, the photographers were on the ground so I flew in and landed, threw my parachute off, still had my uniform on, walked over, put my beret on, walked over to CDF and said, "there is a letter you should read."'

Among other things his letter warned Sir Anthony that the army was losing a lot of gun officers and sergeants, due to its ridiculous posting system.

Harris had $2000 in the bank, a new wife and her old car,

which they drove back to Melbourne to stay with her parents while they figured out the next step.

Harris had ended his army service dangling from a parachute, so it was appropriate that parachuting would provide the springboard for the next phase of his career.

They rented a house in Frankston on the Mornington Peninsula, and Andrew borrowed $4000 from the bank to buy ten training parachutes so that he could set up a parachute training school at a local airfield.

But Harris realised he would need to do more than just train civilian parachutists if he was to make a reasonable living. He hit on the idea of doing the first ever live TV parachute jump into the Melbourne Cricket Ground during the 1979 footy grand final.

He sold the idea to host broadcaster Channel Seven, but when it came time to talk turkey he had no idea of the amount of money he should ask for the stunt.

'I said $30,000 and you pay for the parachutes, and straight away he said, "Deal,"' Harris says. 'We went out and shot all this promo material and they ran it on Channel Seven for four or five years; it was sensational.'

The parachute school flourished and his team worked for numerous media outfits, but his big break came six months later when he received a call from David Frost of Hayden Frost Productions, who asked him if he would teach TV presenter Greg Evans how to parachute for a segment on *The Mike Walsh Show*.

'So Greg Evans sat down, and you know how the military instructs — civilians find that very funny — and he was such a soft cock and he was worried about the way he looked and his make-up,' he says. 'We were typical army training, "For fuck's sake, Evans, get your shit together and don't worry about your make-up, worry about whether you are going to survive the jump or not." We ended up making a very funny segment and he made every mistake you could, but he survived, landed in cow shit, really made a dick of himself.'

It was great television and soon afterwards Harris received a call from Mike Walsh, who wanted him as a regular on the show.

His first stunt was a live parachute jump from the Channel Nine helicopter above Willoughby in Sydney onto the helipad and into the set of *The Mike Walsh Show*.

When he jumped he told the audience to count to ten and he would open his chute on ten. 'If I get to 12 I die,' he said for dramatic effect. He allowed the audience to get to 13 before he pulled his ripcord.

'He [Walsh] was screaming, really screaming, "Andrew, open the parachute, open the parachute!" I went bang on 13 and he said, "Oh, for God's sake! Thank God that happened, don't do that to me again."'

The segment was a huge hit and Andrew Harris, TV star, was born. He recorded a total of 84 segments for the show, ranging from buckjumping at the Booligal Cup race meeting to skiing the Tasman Glacier.

By 1988, Harris was a household name and his business career and family life were steaming ahead. He had two young children, a big house in middle-class Templestowe, a twin-engine aircraft and a farm on King Island in Bass Strait.

He and a mate decided to fly to the farm for a weekend of rest and relaxation. So they went to Moorabbin airport, put in a flight plan and took off for the island, with one thing ringing in Andrew Harris's ears — 'Severe weather warning for Bass Strait.'

It was about nine o'clock on a beautiful clear night in Melbourne, but Harris was thinking about Bass Strait storms and the fact that he had no desire to fly into one. As he approached the island he radioed a mate who had just landed an air ambulance on the airfield.

'He said, "Mate, be super careful, we've just had a wind gust through which I reckon was 80 knots. The predominant wind is coming from the north, but this came from the west, so be super careful."'

They discussed which runway he should use and decided that he would land into the west. An aircraft landing pattern typically consists of a downwind leg in the opposite direction to the landing, a base leg as the plane turns at 90 degrees to the runway before lining up for 'finals' back into the wind towards the runway.

As he turned on the downwind leg Harris copped a blast of wind into his back that was later estimated at 120 knots. 'I'd pulled my throttles back to 80 knots, I had my gear down, I had my flaps down, I'm on the downwind leg and I copped 120 knots of wind straight up the arse with a massive blast of rain. I have never seen it happen in the aircraft before,' he says.

By the time he was on final approach the wind was gusting all over the place. His passenger was starting to panic. 'I said to him, "Mate do me a favour, shut the fuck up, I've always been fascinated with what happens when you die, let me enjoy this experience,"' he recalls. 'I've done everything I can do, we are flat and level, I've got full throttle on, we are going down so fast we are going to hit the ground at 250 knots, we are going to fucking die, this is a four-second conversation. That's all I had, from 1000 feet, that's all I had — four seconds.'

The aircraft came down through some trees and hit a paddock, wings level, at an estimated ground speed of 250 knots, or 460 kilometres an hour. As it slid across the ground Harris recalls thinking, 'Fuck, I've pulled this off.'

Just as he thought luck was on his side, the aircraft lights picked up the dirt wall of a farm dam. The force of the impact was so great that his seat was torn from its mounts and flung through the windscreen, travelling more than 150 metres through the air.

'That's when I thought I'd die. This is the mental process — "I've gone through a windscreen, I've snapped my neck, I'm dead." That was the moment I thought, "Oh, this is what it feels like to die,"' Harris says. 'Well, when I hit the fucking ground I knew I wasn't fucking dead.'

He suffered massive injuries, including compound fractures of both legs and multiple other fractures, and his face was virtually torn off; and for good measure, he was on fire. What was left of the aircraft had followed his body's flightpath and was now heading towards him at a rate of knots.

'I thought, "For fuck's sake, I survived this fucking thing, I might die of injuries, but I've survived and this thing is going to fucking take me out,"' he says.

Fortunately the burning wreckage stopped short, with the passenger hanging out over the front.

'I thought, "I've fucking got to get him, I'm responsible for him," so I went to stand up, but I had compound fractures of both ankles and my legs collapsed. My bones were sticking out through my legs. I thought, "That's not too fucking healthy", so I thought, "OK, I'll do it on my knees,"' he says.

'I got on my hands and knees, same problem, one was OK but the other was completely mangled. So I'm on my knees with one hand, drag myself across the aircraft, got hold of him by the belt, the thing was burning and fucking hot, then the most massive explosion and fortunately, yes, I've got massive scars down my back, but the explosion blew us about ten metres away from the aircraft.'

The passenger had minor burns, severe fractures, including a fractured skull, and serious concussion. Harris's SAS medical training kicked in and he began applying CPR. When a farmer arrived about 15 minutes later, Harris told him to get the passenger to hospital because his breathing had become quite shallow.

Harris spent another 20 minutes sitting in the rain before help arrived for him. He knew he was in strife and he felt his face and found that his eye was resting on his cheek. 'I was just ripped to fucking shreds and I thought, "Fuck, if I don't get help in 15 minutes I will bleed to death, or I will fucking die of injuries."'

He also felt an enormous sadness about his baby son Edward as the extent of his injuries sank in. 'The only thing that came into my mind was my son, I don't know why; I mean I would miss his first birthday. It was the only moment of sadness I could ever remember; I'm not a person that feels sadness.'

Only later did the doctors discover that a large piece of metal had sliced through his ribcage and his lungs and was resting on his spleen.

Six months and 57 operations later Harris was racing cars, and nine months later he was back in the cockpit.

Andrew Harris was awarded the civilian Star of Courage for saving his mate's life that night. When he thinks about how events played out, it distils down to one word — responsibility.

'I was not going to live the rest of my life with his life on my conscience,' he says. 'If someone is in trouble and they are your responsibility — I was flying the fucking aeroplane, so it was technically my fault, but even if it had been none of my fault, it was still my responsibility.'

Harris says responsibility has been a key element of his entire working life, from SAS officer to nightclub bouncer.

'I always felt that responsibility for people I am in charge of and I've always put myself in harm's way to protect them; I've done it all my life,' he says. 'I was responsible for these people. I don't give a stuff about the consequences for me; I will do, calmly and sensibly, the best I can — I don't want to commit suicide — but I want to do it in a way that protects me the best way I can.'

So was he born brave or was it something that he learned?

'I think it's got to be born into you,' he says. 'If you aren't brave, well, that's not your fault. If you are brave that doesn't make you special, I just think there is something. Is it genetic, is it the way you grow up? I don't know, but all the guys I've met who have won a bravery award have led by example, never asked anybody else to do anything, or put others in a situation they wouldn't put themselves in. That is one trait they all have — they seem to have this ability to disconnect their own safety when they are responsible for another human being.'

Harris also recognises that bravery is not universal — just because someone is courageous in one aspect of life doesn't mean that he or she will be able to cope with every situation.

'The most terrifying moment of my life was the first time I was standing there backstage to go and talk on live television,' he says. 'I can never remember having more bubbles in my stomach, being more nervous, being more conscious. So appearing on live television is the most terrifying experience; I would prefer to eat my shit than do that.'

After a year of hell following the plane crash that included bankruptcy (he was not insured for the accident), Harris received a letter from Government House asking him to accept the Star of Courage. He and his wife just sat on the stairs, and for the second time in his adult life — the first had been on the ground in King Island — Andrew Harris wept.

Chapter 5

Eye of the Storm

Major General Peter 'Gus' Gilmore stands perfectly upright, a sea of headstones disappearing into the background behind him, his salute so precise that he looks more like a warrior sculpture than an Australian Army officer. The creases of his shirt are razor-sharp and his uniform impeccable despite the blast-furnace heat and energy-sapping humidity of the Papua New Guinea weather.

It is November 2012 at the beautiful Bomana War Cemetery on the outskirts of Port Moresby, where a small crowd has gathered to pay homage to some very special Australians.

Bomana is one of those solemn resting places for the nation's war dead — along with Gallipoli in Turkey and Kanchanaburi in Thailand — where you can almost feel the spirits of the thousands of soldiers buried in the meticulously landscaped grounds.

Beneath the emerald turf lie 3825 souls, including 3069 known and 237 unknown Australian soldiers, surrounded by the rugged mountains where many of them died. Huge South

American rain trees frame the burial ground, casting welcome shade for visitors.

Major General Gilmore is at Bomana to represent the army and his Special Operations Command (SOCOMD) at a reinterment ceremony for two members of the World War II 'Z' Special Unit, Lieutenant Scobell McFerran-Rogers and Private John Whitworth, and their Indonesian guide Roestan. The three perished in 1945 on the Indonesian island of Sulawesi during a failed rescue mission for downed US airmen.

A team of 'Z' Special operatives had been dropped by flying boat onto the west coast of the island, but were caught in a Japanese ambush. McFerran-Rogers and Roestan were killed during the initial firefight and Whitworth was wounded, captured and later executed by Japanese troops. Their bodies were recovered after the war by US forces and taken to the Philippines before being transferred to Bomana and buried under headstones marked 'known only to God'.

To identify them, Major Jack Thurgar from the army's Unrecovered War Casualties Unit undertook a remarkable piece of detective work involving a complex paper trail and thousands of clues, 67 years after they perished. Thurgar, a former SAS soldier and Vietnam veteran, is a lead investigator and has found the remains of numerous missing Australians from war zones around the world, bringing closure to many families and adding to the nation's historical record.

Also present at Bomana in November 2012 was 92-year-old former 'Z' Special Unit Corporal Henry Fawkes, the sole survivor of the ill-fated mission codenamed Operation Raven 2. He was the last Australian to see both men alive; Lieutenant McFerran-Rogers actually died in his arms all those years ago.

The courage and boldness displayed by Henry Fawkes and his mates from 'Z' Special and other special forces troops, such as the Commandos from the 2/2nd Independent Company in Timor who operated behind enemy lines, provide a rich heritage for modern-day special forces units. This is particularly true of the SAS Regiment, which has inherited the mantle of guerrilla warfare practised so effectively during World War II.

As a former squadron commander and commanding officer of the SAS, Gilmore is acutely aware of the inheritance from men such as Fawkes, who thought nothing of being dropped by parachute or paddling deep inside enemy territory at great personal risk. That heritage was the focus of Gilmore's brief address at Bomana to mark the grave dedication.

Back in Canberra, Gus Gilmore reflects on the deep links between today's special operations troops and those who set the bar so high during World War II and subsequent conflicts.

He says the key to successful special operations is achieving an outcome disproportionate to the investment, citing historical examples of operations conducted by small teams that achieved outstanding results.

He regards Operation Jaywick, the 1942 raid on Singapore Harbour by 'Z' Special, and the achievements of Sparrow Force and the independent Commando companies in East Timor during 1942 and 1943 as classic examples. They involved soldiers who were more mature and better trained than the average digger, including many with special skills or local knowledge.

'They were able to withstand very hard training, so they were physically tough and mentally tough. You just look at some of the training they did for Operation Jaywick in Singapore Harbour, training hard and delivering effect as a result of that training,' Gilmore says. 'They were able to operate in small teams or as individuals, in very non-permissive and hostile environments, sometimes operating alone and, when a number of the team were captured, being able to conduct an escape and evasion independently and having the courage to do that, to see the mission through. All of those things resonate with the character of today's special forces.'

Perseverance and boldness were key traits of both the 2/2nd and Operation Jaywick. In Timor the men cultivated the locals and worked with them to harass a much bigger enemy force and to restrict the enemy's movement through daring guerrilla attacks that achieved results out of all proportion to the forces' small numbers.

Operation Jaywick is regarded as one of the finest special forces missions of all time. As mentioned earlier, the six men from 'Z' Special Unit paddled folboat kayaks 80 kilometres into Singapore Harbour from the mother ship *Krait* to blow up 40,000 tonnes of enemy shipping right under the noses of the Japanese. It was a blueprint for how special forces continue to operate to this day.

Gilmore says audacity was the cornerstone of the mission, from the 8000-kilometre voyage to Singapore in a disguised Japanese fishing boat, to the paddle into the harbour, right into the hornet's nest, to attach limpet mines to the ships.

'The boldness that led to success for that particular operation and then the fact they had to paddle 50 miles south to rendezvous with the *Krait* over a number of days, that extraction in itself shows the toughness of these men,' he says. 'They would have known when they went that they had a very challenging mission that they were unlikely to be successful in, and probably unlikely to return from, because it was so bold and the enemy force was so strong. But they went ahead and did it, they had the courage to do it and then the toughness to be able to extract and successfully complete that mission. The size of the team there actually is telling in terms of how our special forces often operate today.'

Gus Gilmore, who led the initial Australian push into southern Afghanistan alongside the US Marines following the September 11 attacks in late 2001, marvels at the achievements of 'Z' Special Unit and particularly its success in the jungles of Borneo in the latter part of the war. When final accounts were tallied they showed that some 82 'Z' operatives had trained about 2000 local guerrillas and claimed more than 1500 Japanese scalps, literally in many cases.

Fast-forward to 2012 and the operations of the Special Operations Task Group against insurgent leaders across southern Afghanistan and many of the same characteristics are on display.

'They are operations with extreme but very calculated risk,' Gilmore says. 'When our elements are going in to conduct those operations, yes our intelligence is good, but there is always significant residual risk just because of the nature of the area they have to operate in, the unknowns. The courage that those individuals, as part of a team, are displaying I think in some ways is very similar to the twos and threes that were operating in Singapore Harbour or in Sarawak or any of those places.'

While boldness and audacity are crucial elements in a successful special-forces operation, Gus Gilmore believes courage is a common denominator across the entire Australian Defence Force. 'I think any soldier, sailor or airman or woman going from Australia to an unknown situation must be courageous,' he says. 'They would never know what is going to confront them on the ground. Often when they get there, the situation is nowhere near as hostile or dangerous as perhaps it could be, but as I think history tells us, that can swing very quickly. So at an individual level I think there is courage right across the force and we have to recognise that.'

But he acknowledges that the issue of recognition for a particular act of courage can be difficult. 'We all need to recognise that fact and honour their courage; but in doing his job, does an individual deserve additional recognition? That is where we get to the definition of how do you decide that someone has actually gone above and beyond and perhaps sometimes given a bit of extra service,' he says. 'Even those that go above and beyond will often say, "I was doing my job," and I think that is actually true. But there is clearly something that distinguishes the way they are doing their job to the others, and often it's not a matter of choice, it is just the situation that is presented and how an individual responds. The reason they say "I was just doing my job" is because if the boot was on the other foot, they know their mate would do the same for them.'

Gilmore says the circumstances of a particular act of valour are extremely important. 'How dire are the circumstances? As you push towards our highest awards, the situation must be clearly dire, there must be no other avenue, there must be a situation that is sitting on a knife's edge, you'd almost say against the odds, potentially outmatched and proven to be outmatched, and everyone is conscious of where they are sitting.'

He cites the circumstances in which Mark Donaldson won his VC as a classic definition of a dire situation. 'That went over a series of hours, there was a rolling ambush over a long distance of several kilometres. They were trying to break contact and most people had been wounded at least once. They were surrounded on three sides, they tell the story that they went from one side of the car to the other side of the car, and then got about a five-second reprieve before the guns opened up from that side. So there was nowhere to hide and it was a dire situation, and I think that needs to be the environment in which we consider valour.'

Under such dire circumstances the next aspect, according to Gilmore, is that an individual makes a conscious decision to act. 'There may be potentially other alternatives but an individual needs to make a deliberate decision that this needs to be done. It needs to be a conscious decision and that sometimes goes to the heart of cool, clear thinking, but in particular the next point, which is selflessness, and clear selflessness. Essentially it is a choice between him and his mates, or those under his command as a leader,' he says.

'You'll have stories of commanders that are awarded for acts of valour where they move between their men to inspire the team, but once again it's a selfless decision that if they don't do it, then someone else will have to do it, and if they or someone else don't do it, then the dire circumstances will overcome.

'I think it also needs to have a degree of inspiration or audaciousness about it, or must be a breathtaking move and I think if you look at our most recent VC recipients you can see that inspiration in their actions, in what they achieved.'

In each case, their courage inspired the rest of their team and turned the tables on a dire situation. 'I think that act of valour will be the key that turns the lock to regain the initiative to recover the situation,' he says.

Yet as many of the posthumous VCs among the 99 awarded to Australians show, the dire situation is not always reversed by an act of conspicuous valour. But their acts still had those other elements of complete selflessness, deliberate decision, inspiration and audacity, Gilmore says. 'Those type of things are differentiators — those types of things at an individual level, where the individual just has no option but to act independently to close it down.'

Early in the Afghanistan campaign, SAS Sergeant Matt Locke was awarded the Medal for Gallantry after leading a patrol into the freezing mountains, where they played a crucial role in saving first themselves and then a group of US troops whose helicopter had crashed.

'The enemy had made repeated attempts by day and by night to overrun and surround the position, and without regard for his personal safety he led a two-man team to locate and neutralise the enemy in order to regain the initiative and protect his patrol from being overrun,' Gilmore says. 'As a leader, as a sergeant you would expect a leader to do that, that was his responsibility, but it was then followed by another attack. He manoeuvred to attack the observation post with little regard for his own personal safety. He was exposed on higher ground, deliberately exposing himself to achieve the effect he needed. Still under sustained fire, he then directed another indirect fire attack and it eventually allowed for a successful extraction.'

Many aspects of the most gallant acts on the battlefield are breathtaking even for hardened soldiers such as Gus Gilmore.

An improvised explosive device killed Commando Sergeant Brett Wood in Afghanistan in 2011. He had previously been awarded the Medal for Gallantry in an incident in which six of his team were wounded, including himself, and he had been tasked with regaining the initiative against a sizable enemy force.

'He completed that task in this first part of the mission, without hesitation, completing the rapid and aggressive clearance of numerous compounds,' Gilmore says. 'He then displayed extraordinary leadership and courage; he inspired his team and the remaining part of the Commando platoon to repel the attacks. He then led a marksman team to kill seven anti-coalition militia.'

When the bullets are flying and individuals are confronted with death, the decision to act is a very personal one. Regardless of training or a sense of responsibility, when an individual takes a decision knowing it will most likely result in his or her own death, that is extreme valour.

'Those that have been put in that situation and have displayed the bravery in taking that decision and executing that decision, in accepting their responsibility, I think are worthy of the recognition they receive,' he says.

On the broader question of honours and awards, he strongly supports the idea of recognising a unit or sub-unit wherever possible. 'To try to differentiate between one person and the next can be sometimes very difficult.'

Unit awards such as the Unit Citation for Gallantry (UCG) or the Meritorious Unit Citation recognise the efforts of the entire team in achieving their aims and objectives. A classic example was the first UCG awarded to Number 2 SAS Squadron for its work in the western desert of Iraq during and after the invasion of 2003.

'It's the best way to recognise that armies tend to operate as a team, whether that is a team of two people, or a team of a regiment, so I am a real fan of that type of recognition,' says Gilmore. 'It recognises the courage displayed at all levels, it recognises that if put in the same situation, I'm sure that every soldier would react that way.

'Sometimes, though, the nature of the battle or the nature of the engagement doesn't lend itself to that recognition, or the nature of an individual's display of valour is so great, and so irrefutable, that individual recognition is important.'

Individuals receiving gallantry awards always acknowledge the team and invariably say they receive the award on behalf of their mates. At award ceremonies around the nation the message is the same: 'I did this as a soldier, I did what I was trained to do and I did it because I know those to the right and left of me would have made exactly the same decision.' Gus Gilmore says it is a really heartening and fantastic thing to hear. 'Because that is the spirit of soldiering and that's what a soldier does.'

No system of honours and awards is perfect, and many flaws have been uncovered in both the imperial and the Australian systems over the decades. Gilmore acknowledges there will always be a degree of subjectivity and emotion attached to awards, but he argues that there must be a mechanism to ensure that the highest-level awards for valour and gallantry are recognised. As both a recipient (Distinguished Service Cross for leadership in action in Afghanistan, Member of the Order of Australia and US Bronze Star) and as a nominator of troops for awards he is well placed to analyse the modern-day system.

'I do think that the process of an operational commander identifying those individuals who he believes deserve to be nominated for consideration of an award is appropriate,' he says. 'That's the right person to make a recommendation for consideration and I think we do it pretty well. There will always be perhaps some, for whatever reason, that perhaps go less recognised than they should and there may be some who receive higher recognition than others regard as appropriate, but that I think is part of the fog of war and the nature of conflict.

'If you look back to World War I, whole units were killed and there were so many acts of valour that were never recognised, and it could be in today's army that there are actions that actually turn the battle, where individuals took extreme risk, but because of the situation and the fog, others weren't as aware of it as they should have been, of the importance of that action. So in an individual's mind there will always be a degree of frustration. I suppose it does come back to this business that I described, from a commander's perspective. I think it will always be a difficult issue to make sure that those who are most worthy of recognition receive it.'

Gilmore is reluctant to discuss individual cases but acknowledges that during intense contacts such as the battle of Ana Kalay in Khas Oruzgan, every soldier on the ground that day faced death and fought with great courage.

'They knew they were a moment away from a bullet to the left or to the right, so the courage amongst the whole element on the ground was immense, but I think it was the commander's assessment that there were some particular acts that day that were worthy of particular recognition,' he says.

Gilmore is in the unique position of having commanded the vast majority of the recipients of valour and gallantry awards since the East Timor conflict in 1999. From 2001 to mid–2013, awards to members of SOCOMD included two Victoria Crosses for Australia; five Stars of Gallantry; 20 Medals for Gallantry; 34 Commendations for Gallantry; 18 Distinguished Service Crosses; 47 Distinguished Service Medals; and 64 Commendations for Distinguished Service. The true numbers of awards may be 10 to 15 per cent higher because of SOCOMD members' protected identity status and the limited amount of information released about their actions.

Gilmore knows many of them personally and has served alongside and recommended quite a few as well. He doesn't believe there are personal characteristics that identify individuals as most likely to perform acts of outstanding courage, but there are many similarities in those who do.

'We are very fortunate that we select people for certain attributes — mental toughness, physical toughness, their intelligence, their aptitude, their experience — so you would expect there would be some similarities and I think there are,' he says.

'Look at Ben Roberts-Smith and Mark Donaldson, similar but different, and I also look at Star of Gallantry winners and Medal for Gallantry winners and I look at Commendation for Gallantry winners and I look at those who have never been recognised for their bravery and there are, I think, great similarities between them all.

'I don't think there is a characteristic or a trait that I could pick. If there was one, and it's common, it would probably be just a sense that they are very calm and measured and able to assess a situation and maintain that demeanour when the bullets start flying.'

Acknowledgements

Once again a book with my name on the cover would never have been produced without the support, positive reinforcement and hard work of my wife and editor-in-chief Verona Burgess.

There were times when I imagined this one might never be finished, but her prodding and encouragement kept me focused on the end game. Our daughter Lucy and family cat Salem endured my numerous absences and boring phone calls with good cheer, and my step-kids Dan and Jenna were as supportive as ever.

A lot of people helped us with the process and the many people I interviewed gave generously of their time, and for that I say a big thank you.

I am especially indebted to Gary Bornholt for his advice and knowledge.

Special Operations Commander Major General Peter 'Gus' Gilmore, former Commanding Officer of SAS Regiment,

Lieutenant Colonel Paul Burns and Chief of Navy, Vice-Admiral Ray Griggs, were very helpful.

The late Roland Griffiths-Marsh was an inspiration and Douglas Herps a font of invaluable knowledge and insights.

To my sister Jane and to Michael, Alison, John and Karen, big thanks for your hospitality and support.

Janette Doolan worked tirelessly on the transcriptions during a period of unimaginable sadness for her family and we are extremely grateful for her efforts.

My employer News Limited has been as flexible as ever.

To Shona Martyn, Catherine Milne, Katherine Hassett, John Mapps and the team at HarperCollins, thank you once again.

Ian McPhedran, July 2013

Index

Abot oil terminal 271, 275
ADF Gold Group commendation 296
Admiralty House, Sydney 20
aeromedical evacuation (AME) choppers 237, 238
Afghan National Army (ANA) 227–9
  1st Kandak (battalion) of the 6th Brigade 205 Corps 207
Afghanistan 1–4, 199–217, 221–46, 249–52, 256–60, 262, 282, 315, 317–18
  Australian deaths 213
  battle of Ana Kalay 1–4, 223–4, 226, 228–39, 265, 321
  battle of Tizak 256–7, 260, 262, 264
Agostini, Tisha 252, 255
Aitape 18
Akell, Bill 131

al-Qaida 188, 221
Allied Intelligence Bureau 45
ambushes 15, 29, 97, 228
ammunition 14, 16, 19, 99, 118–21, 141–2, 168, 215, 256
amoebic dysentery 53, 55
Army News 304
Army of the Republic of Vietnam (ARVN) 148
Ashmore Reef 289
Ashworth, Lance Corporal James 262
asylum seekers 289–96
Australian forces *see also* Royal Australian Air Force; Royal Australian Navy; Special Air Service Regiment (SASR)
  2/9th Armoured Regiment 125
  1st Australian Task Force 96
  1st Battalion Royal Australian Regiment (1 RAR) 80–1, 95

2nd Battalion 106, 125, 211, 302

3rd Battalion Royal Australian Regiment (3 RAR) 71, 81, 82–7 , 163

5th Battalion Royal Australian Regiment (5 RAR) 96

6th Battalion Royal Australian Regiment (6 RAR) 9, 94, 95, 106, 108, 122, 126–7, 133, 138, 177, 194, 207, 212, 213

Bravo Company 97, 128, 138, 139–40

Delta Company 95, 97, 127, 129, 193

7th Battalion 8

2/8th Battalion 52

9th Battalion 178

2/40th Battalion 36–7

47th Battalion 178

1st Brigade 7

28th Brigade 82

7th Commando Company 19

6th Division 44, 72, 154

9th Division 22, 23

12th Field Regiment of the Royal Australian Artillery 163–4

'A' Field Battery 163

2/2nd Independent Company 35–8, 245–6, 313, 314

2/17th infantry battalion 186

3rd Light Horse Brigade 6

8th Light Horse Regiment (Victoria) 6

9th Light Horse Regiment 80

10th Light Horse Regiment (Western Australia) 6

39th Militia Battalion 73

3rd Training Battalion 23

'M' Special Unit 46

Special Operations Command (SOCOMD) 321

Unrecovered War Casualties Unit 312

'Z' Special Unit 13–14, 22–5, 29, 33, 39, 40–2, 44–6, 48, 49–51, 52, 54, 55–7, 123, 154, 312–15

Australian Army Training Team Vietnam (AATTV) 103, 179, 207, 262

Australian Commonwealth Naval Board 191

Australian Light Armoured Vehicles 208, 209

Australian War Memorial 9, 50, 53, 72

Long Tan Cross 122

Avro Ansons 64

Awala 73

Bagram 221

Bailey, Lieutenant Commander Jody 276

Balado Bridge 64

Balibo 280

Bario 23, 25–7

Barnes, Lieutenant Thomas 14

Barrie, Sergeant Keith 25

Bass Strait 306–7

battle of Ana Kalay 1–4, 223–4, 226, 228–39, 265, 321

battle of Long Khanh 161, 166–73

battle of Long Tan battle of 97–100, 102, 108–11, 120, 122, 124, 129–32, 172

battle of Maryang San 82–7

battle of Tizak 256–7, 260, 262, 264

Bean, Charles 6, 7

Bear Cat 150

Beazley, Kim 152–3

Beevor, Antony 181

Bena Bena 38

Bewes, Private Nathan 213

Bien Hoa province 150

bin Laden, Osama 221

Binh Ba 124

BJ Hart 301

Bleich, Jeff 175

Boer War 79, 163

Bomana War Cemetery 71, 311–13

Bongiorno, Edith 23, 32

Booligol Cup 306

Borneo 42, 47–8, 52, 80, 88 *see also* North Borneo

Bornholt, Brigadier Gary 188–90, 192–6

Boterill, Private Keith 42

Bower, Sergeant Doug 25

Braithwaite, Bombardier Dick 42

Bravery Medal 296

Brazier, Lieutenant Colonel Noel 7

Bremen 66

Bremner, Lieutenant Norman Frederick 178

Bridges, General William 136

British Army 219

   1st Commonwealth Division 82

British Empire Medal 153

British Light Brigade 7

British Special Air Service (SAS) 219, 303

Brown, John 153

Brown, Joshua 288

Brown, Justin 280–8

Brown, Nicole 282, 288

Brown, Sarah 288

Brunei Bay 23

Bryce, Governor-General Quentin 4, 121, 201, 207, 278

Buick, Platoon Sergeant Bob 98, 106–13, 132

   All Guts and No Glory 107

Buna 76

Burns, Lieutenant Colonel Paul 202, 242, 244, 256–65

   Anzac Day address 244–6, 265–7

Burston, Major General Sir Samuel 23

Burton, Corporal Alexander 8

C-47 Dakotas 155

Cairns, Jim 299

Cambodia 151–2

Camp Bastion 252

Camp Doha 286

Camp Martin Cox 150

Camp Russell 250, 256, 260

Campbell, Gunner Owen 42

Canberra Times 304

Cantwell, Major General John 260

Canungra 44, 95, 124, 163
Cap de la Jague 62
Carr, Ivan 175
Chandler, Private John 14
Changi 299
Channel Nine 306
Channel Seven 203, 305
children overboard scandal 188
Chinn, Warrant Officer George
119
Christie, Dave 302
Christmas Island 292
Citizen Military Forces (CMF)
23, 93, 125
Clare, Jason 71
Clemins, Vice-Admiral Archie
158
Clissold, Eugenie 63, 68
Clissold, Pilot Officer George
61–8
Cold War 9
Cologne 67
Commendation for Distinguished
Service 321
Commendation for Gallantry 210,
240, 241, 288, 322
Commendation Medal for Valour
161, 174
Cook, Ainslie 65
Cosgrove, Major General Peter
194, 281, 286
counter-terrorism (CT) 220–1,
303
courage *see* bravery
Crane, Vice-Admiral Russ 296
Crete campaign 66, 154

Crimean War 7
Cusack, Warrant Officer Rod 25
cyanide pills 15, 25, 48

D-Day landings 62, 65
Daily Telegraph 254
Dale, Private Tomas 213
Darby, Flight Lieutenant Jo 294
Dare (East Timor) 36–7
Davis, Sugar 301
Dayak people 154
Davis, Private Graeme 'Doc' 100
de Havilland 82 64
decoration allowance 53
Defence Act 95
Defence Headquarters 303–4
Defence Honours and Awards
Tribunal 189–90, 195
Deh Rawood 213
dengue fever 76
Dennis, Alexander 17
Dennis, Clara 18
Dennis, Don
The Guns of Muschu 20
Dennis, Edgar Thomas 'Mick'
13–21
Dennis, Phil 17
Dennis, Susan Violet 17
Department of Veterans' Affairs
8
Derapet 207, 209, 210, 211, 214
Desfontaines, Edouard 169
Dexter, Captain Dave 39
d'Hage, Adrian Stuart 'Darj'
133–47
Military Cross citation 134

Dili 36–7, 281, 287
  Commando Memorial 36
Distinguished Conduct Medal
    100, 131
Distinguished Flying Cross 121
Distinguished Service Cross 150,
    153, 257, 320, 321
Distinguished Service Medal 121,
    210, 240, 258, 288, 321
Distinguished Service Order 80,
    102, 139, 178
Dohle, Cliff 114, 120, 121
Dohle, Joan 121
Dominion Monarch 63
Donaldson, Emma 4, 201
Donaldson, Kaylee 4, 201
Donaldson, Trooper Mark
    'Donno' 4, 9, 177, 183, 199–
    202, 203, 223, 228, 229, 232,
    233, 238, 240–2, 244, 259,
    261, 316, 321
Dong Tam 150
Douglas Dakota DC3 24
Duchess of Cornwall 78
Duke of Edinburgh 185
Dunn, Mick 144
Dunstan, Corporal William 8
Duntroon *see* Royal Military
    College, Duntroon (RMC)
Dutch Borneo 28
Dutch West Timor 36

Eagleton, Private Ronald 14
East Timor (Timor Leste) 9, 211,
    212, 221, 245–6, 280–1, 284–
    7, 313–14

International Force 280–1
  Portuguese 33, 36–9, 281
Edmeades, Captain Eric 25
Edmondson, Corporal John 186–7
  Victoria Cross citation 186
Eglinton, Ron 112
Eindhoven 61
  Volkel airbase 61, 62, 65
Eisenhower, General Dwight D.
    62
EMUs (Experimental Military
    Unit) 149–51, 153–4
Enoggera Barracks 94
Evans, Greg 305–6
explosive ordnance detection dogs
    3, 224, 233, 243

Falkirk 64
Fallingbostel 66
Fanning, Lieutenant James 210
Farley, Dave 148
Fawkes, Corporal Henry 312–13
Fiji 259
Flinders University 218
Flynn, Errol 155
Fraser Commando School 45, 46
Fraser Island 23, 40, 45, 123
Fraser, Malcolm 299
Front Puffin oil platform 294
Frost, David 305
fuzzy wuzzy angels 70

Gallipoli 5–8, 80, 178, 189, 311
George Cross 299
Geraldton 171
Gillard, Julia 207

Gillespie, Lieutenant General Ken 259

Gilmore, Major General Peter 'Gus' 311–22

Gona 76

Goroka 38

Grandin, Bob 114–20

Grangemouth 64

Greece campaign 66, 154

Greta army camp 72

Griffiths, Sergeant Len 'Griffo' 69–78

Griffiths-Marsh, Corporal Roland 52–8

Griffiths-Marsh, Helen 53

Gubbay, Lieutenant Alan 14

guerrilla tactics 28, 35, 50, 124, 230

Hagger, Private Michael 14

Haiphong 54

Haley, Clare 49

Haley, Frank 'Shagger' 49

Hallam, Sergeant Kel 25, 26

Ham, Paul
  Vietnam: The Australian War 129

Han River 81

Hango 70

Hanover 66

Harbour Defence Motor Launch (HDML) 14, 15

Harris, Andrew 298–310

Harris, 'Bomber' 61–2

Harris, Edward 309

Harris, George 299–300

Harris, Joel 299

Harris, Major Joel 299, 300

Harrison, Major Tom 22, 25, 26–7, 28, 30, 31, 55–6

Hassett, General Sir Frank 86

Hawkesbury Valley 93

Hayden Frost Productions 305

Hayes, Keith 37

headhunters 29, 52

Helmand Province 252

'Hero Corps' 207

Herps, Douglas 44–51

Herps, John 44

Herps, Sophia 44

Hill 317 (Maryang San) 82–7
  the Hinge 83–4

HMAS *Albany* 289–90, 293

HMAS *Albatross* 152, 156, 273, 274, 281

HMAS *Armidale* 189

HMAS *Cerberus* 156, 273, 291, 296

HMAS *Childers* 289, 293, 294–6

HMAS *Coonawarra* 295

HMAS *Hobart* 273

HMAS *Jervis Bay* 285

HMAS *Kanimbla* 249

HMAS *Moresby* 281

HMAS *Nirimba* 281

HMAS *Perth*

HMAS *Stirling* 274, 283

HMAS *Stuart* 272, 276, 277

HMAS *Success* 285–6, 291

HMAS *Sydney* 116, 138

HMAS *Tarakan* 291

HMAS *Waterhen* 282

HMAS *Wollongong* 296

HMAS *Yarra* 189, 191–2

Ho Chi Minh Trail 116, 152
Holsworthy Barracks 163, 221, 249, 254
Holt, Harold 95
Horn of Africa 220, 274
Horner, Professor David 70
Houston, Air Chief Marshal Angus 189, 201
Howard, John 38
Hughes, Bill 80
Hughes, Lieutenant Jim 80–9
Hughes, Major General Ron 80
Hummers 2–3, 199, 224, 228, 229, 233, 235, 237
Hurricane fighters 64

Iban people 28
'ICOM chatter' 225, 228
IEDs (improvised explosive devices) 214, 217, 233, 250, 265, 318
Imita Ridge 73
Imjin River 81, 82
Incident Response Regiment 223, 224, 241
Indian Army 299
Indonesia 95, 280–1, 290, 302
Ingleburn barracks 80
Ioribaiwa 74
Iran 274
Iraq 221, 257, 258, 271, 274, 319
Irian Jaya (West Papua) 302
Isaacs, Sir Isaac 299

J Arthur Rank 46
Jacka, Albert 178, 244

Jacko (explosive ordnance detection dog) 243
Jackson, Brigadier Oliver 114–15, 118, 124–5
Jacksons International Airport 78
Jager, Corporal Sharon 294
Japanese forces 14–28, 33, 37, 70, 312
  camp and march deaths 42–3
  cannibalism 77–8
  headhunters of 29
  snipers 75
Jeffery, Lieutenant Colonel Mike 302
Joye, Col 114, 117, 128
JTAC (joint terminal air controller) Evan 231–2
jungle training 23, 44 see also Canungra
jungle warfare 74–5, 127

Kabul 221
Kanchanaburi 311
Kaot oil terminal 276
Kapooka recruit training centre 161–3, 261
Kapyong 86
Keighran, Corporal Daniel 9, 177, 207–8, 210, 211, 215, 217, 262
Keighran, Kathryn 210
Kelabit, the 22, 26–9
Kelly, Bayne 'Gus' 160–76
Kelly, Margaret 175
Kempsey 61, 63, 68
Kendall, Second Lieutenant Geoff 97

331

Kenna, Ted 177, 182, 185
Keogh, Leading Seaman Matt 289–97
Keswick Barracks (Adelaide) 32
Keys, Sir William 86
Khas Oruzgan 4, 199, 223–4, 227–9, 321
Khemlani loans scandal 299
King's Own Scottish Borderers Regiment 85
Kirby, Private Grant 213
Kirby, Warrant Officer Class 2 John 'Jack' 100–1, 121, 126, 131
Kokoda Track 69–70, 73–8, 254–5
70th anniversary 69–70, 78
Korean 38th Parallel 80, 81
Korean War 9, 79–89
Krait 40, 50–1, 245, 314
Kupang 36

Labuan Island 23, 47
Lae 76
Lafu (Fredolino José Landos da Cruz Buno Silva) 280–1
Landstuhl Regional Medical Center (Germany) 252
Lane, Bruce 114–15, 120
Langer, Private Paul 210, 215
Medal for Gallantry citation 216
Lanigan, Sergeant Sean 210, 211–17
Medal for Gallantry citation 216
Laos 151, 152
Larrakeyah army barracks 285

Lee, John 138
Leonora 35
Liberator bombers 22, 24, 25
Little Pattie 114, 117, 128
Locke, Sergeant Matt 266–7, 317–18
Lone Pine 7–8
Lone Pine War Memorial 7, 8
Long, Bob 31
Long Khanh, battle of 161, 166–73
Long Phuoc 96, 124
Long Tan, battle of 97–100, 102, 108–11, 120, 122, 124, 129–32, 172
awards 101–4, 193
casualties 100
Lysanders 64

McCarthy, Trooper Sean 265–7
McFerran-Rogers, Lieutenant Scobell 312
McKell, Governor-General Sir William 20, 54
MacKinney, Lance Corporal Jared 207, 209, 213, 215
McMahon, Prime Minister William 165
McOwan, Major General Tim 253
McQuinn, Captain Luke 44–5
Mahey, Lance Bombardier Peter 'Bluey' 171
malaria 36, 38, 76
Malaya 88, 95, 106, 125–6
Malino 28
Maluku Islands 25

Martinets 64

Martins, Donnabella 37

Maryang San (Hill 317), battle of 82–7

Mathers, Second Lieutenant Ian 168, 175

Maylor, Rob 227–35, 237–9, 240–1
SAS Sniper 241

Medal for Gallantry 9, 102, 203, 210, 211, 215, 240–1, 258, 277, 278, 317–18, 322

Medal of Honour 150

Mekong Delta 150

Melbourne Cricket Ground 305

Meller, Private Barry 131–2

Member of the Order of Australia 320

Member of the Order of the British Empire 153

Mentioned in Dispatches (MIDs) 102, 121, 131, 150, 153, 173, 190

Mentoring Task Force (Afghanistan) 207, 212, 242
Mentoring Team Alpha 212
Mentoring Team Charlie 213

Meritorious Unit Citation 319

Middle East Area of Operations (MEAO) 274

Mike Walsh Show, The 305–6

Miles Masters 64

Milfield 64

Military Cross 84, 102, 133, 145

military honours 4, 8–10, 319–22
see also by individual name
American 150–1

citations 30–1, 54–5, 134, 159, 178, 179–80, 182, 186, 199–201, 207, 208–9, 216, 258–9, 261, 278–9

Defence Honours and Awards Tribunal 189–90, 195

recommendations 260–1

system of awards 9, 57–8, 85–6, 102–3, 112–13, 130–1, 160–1, 176, 261–3

Military Medal 20, 30, 53, 54, 70, 84, 112, 131, 170

Miller, Keith 164

Mindoro Island 25

mines 139

Mirabad Valley 213

Montgomery, Field Marshal Bernard 62

Moore, Bluey 112

Morant, Harry 'Breaker' 79

Morotai 24, 25, 31

Mount Martha 46–7

Moxham, Lance Bombardier William 42

Muggleton, Regimental Sergeant Major Tom 135

Mullah Bari Ghul 226

Murray Bridge 80

Murray, Jock 56–7

Muschu Island 14–17, 20

MV *Melaleuca* 123

Nadzab 76

National Maritime Museum, Sydney 50

national service 93–5, 125, 160–1, 173–4, 301
  recruit training 161–2
Nek, the 5–7
Nelson, Dr Brendan 51
Neptune bombers 115
New Guinea campaign 14–19, 20, 38–40, 69–71, 73–7
NSW Police 17
New Zealand 16th Field Regiment 82
Newcastle 72
News Limited 209
Nguyen Nam Hung 129
Nicholls, Captain Henry 83–4
Nixon, President Richard 165
Nolan, Terry 164
Noosa Heads 53
North Borneo 22, 25–31, 154 *see also* Borneo
North Vietnamese Army (NVA) 99, 138, 140
  274th Battalion 99, 129
Northam training camp 35
Northern Ireland 227, 228
Nowra 152, 157, 273, 274, 281
Nui Dat 96, 108, 111, 114, 115, 116, 120, 124, 138, 166, 174

O'Brien, Major Owen 119
O'Connell, Pat 84
Oecussi Enclave 280–1, 286, 287
officer training 93–5, 101–2
O'Neill, Professor Robert
  Australia in the Korean War, 1950–53 86

Operation Agus 5 47, 50
Operation Commando 82, 86
Operation Copper 14–15
Operation Enoggera 96, 108
Operation Hobart 99, 108
Operation Jaywick 40, 50, 123, 244–5, 313–14
Operation Katnook 226
Operation Lavarack 133, 138, 139
Operation Market Garden 62
Operation Overlord 161, 172
Operation Plunder 63, 65
Operation Raven 2 312
Operation Resolute 292, 296
Operation Rimau 25, 40–1
Operation Semut 1 22–31, 154
Operation Semut 2 52, 55
Operation Varsity 65
Operation Vendetta 128
Oruzgan province 199, 248
Osmond, Sergeant 'Fatty' 19
Otway, Charlie 35
Otway, Fred 33–40
Otway, Jack 35
Owen Stanley Range 71, 75, 77
Owers' Corner 73

P-38 Lightning fighters 30
P-40 Tomahawk fighter 65
Palmer, Ray 254–5
Palmer, Scott 254
Panzer Group West 62
Papua New Guinea (PNG) 302, 303, 311
Papuan Infantry Battalion 73

334

parachuting 24, 46

Parker, Private Sean 210

Patrol Base Anaconda 2, 199, 224, 233

Patrol Base Wali 212, 214

Payne, Warrant Officer Class 2 Keith 177, 179, 182–5, 185
  Victoria Cross citation 179–80

Pearl Harbor 36

Penang 54

Perry, Acting Sub-Lieutenant Andy 148–55
  Silver Star citation 159

Perry, Dick 154–6

Perry, Rupert 158

Perry, Virginia 158

perseverance *see* bravery

Persian (Arabian) Gulf 271–3, 274

Perth 33, 35, 106, 221, 240, 274, 302

Philippines 25, 312

Phuoc Tuy province 96, 139, 166

Pinjarra 33

Plain of Bah 23, 27

Poate, Private Robert 213

Popondetta 76

Port Fairy 211

Port Moresby 38, 71, 73, 76, 311

Portsea officer training school 125, 302

post traumatic stress disorder 55

POWs 66–7, 299

Prince Charles 78

Puckapunyal 125, 163, 301–2

Qatar 276

Queanbeyan 71–2

Queen Elizabeth II 185

Ranau 42, 44

Raw, Group Captain Peter 118

Reid, General Sir Alexander 299

Reid, Richard 8

Reith, Peter 188

Remembrance Driveway 185

RHIBs (rigid hull inflatable boats) 275–6, 278–9, 286, 288, 290, 292, 293

Rhine campaign 61–3, 65, 66

Richardson, Private Jim 131

Richmond RAAF base 24, 46, 285

Riley, Frank 114, 117–21

Roberts-Smith, Corporal Ben 'RS' 9, 177, 183, 192, 202–6, 256, 259, 260, 261, 262, 321

Roberts-Smith, Major-General Len 202

rocket-propelled grenades (RPGs) 1–2, 204, 215, 223, 225, 233–4, 242, 244

Rodriguez, Sergeant First Class Gregory A 243

Roestan (Indonesian guide) 312

Roses Lagoon 185–6

Royal Air Force (RAF) 219
  59 Operational Training Unit 64
  245 Squadron 62–3, 64, 66
  Typhoon fighters 61

Royal Australian Air Force
(RAAF) 63, 76, 106, 294
9 Squadron 116–17
Iroquois (Huey) choppers 114–
15, 118, 148, 156
RAAF base Pearce 156
training 156
Royal Australian Navy (RAN)
149, 152, 191, 281, 291
aircrew 273
counter-piracy role 274
divers 280–8
RAN Helicopter Flight
Vietnam (RANHFV) 157
rescues 271–3, 275–9, 289–97
Seahawk helicopter fleet 271–5
723 Squadron 281
Royal Marines 227
Royal Military College,
Duntroon (RMC) 80, 134–8
bastardisation 135–6
RSL 86, 146, 190
Rudd government 189
Rudd, Kevin 201
Ruhr, the 62

Sabben, Dave 93–105, 108, 111,
112, 127
Saigon 150, 151, 164, 172, 174
Salvation Army Boys Home 33–4
San Jose (Mindoro Island) 25
Sanananda 74
Sandakan prison camp 42–4
Sanderson, Sergeant Fred 25
Sarbi (explosive detection dog) 3,
233, 234

Scheyville 93–4, 95
School of Artillery 163
Seoul 80, 81
September 11 terrorist attacks 188,
315
Services Reconnaissance
Department of Special
Operations Australia 45
Sharp, Second Lieutenant Gordon
97–8, 100, 108–10, 127
Sheean, Leading Seaman 'Teddy'
189, 190, 191
Short, Private Nelson 42
SIEV (Suspected Irregular Entry
Vessel) 36 289–95
Silver Star 150–2, 158
Sime, Leading Seaman Ben
271–9
Sime, Stacey 274
Simeni, Francis 70
Simmonds, Clive 218
Simmonds, Lia 221
Simmonds, Margaret 218
Simmonds, Sergeant Troy
'Simmo' 1–3, 218–25, 227,
229, 233–4, 235–8, 240–2,
243, 245–7, 265
Simpson, Private John Kirkpatrick
189, 190–1
Singapore Harbour 25, 40–1, 123,
313, 314
Singleton 163
'Sleeping Beauty' motorised
submersible canoes 40–1
Slim, Field Marshal William J
180

Smith, Felicia 123
Smith, Major Harry 95–6, 97–8,
101, 102–3, 106, 107, 108–9,
111, 112, 118, 122–3–32,
193–4
Somalia famine 220
Sparrow Force 36–8, 313
Special Air Service Regiment 1,
9, 13, 80, 88, 199, 202–3, 207,
219–23, 242, 244, 248, 256,
257, 259, 299, 302, 313
free-fall parachutists 220, 303
medics 220
Number 2 SAS Squadron 220–
1, 245, 319
1 Troop Number 3 SAS
Squadron 223–4
'reo' (reinforcement cycle of
training) 220, 249
2nd Commando Regiment
248
selection 302–3
signallers 220
TAG (Tactical Assault Group)
East 221
TAG (Tactical Assault Group)
West 220–1
water operators 220
Special Operations Executive 47
Special Operations Task Group
315
Spitfires 64
Stalag XI-B 66
Stanley, Captain Morrie 110,
129
Star of Courage 299, 309–10

Star of Gallantry 9, 102, 210, 262,
321
Sticpewich, Warrant Officer Bill
42
storpedoes 23
Suai 285
Sukarno, President 95
Sulawesi 154, 312
Swanbourne 221
Sydney Olympic Games 147,
220–1
Synnott, Admiral Sir Anthony
304

Taliban 1, 224–6, 229–30, 245
Tamworth 63
Tan Son Nhut airbase 164, 174
Tarakan 31
Tarin Kowt 2, 213, 238, 249, 256
see also Camp Russell
Tasman Glacier 306
Tedman, Lieutenant Commander
Peter 286, 288
Templeton's Crossing 70, 75
Ternhill 64
terrorist attacks 271–7

Thomlinson, Damien 248–55
Thurgar, Major Jack 312
Timor Leste see East Timor
Timor Sea 289
Tobruk 186
Tokyo 70
Tongs, Bede 70–1
Townsend, Lieutenant Colonel
Colin 126, 194

Townsville 20, 158, 163, 284, 291

Tredrea, Sergeant Jack 'Snow' (Chuon Doc) 22–32

Military Medal citation 30–1

Trinity Grammar School, Sydney 94

Trooper G 238

Trooper H 234–5, 241

Trooper J 238

Tubb, Lieutenant Fredrick 8

Tunn, Lieutenant John Patrick 178

Typhoon ground attack fighter-bombers 63, 64, 65–6

Unit Citation for Gallantry (UCG) 102, 112, 192, 257–8, 319

United Nations Multinational Force 79

US Army Special Forces (Green Berets) 230

US Black Hawks 203–4, 238

US Bronze Star 320

US Cobra gunships 170

US Fifth Air Force 76

US Presidential Unit Citation 102, 112

USS *Blue Ridge* 158

USS *Firebolt* 271, 275, 276, 277

University of Adelaide 218

V-2 rockets 62

valour *see* bravery

Vampire jets 156

VE (Victory in Europe) Day 68

Victoria Cross (VC) 4, 8, 9, 53, 88, 101, 102, 103, 131, 150, 177, 182–7, 199–206, 207, 240, 242, 244, 259, 262–3, 316, 321

Vietcong 108, 138

275VC Regiment 99

D445 VC Provincial Battalion 99, 128

Vietnam Gallantry Cross with Palm Unit Citation 102, 112

Vietnam War 9, 80, 88, 96–105, 108–11, 126–7, 133–8, 221, 262, 285, 302

body count 139

public attitude to 146, 165

'scorched earth policy' 96–7

treatment of veterans 152

212th Company of the 1st Mobile Strike Force Battalion 179

von Dawans, General 62

Vung Tau 98, 107, 114, 115, 116, 138, 150, 173

Walker, Max 155

Walklate, Lance Corporal Spencer 14

Wallace, Norm 40–4

Walsh, Corporal Ray 'Walshy' 170

Waterhouse, Jack 137

Waterhouse, Margaret 137

Waterside Swimwear 300

weapons 14–15, 16, 28
AK-47 1
Austen (Australian Sten) sub-machine gun 14, 16
blowpipes 28, 32, 49, 53
Bren machine gun 28, 50
Oerlikon 20 mm anti-aircraft guns 63
Owen sub-machine gun 16, 28
parang knives 32, 49
poisoned darts 28, 53
Weber, Sergeant Malcolm 14
Weir, Peter 6
West Timor 280–1, 287
Western Front 6
Wewak 18, 20, 38, 182, 302
Wheatley, Kevin 'Dasher' 88
White, Peter 152, 153
Whitlam government 299
Whitworth, Private John 312
Wickham, Brian 128
Wilsons Promontory 35
Winjeel training aircraft 156
Wood, Commando Sergeant Brett 318